Economy/Society

Sociology for a New Century

A PINE FORGE PRESS SERIES

Edited by Charles Ragin, Wendy Griswold, and Larry Griffin

Sociology for a New Century brings the best current scholarship to today's students in a series of short texts authored by leaders of a new generation of social scientists. Each book addresses its subject from a comparative, historical, global perspective, and, in doing so, connects social science to the wider concerns of students seeking to make sense of our dramatically changing world.

TITLES OF RELATED INTEREST FROM PINE FORGE PRESS

An Invitation to Environmental Sociology *by Michael M. Bell*
Global Inequalities *by York W. Bradshaw and Michael Wallace*
Schools and Societies *by Steven Brint*
Economy/Society *by Bruce Carruthers and Sarah Babb*
How Societies Change *by Daniel Chirot*
Ethnicity and Race *by Stephen Cornell and Doug Hartmann*
The Sociology of Childhood *by William A. Corsaro*
Cultures and Societies in a Changing World *by Wendy Griswold*
Crime and Disrepute *by John Hagan*
Gods in the Global Village *by Lester R. Kurtz*
Waves of Democracy *by John Markoff*
Development and Social Change *by Philip McMichael*
Aging, Social Inequality, and Public Policy *by Fred C. Pampel*
Constructing Social Research *by Charles C. Ragin*
Women and Men at Work *by Barbara Reskin and Irene Pakavic*
Cities in a World Economy *by Saskia Sassen*
Gender, Family, and Social Movements *by Suzanne Staggenborg*

Economy/Society:

Markets, Meanings, and Social Structure

Bruce G. Carruthers
Northwestern University

Sarah L. Babb
University of Massachusetts—Amherst

PINE FORGE PRESS
Thousand Oaks ◆ London ◆ New Delhi

For information, address:

 Pine Forge Press
A Sage Publications Company
2455 Teller Road
Thousand Oaks, California 91320
(805) 499-4224
E-mail: sales@pfp.sagepub.com

Sage Publications Ltd.
6 Bonhill Street
London EC2A 4PU
United Kingdom

Sage Publications India Pvt. Ltd.
M-32 Market
Greater Kailash I
New Delhi 110 048 India

Production Editor: Wendy Westgate
Production Assistant: Nevair Kabakian
Designer: Lisa S. Mirski
Typesetter: Marion Warren
Indexer: Molly Hall
Cover: Ravi Balasuriya

Printed in the United States of America

08 09 10 11 12   8 7 6 5 4 3 2

Library of Congress Cataloging-in-Publication Data
Carruthers, Bruce G.
    Economy/society: Markets, meanings, and social structure/
By Bruce Carruthers and Sarah L. Babb
        p. cm.
    Includes bibliographical references and index.
    ISBN 978-0-7619-8685-0 (cloth : acid-free paper)
    ISBN 978-0-7619-8641-6 (pbk. : acid-free paper)
    1. Economics—Sociological aspects. 2. Sociology. 3. United
States—Economic conditions—1981- 4. United States—Social
conditions—1980- I. Babb, Sarah. II. Title III. Series.
HM548 .C37 2000
306.3—dc21   99-6359

Contents

ABOUT THE AUTHORS

Bruce G. Carruthers is Associate Professor in the Sociology Department at Northwestern University. He did his undergraduate work at Simon Fraser University in Canada, received a master's degree from Rutgers University, and earned his Ph.D. from the University of Chicago in 1991. He has previously written two books, *City of Capital: Politics and Markets in the English Financial Revolution* (1996) and *Rescuing Business: The Making of Corporate Bankruptcy Law in England and the United States* (1998), as well as numerous articles. He has been teaching courses in economic sociology to Northwestern undergraduates for the past seven years.

Sarah L. Babb is Assistant Professor of Sociology at the University of Massachusetts at Amherst. She received her B.A. in philosophy from the University of Michigan in 1988 and her Ph.D. in sociology from Northwestern University in 1998. She is the author of several articles in historical and economic sociology, published in journals that include the *American Journal of Sociology, American Sociological Review,* and *Estudios Sociológicos.* Her recent work looks at how the economic policies of developing countries are shaped by international pressures and economic ideas, focusing particularly on the case of Mexico. She was the recipient of the American Sociological Association's annual dissertation award for the year 1999.

ABOUT THE PUBLISHER

Pine Forge Press is a new educational publisher, dedicated to publishing innovative books and software throughout the social sciences. On this and any other of our publications, we welcome your comments, ideas, and suggestions. Please call or write to:

Pine Forge Press
A Sage Publications Company
2455 Teller Road
Thousand Oaks, CA 91320
(805) 499-4224
E-mail: sales@pfp.sagepub.com

Visit our World Wide Web site, your direct link to a multitude of on-line resources: www.pineforge.com

Foreword

Sociology for a New Century offers the best of current sociological thinking to today's students. The goal of the series is to prepare students, and in the long run, the informed public, for a world that has changed dramatically in the last three decades and one that continues to astonish.

This goal reflects important changes that have taken place in sociology. The discipline has become broader in orientation, with an ever-growing interest in research that is comparative, historical, or transnational in orientation. Sociologists are less focused on "American" society as the pinnacle of human achievement and more sensitive to global processes and trends. They also have become less insulated from surrounding social forces. In the 1970s and 1980s, sociologists were so obsessed with constructing a science of society that they saw impenetrability as a sign of success. Today, there is a greater effort to connect sociology to the ongoing concerns and experiences of the informed public.

Each book in this series offers a comparative, historical, transnational, or global perspective in some way, to help broaden students' vision. Students need to be sensitized to diversity in today's world and to the sources of diversity. Knowledge of diversity challenges the limitations of conventional ways of thinking about social life. At the same time, students need to be sensitized to the fact that issues that may seem specifically American (e.g., the women's movement, an aging population bringing a strained social security and health care system, racial conflict, national chauvinism, etc.) are shared by many other countries. Awareness of commonalities undercuts the tendency to view social issues and questions in narrowly American terms and encourages students to seek out the experiences of others for the lesson they offer. Finally, students also need to be sensitized to phenomena that transcend national boundaries, economics, and politics.

Economy/Society: Markets, Meanings, and Social Structure fulfills the goals of the series by offering an accessible introduction to the various institutional arrangements that govern economic activity. Bruce Carruthers and Sarah Babb show that economic exchanges are deeply embedded in social relationships. Moreover, they demonstrate that an understanding of how the economy is socially constructed offers rich and novel insights into such topics as advertising, consumer behavior, the diffusion of innovations, conflicts at the workplace, social inequality, and the economic development of nations.

Understanding how economic activities and institutions are shaped by social structures is important because these insights help us to understand the variability and mutability of the economy. Markets, for example, do not appear in mature, viable form at the drop of a hat or on command. Markets develop slowly, if at all, depending on the social infrastructure and culture. In that sense, markets are very much embedded in other social institutions. Consider how difficult the transition to capitalism has been in the former Soviet Union, where the development of markets has been hindered by greed, crime, predation, a lack of faith in contracts, and the absence of a supporting legal system. In contrast, look at how fast electronic markets have developed in the United States as, contrary to the expectations of many, consumers have moved readily to purchase items via Amazon.com or eBay. Confidence, technological know-how, and faith in the reliability and accountability of the enterprises are all essential elements in supporting economic exchange, and these social factors are distributed unevenly across time and space.

The core topics in this engaging book—markets, networks, the workplace, social stratification, economic development, and globalization—are approached with a keen sociological lens. This lens reveals how these diverse economic phenomena are embedded in society in a myriad of ways, some readily apparent, others much less obtrusively. Along the way, the analytical focus reveals how consumption becomes a status competition, how jobs are secured through acquaintances and not close friends, how gender and race shape relations in the workplace, and how international production and trade are challenging the sovereignty of the nation-state. This book displays the authors' vivid sociological imagination—it tackles big issues and real problems with analytical power and lively ideas. Students, scholars, and, yes, even economists will both enjoy and be rewarded for their time spent with *Economy/Society*.

WALTER W. POWELL
Stanford University

1

The Embeddedness of Markets

In a chapter titled "Closing the Deal (Getting Him to the Altar)," a recent book for husband-hunting single women observes that "getting the man you want to propose and then to turn that proposal into an actual wedding date [is] a feat some women say can be tougher than any corporate transaction" (Fein and Schneider 1997:99). The chapter then proceeds to outline strategies that women can employ to get "a good deal" on the "marriage market." Although the book is about matrimony, the authors write as if they were a pair of economists! The idea that there are "markets" in seemingly noneconomic areas, such as love and marriage, has become quite widespread in recent years, and not just in popular advice books. Today, even personal matters such as selecting a spouse are conceptualized as market transactions into which "buyers" and "sellers" enter with their preferences and resources and leave with their individual utilities maximized.

Mirroring the spread of economic ideas and market metaphors, economists have increasingly begun to look at issues and problems previously reserved for political scientists, anthropologists, psychologists, and sociologists. Various social institutions such as marriage, crime, discrimination, politics, and religion are being analyzed as if they were markets. One economist particularly famous for studying nonmarket institutions is Gary S. Becker from the University of Chicago, winner of the 1992 Nobel Prize in economics. Becker views education, for example, as a form of capital in which people invest; by investing in their stock of "human capital," individuals increase their future earnings; thus, they earn a "return" on their investment. Moreover, just as in the popular account, Becker views marriage and childbearing as occurring in a kind of market: "When men and women decide to marry, or have children, or divorce, they attempt to raise their welfare by comparing benefits and costs. So they marry when they expect to be better off than if they remain single, and they divorce if that is expected to increase their welfare" (Becker 1993b:395-96).

We propose to stand Gary Becker on his head (so to speak). Instead of offering interpretations of *social* behavior through the lens of *economics*, this book looks at *market* behavior from the perspective of *sociology*. Instead of viewing social institutions as akin to markets, we examine markets as social institutions (Swedberg 1994). Economic models of marriage, childbearing, crime, education, and other social phenomena can provide us with useful insights. However, they tend to assume—or at least imply—that something like market rationality is a fundamental part of human nature. The idea of the rational individual maximizing his or her own utility in the marketplace seems completely natural to us today. How could people ever behave differently? And if such behavior is second nature in markets, it seems logical to expect it in other areas of social life, such as marriage and education.

The central message of this book, however, is that markets are not natural or inevitable. Rather, they are **social constructions** (Fligstein 1996). Markets, like all social constructions, do not appear or arise automatically. And they do not everywhere look the same. Markets are real in the sense that they have real and important consequences for human behavior. But they are not something humans have no control over; they are not natural in the same sense that the weather, or human biology, is a part of nature. Rather, markets can be shaped this way or that in different societies.

Markets and Their Alternatives

The socially constructed character of markets is illustrated by the fact that unlike economies, which are an inevitable feature of human societies, markets are only one of an array of institutional possibilities. Since every society must produce, distribute, and allocate the goods that people need to live, all human societies have an economy of one sort or the other. But economies can be organized in many different ways, as any anthropologist or historian can tell you (Collins 1997). In other words, the basis on which economic activities occur can vary widely. For example, economic production occurs within subsistence economies, in which families produce all—or almost all—of what is needed for household consumption. In traditional hunter-gatherer societies, people live in small family-based communities in which men hunt and women gather wild roots, seeds, and other vegetable products. Nobody buys or sells anything, and there are no markets to speak of.

NOTE: **Boldface** terms in the text are defined in the glossary/index.

Besides markets, another way to exchange and distribute goods is through gift giving. Anthropologists have long noticed that in traditional societies, gift giving plays a crucial role in exchange—often much more important than exchange through markets. In the words of one famous anthropologist discussing the Maori of New Zealand, "Gifts were presented in the event of births, marriages, deaths, exhumations, peace treaties and misdemeanors, and incidents too numerous to be recorded" (Levi-Strauss [1949] 1996:18).

During the Middle Ages, luxury goods were distributed over long distances in three different ways: market exchange, gifts, and theft (Grierson 1959). Market exchange, the method most often studied by economists, was in fact the least important of the three. Most of the valuable goods that circulated did so because they were given as gifts or stolen as booty (Spufford 1988). When thinking about how French gold coins ended up in a medieval Danish hoard, we might be tempted to suppose that traders from Denmark exported goods to France and were paid in cash. Far more likely, however, is the possibility that Vikings simply stole the coins during a raid on the French coast and took their loot back home to Denmark. In this historical period, theft and gift giving governed the circulation of precious goods much more than did market exchange.

Traditional obligations between people at different levels in the medieval social hierarchy also regulated economic activity. During the Middle Ages in Europe, economies were governed through an economic system known as feudalism. In a feudal economy, serfs worked the land of the lord of the manor according to a set of long-held traditions (with the threat of coercion lurking in the background). In return, the lord was supposed to protect the serfs, dispense justice, and provide for the local church. Thus, agricultural produce and other staple goods were distributed in the local economy, but not through market exchange. The serfs were not paid wages for their labor, and the lord was not paid for his protection: Their symbiotic relationship was based on tradition, not on the market.

A market is but one institution for governing economic activity, although it is the one most familiar to us today. In markets, goods are exchanged voluntarily on a bilateral basis rather than yielded under the threat of unilateral coercion, given as gifts, or offered in satisfaction of a traditional obligation. Market exchanges occur between individuals motivated by the satisfaction of their own desires but constrained both by their budgets and the rules of the marketplace. Markets are an old and well-known form of economic activity, although they have not been ubiquitous. Archaeological and historical evidence from Africa, Europe, and the Americas documents the existence of ancient transcontinental trade networks (Abu-Lughod 1989).

Although market exchange is an ancient form of organizing economic activity, the economic system of capitalism is actually quite recent. Whereas earlier in human history, markets coexisted with other forms of economic governance (e.g., traditional obligations, gift giving, theft, etc.), under capitalism, markets become dominant. This is not to say that all other bases of economic behavior have completely disappeared under capitalism: Gift giving plays a central role in stimulating the American economy, especially around Christmas, and the circulation of goods and money within families continues to occur largely outside of markets (parents typically don't sell breakfast to young children or charge them rent). Furthermore, markets are regulated by various formal and informal institutions. Nevertheless, markets generally play a much bigger role in people's lives today than they have at any other period in human history.

Under contemporary industrial capitalism, almost all of the things we use in our everyday lives are acquired through markets—food, clothing, shelter, transportation, entertainment. To purchase these things, most of us earn a living by getting a job in the labor market. With the widespread entrance of women into the paid labor market, one last bastion of non-market economic activity is being undermined: namely, the contribution of the housewife to the national economy. As a result, many goods and services—such as meals, child care, and housework—that only 30 years ago were provided within the family (usually by Mom and for no pay), are today being provided to upper-middle-class households through a paid labor force of cooks, babysitters, and cleaners.

Like gift giving in hunter-gatherer societies, markets enter our lives today in ways "too numerous to be mentioned." Given the near-complete penetration of market relations into our modern economic lives, it is not surprising that we tend to use the market metaphor for other areas of social life, such as dating and marriage. However, in applying this market language elsewhere, we tend to forget that markets themselves are not inevitable but, rather, represent one of many possible economic arrangements. This book considers markets as social institutions and calls the "naturalness" of markets into question. Our argument is informed by two general observations. The first is that markets have certain preconditions without which they cannot function. The second is that markets function very differently at different times, in different places, and in different spheres of economic life.

Markets and Their Preconditions

Markets involve a form of social activity that is possible only under certain specific circumstances. Markets don't appear out of thin air but depend on an institutional foundation (Collins 1992; Weber 1981). Four key elements constitute that foundation: property, buyers and sellers, money, and information. Markets depend on the existence of property. Market exchange cannot occur unless there is something to exchange, and what people buy and sell in markets are not things or objects themselves but rights over those things. Today, the idea of private property has become so commonplace that we tend to take our ownership of property for granted. If I buy a car, I assume that it is my car and that nobody can take it away from me; my ownership of the car seems obvious. If my car were stolen, however, my property rights would be violated. And although I would no longer possess the car, I would still own it (the thief, in contrast, possesses the car but doesn't own it). What makes the car mine is a set of property rights, which apply because I live in a society that recognizes private property rights and enforces them through an effective legal system.

In the United States today, if my car is stolen I can call the police to help recover it, and if caught, the thief will be prosecuted in court. But in many other societies in history, my rights over my car (or a similar object) would not have been so secure. In some countries, I might not even be able to use the law or the police to recover my stolen property because I belonged to an oppressed ethnic minority. In other countries, and at other times in history, law enforcement officials might actually use their coercive powers to take my property for themselves. In general, markets perform poorly in places where private property rights are insecure (why should I invest in a factory if it can be taken away from me?), and insecure property rights are cited by economists as a factor contributing to economic underdevelopment.

Property rights are not "natural"; they are a social construction—the creation of groups of human beings. And property rights evolve over time. In the United States today, property law is being extended to encompass things such as software, databases, and computer operating systems (Nimmer and Krauthaus 1992). A century ago, such forms of property didn't even exist. But whatever tangible and intangible things that property law covers, without reasonably secure property rights, markets cannot function.

Another precondition for markets is the existence of buyers and sellers. This precondition seems easily met today, but during earlier historical periods, the absence of buyers and sellers limited how much economic activity could be conducted in markets. Throughout much of human history, people have hunted, gathered, and grown the food they ate, making their own clothes, and constructing their own shelters—all things that today we are used to receiving through markets. People who make their own clothing or provide their own food don't need to buy in the market. Thus, a grocery store that opened in a community of subsistence farmers would probably fail due to the lack of buyers. Even today, the importance of advertising serves as a reminder that the existence of buyers for a product cannot be taken for granted. Entrepreneurs and inventors must hire teams of marketers and advertisers, or their product will never be sold.

If buyers cannot be taken for granted, then neither can sellers. The fact that someone wants to buy doesn't mean that there is someone else who wants to sell. The experience of employers in colonial sub-Saharan Africa during the late 19th and early 20th centuries illustrates the point. European firms established extractive enterprises to exploit Africa's natural resources—mining for gold, diamonds, and copper and producing cash crops such as rubber and kola nuts. They needed workers to labor in the mines and plantations, so they tried to hire the indigenous population. The mine and plantation owners wanted to "buy" in the labor market, but the indigenous population, who were mostly subsistence farmers and hunter-gatherers, didn't want to "sell." Working in a mine was dangerous, unpleasant work, and they didn't need the money.

One solution was to force natives into the cash economy by requiring them to pay taxes in cash. Colonial governments instituted new taxes, and to acquire the necessary money, indigenous people had to offer themselves as wage laborers to the mines and plantations (Arhin 1976:460). Thus, colonial governments found a way to create "sellers" in the labor market.

The need for buyers and sellers draws our attention to another precondition for markets: namely, a medium of exchange. During earlier periods of human history, exchange took place through barter, or in-kind exchange: a sack of wheat for a baby goat and so on. In-kind exchange is restricted, however, by the need for a "double coincidence of wants"; the person with wheat has to want a goat, and the goat owner has to want wheat. Otherwise, the deal doesn't go through.

Gradually, however, a diversity of different forms of money emerged, from gold and silver in Europe and parts of Asia, to cowry shells in parts of Africa, to cacao beans in the trading region of the ancient Aztecs. The value of these earliest forms of money derived from the value of the objects serving as money: A gold coin, for example, possessed value because gold possessed value. The first forms of paper money were essentially "IOUs"—pieces of paper that certified that they could be redeemed for a certain quantity of precious metal. Today, however, we have become accustomed to "fiat money," or money that is valuable simply because we all agree that it is worth something. Fiat money is the ultimate social construction, because its value depends only on our collective beliefs regarding its worth.

A final precondition for the functioning of markets is reliable information. People won't buy or sell things if they don't know enough about them. The absence of accurate information presents an enormous obstacle to markets. For example, people would hesitate to buy gold jewelry if they didn't know how pure the gold was (10-, 14-, 18-, or 24-carat gold). Shoppers might not purchase hamburger at the supermarket if they weren't sure that it was pure and uncontaminated by germs. And almost no one purchases a used car, sight unseen. Information tells market participants about both the quantity and the quality of the goods they buy and sell (as in three pounds of USDA-inspected hamburger with only 10% fat content).

The importance of information for markets is reflected in the role that governments play in providing that information. For centuries, rulers have recognized that they can help markets grow and flourish if they offer standards for information. Kings and princes would often establish standardized weights and measures so that in the markets, merchants could be sure that a pound measure really weighed a pound or that 100 yards of thread really was 100 yards long.

The Embeddedness of Markets

This book introduces the field of economic sociology. One of the central insights of economic sociology is that markets are **embedded** in nonmarket social relations (Granovetter 1985). By *embedded* we mean that markets coexist with, are shaped by, and depend on, other social relations. Market relations constitute but one way for human beings to interact with one another. Social relationships consist of many other types of human interaction, including participation in a religious community, belonging to a family or having a network of friends, having political allegiances and animosities, professional interactions among co-workers, citizenship in a country, and so on. Economic sociologists study the different ways that markets are influenced by these other kinds of social relationships (Carruthers 1996).

Earlier, we mentioned the four different preconditions needed for markets to exist and operate. In general, these are not met by the markets themselves but, rather, must be satisfied in some other fashion. Markets don't automatically engender secure property rights, provide accurate information, offer a medium of exchange, or generate sufficient numbers of buyers and sellers. Frequently, government plays some kind of role in the satisfaction of these preconditions (Fligstein 1996). Governments promulgate and enforce formal property rights (North 1981). The legal system also offers contract law so that people who wish to transact with each other can create legally binding agreements. A formal contract law that makes it harder for people to break their promises or to fail to live up to their commitments helps to encourage market activity. In **capitalist** countries, legal systems offer bankruptcy law—a way for inefficient or unprofitable companies to be "killed off" (Carruthers and Halliday 1998).

Currency, whether paper or coin, is issued by a government mint or central bank. Governments set standards for information about commodities that market participants need. And as the example of colonial Africa reveals, governments can even get into the business of ensuring that markets have sufficient buyers and sellers. The important role played by governments in meeting market preconditions ensures a strong link between politics and the economy, even when overt public involvement or government regulation is minimal (Campbell and Lindberg 1990).

Formal government action (laws, policies, etc.) often satisfies these market preconditions, but it is not the *only* way to do this. **Informal social relations**—the kind that are not written down and codified—are also used frequently to solve the problems of markets. In today's New York City diamond market, people trade small, easily concealed, highly valuable commodities. Trust is a problem in such a market. If you are a diamond dealer, how can you ensure that your employees will not slip merchandise into their pockets? After all, if employees are self-interested profit maximizers, theft of the merchandise may be the most rational thing for them to do. Or you may have problems with suppliers who agree to sell so many diamonds to you at an agreed price but then back out of the deal when they get a better offer elsewhere.

Diamond merchants in New York can use the legal system, which protects private property rights and offers an effective contract law to make agreements binding. Remarkably, however, this formal apparatus is seldom used (Bernstein 1992). In fact, diamond merchants almost never use the courts to settle disputes or enforce agreements. How can the diamond market continue to function? Why doesn't the diamond trade collapse in a heap of unsettled disputes and pervasive mistrust?

The answer lies in the ability of people to use informal social relations instead of formal institutions. In New York City, the diamond market is overwhelmingly dominated by Hasidic Jews, who run their firms as family businesses—a tradition portrayed in the 1992 movie *Strangers among Us*. In the Hasidic diamond merchant community, employer–employee trust is created through the strength of family ties but also through common membership in a close-knit, deeply religious community in which stealing from other family members for personal gain would be unthinkable.

The diamond market in New York is embedded both in family networks and in a specific ethnic-religious community. Diamond traders who break their promises or who act dishonorably won't get sued in court, but they will acquire a reputation that, in such a small group, leads inevitably to commercial failure. Reputations travel quickly and easily through the tightly knit community. Other diamond traders will simply not deal with someone who has a bad reputation, effectively freezing them out of the market. Informal ethnic-religious social ties thus can be mobilized to punish rule breakers as effectively as if they had been taken to court.

Thus, some markets are embedded in formal social institutions (such as the law), whereas others are embedded in informal ones (such as family, ethnic community, or friendship networks). Whether formal or informal, institutions help provide critical market preconditions. At the same time that markets are embedded in *institutions*, they are also embedded in *culture*, or sets of meanings. The embeddedness of markets in culture is well illustrated by the role of advertising in creating a group of buyers for a given consumer product. As we discuss in Chapter 2, advertisers draw on preexisting cultural meanings (e.g., what it means to be a successful and attractive man), and link those meanings to the product being advertised (e.g., a sports car with a powerful engine) so that members of a particular culture want to buy it. Together, institutions and cultural meanings constitute two different sorts of nonmarket social relationships in which markets are embedded.

The Consequences
of Markets

What difference does it make that in our society so much of the economy is governed by markets? If we look around today's world, it seems that markets are spreading all over: Many countries are switching from **socialist** economies to capitalist ones. Within capitalist nations, markets are being deregulated, and publicly owned industries are being privatized. If markets have consequences, then the spread of markets means those consequences are becoming increasingly significant.

In Chapter 5, we will focus on the consequences that pertain to economic inequality. Markets distribute goods, but they also distribute wealth, income, and jobs in a highly uneven manner. We shall examine the extent of economic inequality and how it has changed over time. And we shall look at different forms of discrimination that occur in markets and their role in the creation and maintenance of inequality.

Through their actions, markets can reduce, reinforce, or exaggerate other social differences. The case of gender illustrates this point. In every society, social and cultural differences (in addition to biological differences) distinguish men from women. When added to these social differences, economic differences can make the distinction between male and female even sharper. In the contemporary United States, for example, men and women have very different labor force experiences, and consequently, men on average earn substantially higher incomes than do women. The U.S. labor market exaggerates the difference between men and women.

The Variety of Capitalisms

Economists—both classical and contemporary—have tended to conceptualize capitalism as a single economic system. In the 18th century, Adam Smith praised the virtues of "homo economicus," or "economic man," a universal character who behaved in a rational, self-interested way, regardless of residence, social background, historical period, or cultural context. A century later, the revolutionary Karl Marx described what he saw as the defining features of capitalism in his masterwork, *Capital*. Today, economic advisers from the West consult with Eastern European nations on how to shift from a socialist to a capitalist economy, offering plans and advice that at least initially were premised on a "one-size-fits-all" theory. Over the years, economists have come up with useful generalizations about capitalism as an economic system.

The fact that capitalism possesses some core features does not, however, mean that markets are always and everywhere the same. In fact, even in the same city we can see very different kinds of markets at work. In New York City, for example, financial markets governed by formal organizations such as the New York Stock Exchange, with oversight by the Securities and Exchange Commission, can be found on Wall Street, while markets governed by informal, family-based institutions can be found only a short distance away, where Hasidic Jews have their diamond stores. In midtown Manhattan, there are huge department stores run according to formal bureaucratic rules, such as Bloomingdale's and Macy's. Meanwhile, down on Pearl Street in Chinatown, family-owned businesses work according to a very different set of organizational principles.

Just as we can see differences at the level of markets in the same city, or even in the same industry, we can also discern macrolevel differences in markets across different countries. Some very good examples of such variation can be found in labor markets. In contemporary Germany, for example, blue-collar job markets tend to be governed by formal institutions. German companies have apprenticeship programs in which entering employees receive high levels of training that prepare them for a variety of skill-intensive tasks within specific industries. As a result, German workers tend to stay with the same company over their entire working lives, moving up within the company. In contrast, in the United States, working-class people generally have less specialized education and tend to move frequently between jobs and firms (Hollingsworth 1997; Piore and Sabel 1984).

In their search for new jobs, American workers sometimes rely on social networks; they hear about a job opening through a friend of a friend or the brother of a neighbor, for example (Granovetter 1974). The embeddedness of U.S. labor markets in informal social networks helps solve problems of information, such as how to find reliable employees. However, such forms of embeddedness can have negative side effects, such as the perpetuation of discrimination in hiring—a problem we discuss in Chapter 5.

These national differences in the institutions and traditions governing labor markets are often a by-product of the distinct problems faced by different nations in the process of economic development (discussed in Chapter 6). They can also be traced to cultural differences—for example, different culturally based perceptions of what is appropriate or inappropriate, right or wrong (or "legitimate," as sociologists like to say). It may be that U.S.-style labor markets would never work in Germany because people would perceive them as too arbitrary; conversely, the German model of lifetime employment might be perceived in the United States as inhibiting an individual's freedom of choice. Whether problem based or culture based, such cross-national differences are deep and pervasive enough that some sociologists have begun to speak of a multiplicity of "capitalisms" rather than "capitalism" in the singular (Hollingsworth and Boyer 1997).

The plurality of "capitalisms" highlights a final theme running throughout this book: namely, the process of globalization that has increasingly affected our political, social, cultural, and economic lives (the main topic of Chapter 7). Now that capitalism has become a truly international economic system, will different forms of capitalism around the world come to look increasingly similar? What does globalization mean for the evolution of different forms of embeddedness? Finally, how have global capitalism and local culture adapted to one another? This latter issue is discussed in the following chapter, which deals with the embeddedness of commodities in systems of social meaning.

Outline of the Book

Roughly speaking, the organization of this book is from the micro to the macro—progressing from topics that concern individual economic behavior to those that focus on the economic development of nations and the international economic system. We begin with a chapter on the cultural meanings of commodities, why such meanings matter, and how they are shaped through marketing and advertising. Such meanings are an important determinant of market demand. Chapter 3 considers the role that social networks play in markets. Networks operate at multiple levels, ranging from the personal networks that link friends or family together, to the formal interorganizational networks that join one corporation to another. Networks create a particular structure within markets.

Chapter 4 discusses organizations in the economy. Large corporations have come to dominate many of the leading sectors of the modern economy. The chapter addresses the consequences of this important change. Chapter 5 deals with the issue of economic inequality. Among other things, markets create economic differences: How substantial are these differences? Who do they benefit? Do they vary over time or from one country to the next?

Chapter 6 deals with the question of economic development. How do market economies change over time? Are all nations developing in the same direction, or at the same speed? What causes development, and how is it influenced by involvement in the global economy? Finally, Chapter 7 analyzes the global economy. More so than in the past, national economies participate in a global economy that knits together markets from all over the planet. What kind of a difference does this global scale make? Is it leading to an increasing homogenization of markets as products spread throughout the world?

2

Marketing and the Meaning of Things

What exactly does a teenager get when she lights up a cigarette? Physically, she sets fire to dried vegetable matter (combined with some other ingredients) wrapped in a paper tube and inhales the smoke through her mouth. The process continues until the fuel is completely burned. She might just as well stick her head in a lit fireplace and breathe in. And in the long run, if the teenager continues to smoke, she will substantially increase her risk of a whole list of physical maladies, starting with lung cancer. Physically speaking, cigarettes seem much more a "bad" than a good.

So why do teenagers and so many others continue to consume cigarettes? What benefits do they get? Part of the answer is physiological: Research shows that cigarettes produce a "high" that results in a physical addiction. The other part of the answer, however, is sociological: Cigarettes possess a symbolic meaning conveyed to those who consume them and to others. Anyone familiar with U.S. cigarette advertising, or with the way they have been portrayed in countless movies and TV shows, knows that cigarettes connote "cool." In the collective imagination, lighting them up provides wonderful opportunities for pregnant pauses in meaningful conversations, for expert displays of virtuoso dexterity with a lighter or case, a way for handsome men to satisfy the whims of beautiful women, a way for groups of guys to express their solidarity with each other in times of trouble (consider classic war movie scenes in which during a pause in the battle soldiers share their cigarettes or give one to a wounded comrade), and a way for a handsome man with a weathered and deeply creased face, on horseback, to express his rugged individualism (as in the Marlboro ads; for a typical Marlboro ad, see Sidebar 2.1). For many teenagers, cigarettes connote adulthood, so to consume them makes a public statement about autonomy, maturity, and independence.

SIDEBAR 2.1

Cigarette Imagery

Exhibit 2.1 shows a recent ad for Marlboro cigarettes. The ad is much more picture than text, selling the product using a visual argument rather than one based on words. The picture almost speaks for itself: two cowboys settling down after a hard day in the saddle. The sun has already set as they relax, drink their coffee, and smoke their cigarettes. The consumer is invited to believe that purchasing Marlboro cigarettes will transport him or her to a mythical country "where the flavor is." The ad underscores the connections between cigarettes and relaxation, on the one hand, and cigarettes and coffee, on the other.

The apparently considerable distance between the physical properties of cigarette smoking (small controlled conflagrations generating carcinogenic fumes that the consumer inhales) and its symbolic properties (cool, mature, individualist, etc.) is not unique. Nor is the fact that in many consumers' eyes, the symbolic meaning of cigarettes seems much more important than their physical features. The entire world of consumer goods is fraught with cultural meaning and symbolism. And to understand why consumers buy cigarettes and other goods, and to know how producers sell such goods, economic sociologists focus on the ways in which commodities are *embedded in systems of cultural meaning.*

The modern world is filled with commodities. A typical American supermarket chain offers about 75,000 items in a single store, and even a small neighborhood hardware store contains approximately 40,000 different items. Revlon makes 158 shades of lipstick, and Seiko alone produces over 3,000 different kinds of watches (Twitchell 1996:99). If you consider all the different commodities sold in all the different stores (hardware stores, department stores, grocery stores, shoe stores, etc.), the number of commodities that modern consumers have to choose from is simply staggering. And this number is constantly changing as new brands are brought onto the market and old ones are retired. In the decade from 1980 to 1990, grocery store shoppers had to choose from among an additional 84,933 new products (Lebergott 1993:18). Shoppers face a bewildering universe filled with things for sale.

In emphasizing the importance of the meaning of commodities, we need to update the utilitarian picture of commodities as essentially objects with physically useful characteristics. To be sure, a carpenter buys

EXHIBIT 2.1

nails because they can join together two pieces of wood, but commodities have symbolic uses as well. For male auto enthusiasts, a brand-new red Corvette Stingray is not merely a means of transportation but an emphatic statement about male identity, achievement, and success. If transportation were all that cars were about, a Ford Escort would do as well as a 'Vette. In the real world of commodities, however, nobody would mistake these two cars for each other: Their meanings are too distinct.

One of the first social scientists to remark on the role of commodities in modern life was Karl Marx. In his famous discussion of commodity fetishism, Karl Marx claimed that in a capitalist economy commodities weren't just useful things, they possessed another more mysterious kind of value. "The mysterious character of the commodity-form consists therefore simply in the fact that the commodity reflects the social characteristics of men's own labour as objective characteristics of the products of labour themselves" (Marx 1976:164-65). Commodities give to social relationships a physical form. In Marx's analysis, commodities consist of much more than just a set of useful features: They embody social relationships. But for Marx, this additional complexity applied only to commodities in a capitalist society.

Marx believed that under capitalism, relationships between human beings were distorted to appear as if they were relationships between things. The current sociological view of commodities under capitalism, however, is somewhat different. Rather than viewing commodities as *distorted* social relations, the embeddedness approach of this book conceptualizes the commodity as being both *dependent* on social relations and *constitutive* of social relations. Commodities depend for their very existence on systems of cultural meaning, but they also help create new meanings and reinforce social relationships. The complexities of the relationship between commodities and society are explored in the following section.

People whose job it is to sell commodities certainly appreciate the importance of symbolism. Marketing and advertising professionals devote considerable effort to shaping the symbolic meaning of commodities to sell more of them. The inventors of the Energizer Bunny, that stuffed toy animal powered by batteries that marches across the TV screen, employed a rich set of meanings and connotations that made it the centerpiece of an effective marketing campaign (Fowles 1996:1-8). Marketing professionals have even devised complex conceptual schemas with which to analyze the multiple meanings of commodities and how those vary from one culture to the next (de Mooij 1998:116-19). In some countries, for example, the horsepower of a car's engine is a highly salient feature, so effective advertising stresses an engine's power. But in other countries, horsepower really doesn't matter to consumers, so car advertisers focus on other features (de Mooij 1998:145-47).

In this chapter, we analyze the symbolic aspects of goods: how they acquire meanings, what meanings they possess, how such meanings are shaped, and the role these meanings play in the lives of consumers. These meanings concern social status, lifestyle, and self-image, among other things. They change over time and vary from one context to the next. Through the cultivation of a specific brand image, manufacturers try to manipulate the meanings their products possess (although they aren't always successful). What strategies do they use, and which ones work? Sometimes, commodities assume such importance in the lives and minds of people that we will talk about "consumerism." By historical standards, consumerism is a relatively recent occurrence (although perhaps not as recent as you think). How did consumerism emerge? What are its consequences?

The meanings of commodities are both powerful and pliable. They motivate the consumer to want to acquire a particular commodity: To drink Gatorade is to enjoy an association with superstar athlete Michael Jordan (to "be like Mike"), who has endorsed the product. A less emphatic meaning, or a less desirable association, would lead to fewer sales (suppose Gatorade was instead endorsed by a superstar sociologist such as Arthur Stinchcombe). And in some countries, the entire genre of celebrity endorsement simply doesn't work very well. Testimonial ads are common in the United States, Britain, and Germany but rarer in other countries (de Mooij 1998:162).

Indeed, meanings can change even as the physical properties of the commodity hold constant. Consider the different, and somewhat inconsistent, meanings of Listerine, which today is a nasty-tasting mouthwash that "kills germs by the millions." When first invented, the Listerine formula started out as a cure for athlete's foot and dandruff, not something you would normally consider putting in your mouth (Settle and Alreck 1986:101). And although Listerine hasn't changed, what it means and what you do with it has. Similarly, Pepsi-Cola started out as a beverage celebrated more for its medicinal qualities (it was supposed to help with digestion) than its taste. Pepsi's brand image, like Listerine's, has over time changed more substantially than the actual physical product.

The meaning of things can be surprisingly complex and nuanced, changing from one context to the next and subject to manipulation. This means we have to update simple notions of consumer sovereignty, a perspective that sees the economy as fundamentally driven by the autonomous preferences of consumers. It is simplistic to claim that manufacturers and distributors only satisfy the needs and meet the demands of consumers. They do not passively respond to consumer preferences. If the symbolic import of commodities can be deliberately shaped, through advertising for example, then consumer preferences also can be influenced. One sociologist regards advertising as part of the culture industry, whose job it is to "refram[e] meanings in order to add value to products" (Goldman 1992:5).

Meanings can be private or public, and most commodities involve a combination of both. Commodities involve varied associations with the symbolism of gender, status, class, ethnicity, and power, among other things. Their meanings may be rooted in relationships between particular people (consider, for example, the private meaning of an old bundle of dried flowers, originally used as a bridal bouquet, for a married couple) or relationships between groups of people (e.g., the meaning of the Statue of Liberty as a gift from the people of France to the citizens of the United States).

Meanings are not unimportant or epiphenomenal. The meaning of things plays a central role in modern capitalist economies. Such meanings influence who buys what commodities and why. They affect how commodities are advertised and marketed. They even help to determine the physical shape and color of commodities (consider how different men's and women's razors are, even though they are both used to remove body hair—a man's razor would never be colored pink). Modern markets are filled with meaning.

Things and Meaning

Consider a bar of soap, the kind you keep by the bathroom sink to wash your hands and face. How much meaning could such an innocuous object contain? While it may be tempting to answer "not much," or even "none," in fact, even soap can embody a rich set of symbols. Think about a particular brand of soap, perhaps the kind you can purchase at the Body Shop. By itself, Body Shop soap cleans like any other soap. But through some clever marketing, packaging, and advertising, the Body Shop immerses its soap in a complex set of messages about the environment, personal empowerment, and progressive politics. As they say at the Body Shop website on the Internet (http://www.the-body-shop.com), "We are committed to animal protection, environmental protection and respect for human rights." These meanings allow Body Shop customers to do more with soap than just clean their faces: By using these products, they can make a statement about what kind of person they are and what kind of politics they embrace.

The new Body Shop product line, Hemp, not only creates a single marketing theme that subsumes a whole range of products (consumers can use the soap, lip conditioner, moisturizer, and hand cream), but through the explicit reference to marijuana, it signals a rebellious 1960s revival, countercultural image attractive to young adults. Hemp soap, the Body Shop tells its customers, isn't just any soap: "Not only does hemp seed oil provide outstanding emollient qualities, it is also a star performer where the environment is concerned. Requiring minimal use of pesticides, herbicides, fertilisers and low-maintenance man-power, hemp is a 'plant from the past with hope for the future!'" Hemp soap is as good for a customer's self-image as it is for her complexion.

To suppose that people purchase Body Shop soap only because of how well it cleans their skin is to overlook the powerful image that comes with the soap. The image and symbolism is, strictly speaking, quite irrelevant to the physical task of removing dirt and dust from human skin. After all, the recyclable packaging and principled rejection of animal testing don't make the soap clean any better. But they do help to construct a message that certain consumers may find attractive. Different personal care products will involve different messages (some signal status, elegance, and sophistication rather than environmentalism—e.g., Chanel No. 5), but it is clear consumers are purchasing the message as much as the physical object.

How can we be sure of the importance of symbols? Imagine a new Body Shop product line and marketing campaign that changed the message but not the soap: "Aryan Nation Soap—Cleans and Whitens!" Perhaps the soap would come in a swastika shape rather than the familiar bar. Although containing the same ingredients and cleansing as well as ever, the new product would send a loud message that almost all consumers today would find morally objectionable, and they wouldn't buy it (German consumers in the 1930s might have felt differently). The political backlash would probably force the manufacturer to withdraw the product from the market.

Commodities acquire meaning not only because of what producers claim about them and how they are packaged but also by virtue of who sells them. Many ads for high-fashion garments or perfumes proudly announce which stores sell the goods. An ad for Guerlain perfume lists a set of high-status stores that carry it: Nordstrom, Bloomingdale's, Jacobson's, and Lord & Taylor. The prestige of the retail venue confers status on the commodity. Imagine what you might think of Guerlain perfume if it were sold "exclusively" at Wal-Mart, Target, or Sears! A high-status good should be sold only through high-status retail outlets: To do otherwise is to compromise the message.

Commodities such as soap, cosmetics, and so on, possess public meanings that their producers have deliberately cultivated. Other commodities have been imbued with a meaning that appears to be much more "personal" and "private." For instance, one ad says, "Being a Mom . . . It's never having a minute . . . yet always making a moment. Through a hug . . . a whisper. By just being there. It's giving your best. It's why you feel good about creamy Jif. It's made from the very best peanuts. . . . Hot roasted, to bring out more fresh roasted peanut taste than any other leading creamy brand. And nothing less will do. For more fresh roasted peanut taste, Choosy Moms Choose Jif" (*People Magazine*, August 31, 1998:17). The deeply personal relationship that moms have with their children has somehow gotten mixed up with peanut butter. The ad doesn't provide technical information on the nutritional aspects of Jif peanut butter, although one might argue that such information more accurately portrays exactly what Jif moms are feeding to their children. Rather, the ad suggests that being a good mom entails giving Jif to the kids. The ad is about the personal relationships of the consumer rather than the commodity itself. Motherhood is used to sell peanut butter.

In general, whether we consider food, beverages, personal care products, or automobiles, it is hard to think of a commodity sold to consumers that hasn't acquired some distinctive image or meaning. Even ads that provide seemingly technical information on the objective performance characteristics of a commodity are nevertheless trying to create a unique image. Consider products such as sports watches and sports cars. An ad may point out that a watch is waterproof to a depth of 600 feet below the surface or that a car can accelerate from 0 to 60 miles per hour in less than five seconds. Such ads focus on the extreme performance of the commodity as a way to create an association with excellence, high standards, and technical virtuosity.

These ads also invariably neglect to point out that most sports car owners drive their vehicles at an average speed of less than 30 miles per hour during rush hour traffic and that the capacity to accelerate so quickly is simply irrelevant in ordinary driving. Four-wheel drive sports utility vehicles cross parking lots more often than rivers and hills. Similarly, sports watch owners seldom get into water deeper than a swimming pool, so the capacity to resist water pressure that would crush a navy submarine doesn't really matter. But the potential performance of these commodities confers meaning, even if those capacities are never exploited in actual use.

The association of distinctive meanings with particular commodities gives to consumers the opportunity to embrace or acquire those meanings through the purchase of the commodity. To buy the good is to buy the meaning, so goods become a way to say things about oneself. By buying Jif peanut butter, a woman can make a statement about what kind of mother she is. She can feel good about herself. Ownership of Ralph Lauren clothing enables a man not only to possess khaki pants and woolen sweaters but also to acquire an easily recognized sense of style. Between grooming products, clothing, shoes, accessories, cars, tobacco products, and alcoholic beverages, consumers face a whole repertoire of commodities and messages: They can use these to tell the world what kind of a person they are or aspire to be.

Commodities as Gifts

The meaning of things matters not only as a way for people to express aspects of their own selves (their personalities, for example, or self-images) but also as an expression of relationships between selves (friendship between two people, for instance). Commodities can play an important role in designating and maintaining social relationships (Douglas and Isherwood 1978:60). Such expressions have a cumulatively substantial impact on the economy: Consider the commercial importance of Christmas. People purchase presents for their families and perhaps some close friends, but together, all the buying really adds up. Gift purchases during the winter holiday season make up a substantial proportion of retail sales and can make or break a U.S. retailer's annual bottom line. In 1990, American consumers spent $72 billion on Christmas purchases, an average of about $770 per household (Offer 1997:465).[1] The Christmas shopping season alone is bigger than the gross national product of many countries!

As gifts, things acquire a meaning by virtue of the kind of social relationship they reflect. What might be a "perfect" gift for one relationship is a catastrophic choice for another. And what sometimes makes a gift a failure is not that the recipient doesn't like the present but, rather, that the object given is "inappropriate" to the relationship between the giver and recipient: It means the "wrong thing" or sends the "wrong signal." For instance, a businesswoman who received a black silk bra and panties from a male business associate would probably become uncomfortable and reject the gift, not because she doesn't like beautiful underwear but because the gift is much too intimate to accept from a relative stranger. She would feel very differently about the same gift from a husband or fiancé.

Gifts must be "proportional" to the relationships in which they are embedded. Their meaning has to correspond to or be consistent with the nature and strength of the connection between the giver and receiver. Within a romantic relationship, for example, gifts tend to become more costly and more intimate as the relationship develops and deepens over time (Belk and Coon 1991). Gift giving and gift acceptance are not just about individual likes and dislikes but also about social relationships between individuals. The social meaning of a gift matters much more than its individual utility.

---

[1] Another study underscores the importance of Christmas. According to Cheal (1988:82), almost half of all the gifts given during the year were given at Christmas.

One telling indication of the importance of meaning for gifts is the role of money. Cash, as generalized purchasing power, can be used to buy anything. It is extremely useful. Yet however great its utility, money often performs poorly as a gift because it sends the wrong message. Suppose today is St. Valentine's Day, and you wish to give your sweetheart a special gift. First you think that spending $50 on a bouquet of red roses might be nice, but then it occurs to you that flowers are not very useful and that your girlfriend might prefer something else instead of roses. So you conclude that $50 cash would be a better gift. Wrong. Red roses symbolize romance, cash does not. Cash may be more useful, but it has the wrong meaning for a romantic relationship. On St. Valentine's Day, it makes a lousy gift.[2]

Consider another situation involving the favors that good neighbors might perform for each other. Such favors (lending a tool, helping to carry furniture, sharing flour, eggs, or sugar when needed) are like small gifts and generally incur an obligation to reciprocate: If your nice neighbor does something for you, you feel obliged to return the favor at some future opportunity. How should the recipient of a favor reciprocate? One study (Webley and Lea 1993) found that most people regarded money as an inappropriate payment for such favors and that they would rather compensate their neighbors in some other fashion. If friends invite you over for dinner, you are more likely to reciprocate by having them to dinner sometime in the future than by repaying them with cash. Sidebar 2.2 presents a recent ad that reflects the complexity of money in relation to gifts.

SIDEBAR 2.2

Selling Money

A recent MasterCard ad (see Exhibit 2.2) illustrates beautifully the uneasy place of money in gift giving. MasterCard makes a virtue of a necessity: The ad markets credit cards—a form of money. But it shows how plastic money can be used to obtain an experience beyond price. The text of the ad enumerates and gives the exact prices of all the things that a daughter purchased with her MasterCard: the plane tickets for herself and her mom, the train ride, pints of ale for the two of them. But all these gifts add up to something priceless: "finally understanding where your mother was coming from."

---

[2] For a discussion of the social constraints on money, see Zelizer (1993).

EXHIBIT 2.2

Gift giving in contemporary society is not something that happens only within the intimate relations of lovers, spouses, or family. Nor does it occur only within densely interlinked communities such as neighborhoods or small towns. Gifts are a common feature of American business life (and are even more important for business in places such as Japan). Salespeople use gifts and other forms of hospitality as a way to build and maintain relationships with their customers (e.g., business lunches and dinners). Business conventions are orgies of gift giving, with sales reps giving away free samples, T-shirts, hats, and other promotional items as a way to build goodwill with potential customers. As we will see in

Chapter 3 on networks, relationships are as important in business as they are in personal life. Consequently, gifts can be important for building relationships in business.

Consumerism

We have seen that commodities allow consumers to express their values and make public statements about self-image, social status, and personal identity. When used as gifts, commodities also enable people to express their feelings about relationships with others. Commodities can be used by their owners to align themselves with social groups and publicly declare their allegiance (consider how many students wear T-shirts, sweatshirts, or hats bearing the insignia of the college they attend). But why do this through the medium of purchasable things? Why not simply express these characteristics, values, and allegiances directly? After all, an individual could just as well express his or her personality by behaving in a particular way or through some creative act. To answer these questions, we must address the historical emergence of **consumerism** and why it is that so much personal expression is now channeled through the unending purchase of commodities.

Change is an important part of consumerism. Consumers' demands ebb and flow quickly and don't remain stable for long. What was fashionable or desirable last year is no longer fashionable this year, so all those who wish to remain current in their dress must purchase new wardrobes. Bell-bottom jeans were trendy in the late 1960s, became unfashionable during the 1970s and 1980s (so much so that no one would be caught dead wearing them), but are now making a comeback. Without such changes in fashion, people could simply buy the same kind of clothes (or cars or food etc.) for their entire lives. For no apparent reason, hems go up and down, lapels widen and shrink, collars wax and wane, and fabrics and colors change in ways that has no effect on the ability of clothes to keep their wearer warm and dry. Such change does, however, determine what styles are fashionable, and thus in great demand, and what are obsolete.

The Growth of a Consumer Society

Consumerism didn't appear instantaneously or completely at a given point in time. Rather, it has emerged piecemeal, developing more quickly in some parts of the world than in others and in some markets before others. Some of the key elements contributing to its emergence included a general rise in productivity, personal incomes high enough to afford more than just the bare necessities of life, and a willingness to put those higher incomes into more consumption rather than more leisure time (i.e., spend more rather than work less). Let us consider each of these key elements in turn.

In both agriculture and manufacturing, the U.S. economy enjoyed long-term productivity growth in the 19th and 20th centuries. It takes far fewer people today to mine a ton of coal, grow a bushel of potatoes, or forge a ton of steel than it did a hundred years ago. Increased productivity has allowed American workers to enjoy higher wages; not only do they produce more, they have more to spend. But this very success threatened to create a new problem: overproduction. Unless the demand for coal, wheat, and steel expanded along with the supply of these products, the increased efficiency would result in excessive supply; it would be too easy to produce too much of these things. Obviously, the overall demand for a product such as potatoes will expand along with the U.S. population, but the per capita demand cannot grow too much; after all, people can eat only so many potatoes before they get full. Similarly, there seems to be a ceiling on the amount of coal or steel households need.

The increased willingness and ability of American households to consume more helped to solve this rather fundamental problem. Productivity growth over the 19th and 20th centuries meant that fewer and fewer people could produce more and more goods. If demand didn't increase with supply, factories would develop excess capacity and fall idle. But with symbolic goods, demand becomes nearly limitless (Cross 1993). If people care deeply about having the latest car and if fashion governs car designs like it does clothing, then the demand for cars will be renewed with every new season (and model). Planned obsolescence through the steady introduction of innovations in technology and style (never-ending "improvements") means that consumers will always fall behind in the things they own and will have to "catch up" by purchasing new things (Marchand 1985:156).

The "meaningfulness" of commodities therefore serves a very useful purpose. If consumers acquire commodities only because of their physical utility, before too long the consumer has had enough. Demand is capped by a person's finite demands for whatever the commodity provides. The situation is rather like sitting down to dinner and eating: The capacity of a stomach sets a fixed limit on how much even a hungry person can eat. But if commodities instead offer symbolism and meaning, consumer appetites become nearly insatiable.

Clothing is purchased for its fashion more than its utility, and people discard unfashionable clothes long before they are worn out (indeed, secondhand clothing stores are filled with useful but out-of-fashion clothes). By annually updating the symbolism of clothes (this year's fashions replace last year's), the fashion industry ensures that the meaning of "trendy" or "fashionable" will always be changing, so people who wish to wear trendy clothing will always be heading back to the stores to buy more. Neither they nor their wardrobes can ever sit still.

One of the first places to witness a consumer boom was 18th-century England, where relative to preceding centuries, men, women, and children enjoyed access to a greater number of goods than ever before. The spending boom started, as one might expect, among the wealthy classes, who had the disposable income to devote to consumer goods. Of course, in the 18th century, people couldn't purchase consumer electronics, automobiles, or most of the other goods we associate with modern consumerism. But other kinds of goods reflected the concern for variety and timeliness that we now associate with "fashion."

Today, when we use the term fashion in ordinary language, we normally suppose it to apply to clothing. Of course, fashions and trends occur in many realms, not just in dress, but the common association between fashion and clothing may reflect the historical fact that clothes were among the first mass consumer products (McKendrick 1982:53). Beginning in the 18th century in England, standards for adult dress (including shoes, hats, and hairstyles) changed on an annual basis and clearly marked a distinction between those who were fashionable and those who weren't.

Dress in England during this period reflected more than just the personal or idiosyncratic preferences of the wearer for certain colors, fabrics, cuts of garments, length of hem, and so on. Then, as today, dress reflected membership in a social group, or aspirations thereto. Fashion is partly about fantasy (who you would like to be) and partly about reality (who you really are). The leading fashions were those of the aristocracy, who distinguished themselves from nonaristocrats on the basis of how they dressed: the expense of the materials, the beauty and style of the designs. Indeed, in earlier periods sumptuary laws actually stipulated who could wear what kinds of clothes: Only the elite were allowed to wear certain colors, fabrics, or styles, and more generally, personal appearance was legally regulated. In classical China, for instance, the color yellow was reserved for the Emperor alone. In the Roman Empire, only the Emperor or his family members could wear purple clothing (McKendrick 1982:37).

Aristocrats engaged in the kind of **conspicuous consumption** that affirmed not only a personal appreciation of fine objects but that also publicly signaled membership in an elite social group. And if the elite could be relied on to pursue distinction through consumption (and possessed both the taste and financial means to do so), others reliably attempted to emulate them. Thanks to a general rise in incomes, members of the middle class in 18th-century England had the disposable income necessary to ape the rich.[3] A small number of aristocrats set the fashion trend, and a much larger number of people of middling status tried to follow the trend, using fashion to express their social aspirations. It also helped that such a large proportion of the population lived in one big city, London. This geographic concentration made it easy for trends and fashions to get established. Some merchants deliberately cultivated wealthy patrons, knowing that if they adopted what the merchants had to sell, others would be sure to follow (McKendrick 1982:76-77). Even provincial newspapers regularly reported the latest in fashion news to readers outside London.

The consumer revolution involved changes in the demand for goods. But the effects were equally important on the supply side, for an enormous amount of trade, and a substantial amount of employment, was devoted to satisfying the expanded and ever-changing demand for consumer goods. The textile industry, which helped to meet the demands of fashion, employed many thousands of people in London alone. Importing cloth, weaving, sewing, dyeing, and tailoring were just some of the activities needed to meet demand (Earle 1989:21). Consumerism created jobs for many people.

This 18th-century pattern, in which consumption mirrored the status hierarchy of a society, has been re-created countless times. Consider the ways in which the social elite in the United States today consume goods (e.g., haute couture fashions, luxury automobiles, rarified wines and spirits, holidays at exclusive resorts) that signal their high status. Social climbers and those who aspire to distinction model their own consumption patterns after those of their social betters. Instead of haute couture, they buy designer label clothing off the rack. Instead of a Rolls Royce, they purchase a BMW or Mercedes Benz. The pattern of elite consumption followed by emulation sets off a never-ending dynamic in which the elite first consume exclusive goods to underscore their elite status and then the nonelite copy the elite. But as soon as they do so, to remain ex-

---

[3] Of course, emulation didn't necessarily operate in a simple or straightforward manner (see Weatherill 1986).

clusive, the elite are forced to change what they consume. Once everyone drinks imported beer (or wears designer jeans or has a digital watch or owns a stereo), it can no longer serve as a status good. To remain fashionable, fashion must always move on.

As this pattern unfolds, producers are in the enviable position of facing demand that is never fully satisfied. Black-and-white televisions were once prestige goods available only to a wealthy few. Now almost every American household has a TV, but rather than become satisfied, American consumers have come to demand more: color TVs, TV-VCR combinations, TVs with stereo sound, big-screen TVs, and so on. Consumerism involves demands that evolve over time and, consequently, the need for additional production continues.

Consumerism in the 18th century revolved around textiles and clothing, household items (furniture, kitchenware), and food (sugar, tea, coffee, chocolate). For instance, the average per capita consumption of sugar in England rose from about 6 pounds in 1700 to 24 pounds in the 1790s (Shammas 1993:182). Eighteenth-century England was probably the first place where edible luxuries (such as tea, coffee, and chocolate) became items of everyday consumption (Mintz 1993). Meat was a status good, and people higher up the social ladder simply ate more of it (Earle 1989:273).

Consumerism in the 20th century involves these items as well, but now includes a very different set of commodities, what economists term "consumer durables." This category includes more expensive items such as consumer electronics (TV, stereo, radio, VCR, home computer), cars, refrigerators, air conditioners, washers and dryers, microwave ovens, boats, and recreation and entertainment expenditures (vacations, sports, restaurants). Virtually all these commodities are subject to the same kind of annual changes in fashion that encourage consumers to buy new models, year after year. "New and improved" versions, complete with additional features, get produced every year and sold to consumers who eagerly seek the status associated with being fashionable.

Clothing continues to be a way to symbolize a variety of meanings: some associated with group membership, others with personal characteristics. One scholar has gone so far as to claim that modern American dress is virtually like a language: Its purpose is primarily communicative (Rubinstein 1995). Perhaps the most obvious example of the deliberate use of clothing to distinguish membership in groups is the uniform. Wearing distinctive and standardized clothing communicates that a person is a soldier, policeman, priest, nun, sailor, gang member, or nurse. Even without official uniforms, people can say a lot about themselves through their clothing. On ceremonial occasions, people often wear clothing that is manifestly symbolic (think what the whiteness of a bride's gown is supposed to signify and what it would mean if she wore a red dress on her wedding day). And of course, clothing continues to be suffused with gender differences.

One driving force behind the spread of consumerism has been the **commercialization** of major holidays. This has both encouraged widespread gift giving and connected it with the purchase of commodities. If it truly is the thought that counts, why do we spend so much money at Christmas buying the right gift for our loved ones? Why not just express the thought directly and not bother with commerce?

The commercialization of holidays didn't happen accidentally, or overnight. Some holidays, Christmas for example, preceded commercialization and were simply co-opted. Traditionally, the New Year had been the occasion for European aristocrats to give gifts. But in England and the United States during the 19th century, Christmas emerged as a distinct opportunity for gift giving, and the middle classes (as well as the merchants who sold to them) were eager to emulate their social betters. Both Santa Claus (a 19th-century invention) and the Christmas tree became key symbolic elements in seasonal patterns of gift purchasing and giving.

Other holidays, such as Valentine's Day, were transformed in meaning and expanded in importance. Originally, St. Valentine was just another Christian martyr, and his holiday in early 19th-century America was no special event. But starting in the 1830s and 1840s, this saint's day began to involve giving and receiving love messages written on fancy-colored paper. These came to be the mass-produced cards we know today, and as the holiday became more elaborate, confectioners promoted their goods as suitable offerings.

While some holidays were co-opted, holidays such as Mother's Day and Father's Day were practically invented in the 20th century by the greeting card, florist, and confection industries to promote sales of cards, flowers, and candy (Schmidt 1995). Whether through co-optation or invention, the overall effect was to make holidays an opportunity not only to celebrate with one's family and friends but also to purchase large quantities of consumer goods. The commercialization of public sentiment, and the overt use of these holidays for crass monetary purposes, often threatens to undermine the authenticity of the occasion; the true "spirit" of Christmas (or Easter, Hanukkah, etc.) isn't about material wealth. But holidays that were co-opted for commercial purposes, and even those that were invented for commercial purposes, nevertheless remain opportunities for the expression of genuine sentiment: Children can really express their love for their mothers even though Mother's Day was an invention.

Consumers and Debt

Another key factor in the rise of consumerism has been the invention and spread of new ways to help consumers purchase commodities they can't otherwise afford. For producers to sell their goods, consumers have to be able to buy. Purchases can be financed in three ways: out of income, from savings, or by going into debt. Rising incomes can generate increased spending, but rising savings entail reduced spending (to save for the future, one has to spend less now). Debt, however, allows people who do not have savings to spend more than their income.

In the 1920s, new forms of borrowing allowed many consumers to purchase durable goods and so unleashed a "consumer durables revolution" (Olney 1991). In the early 20th century, credit cards didn't exist. And banks, which were in the lending business, generally didn't make loans to consumers (rather, they lent their money to businesses). A consumer who wished to make a large purchase would have to save long enough to accumulate the necessary money and then pay cash. For a really big expense, such as buying a car, this meant consumers would have to save for a long time. In 1922, for example, a new Dodge automobile cost $980, or about 42% of an average household's annual disposable income. Given how much the typical household saved, it would take more than six years to accumulate enough to make the purchase in cash, even if the household devoted all its savings to buying the car (Olney 1991:102-5).

After World War I, spending in the United States on consumer durables (goods that typically last longer than three years) increased dramatically. American families were allocating more of their incomes toward purchasing major durable goods (such as cars, furniture, etc.), and their spending almost tripled in the first 20 years of this century. American families were also saving less, so more of their overall income went to consumption.

Many of these consumer durable goods were purchased with credit, as more and more Americans embraced a "buy now, pay later" strategy. Not surprisingly, consumer indebtedness rose from about 4.5% of annual income in 1900 to over 11% in 1939 (Olney 1991:92). Without the development of new ways for consumers to borrow to pay for their purchases, sales could not have grown as much as they did. During the 1920s, about 70% of all new car sales, 70% of furniture sales, 75% of radio sales, 90%

of pianos, and 80% of household appliances were purchased with credit (Olney 1991:95).

Early forms of consumer credit were tied to the purchase of specific items; sellers would let consumers borrow money only if they bought the seller's products. Later forms of consumer credit included the credit card, which could be used to purchase any item the consumer wished to buy. Such generalized credit gave an additional boost to spending for all types of products. Overall, the growth of all forms of consumer credit helped to finance the growth of consumerism.

Advertising

One especially important factor contributing to consumerism was the emergence of the advertising industry in the early 20th century. Large-scale advertising was used to mass market goods to consumers. Not only could more Americans afford to buy commodities (thanks to new creative financing), but their knowledge and perceptions of those commodities were actively shaped through advertisements. If modern commodities possess complex meanings, as we have argued earlier in this chapter, then those meanings are not left to chance. In many respects, modern advertising is chiefly concerned with the creation of suitable meanings and their attachment to commodities. Its ability to do this forces us to revise the picture offered by economists of a sovereign consumer whose tastes drive the market.

One way to measure the importance of image making to the success of a product is to consider the amount of money expended on marketing and promotion. Two alternative strategies can be used to increase sales: (1) invest in product improvements or (2) spend more on advertising. While manufacturers do alter their products, they spend as much money, if not more, advertising the improvements as they do making them in the first place. In the early 1990s, for example, about 40% to 50% of the price of a name brand cereal represented manufacturing costs. The rest of the price covered advertising, promotion, and profits (Bruce and Crawford 1995:253). This cost breakdown suggests that as a commodity, breakfast cereal is about one-half nutritional reality and one-half image. The same is true of perfume: Most of the price goes to cover packaging and marketing rather than to the cost of manufacturing the actual perfume itself.

According to Olney's figures (1991:137-38), total business spending on all forms of advertising grew substantially in the early 20th century. From about $200 million in 1880, this figure rose to $542 million in 1900, then to $2.935 billion in 1920, and reached $3.426 billion in

1929, just before the stock market crash that marked the beginning of the Great Depression. Not only did advertising increase dramatically, but its content changed. Rather than provide detailed descriptions of the particular commodity being promoted, advertising increasingly focused on the beneficial consequences for the purchaser: youthful appearance, happy family life, attractiveness to members of the opposite sex, and so on.

Through advertising, producers hoped to create a **brand image,** a set of stable meanings attached in the minds of consumers to a particular commodity. Even before conjuring up the image, however, producers had to create a brand name for their goods. The number of brands and names registered with the U.S. Patent Office grew from 121 in 1871 to over 10,000 by 1906. At the start of the 1920s, this number had climbed to 50,000 (Norris 1990:19). Soap was no longer just generic soap; it was Ivory Soap or Pears' Soap (or in the 1990s, Body Shop soap). And having been given a brand name, it could also receive a distinctive brand image. Even natural products such as fruit were branded and promoted through national ad campaigns: Oranges weren't just oranges anymore; they were Sunkist (Marchand 1985:5).

Once branded with an image, it became easier for commodity producers to avoid direct comparisons and thus price competition with their business rivals. Advertising helped to differentiate products so that in the minds of consumers, there really were no substitutes. So important did these national brand images become that even during World War II, when because of wartime rationing many firms had little to sell to the mass market, companies still advertised to maintain these images (Pollay 1985:32).

Brand images and brand loyalties can be surprisingly durable. Many of the leading brands of 1925 (e.g., Kellogg cereal, Kodak cameras, Goodyear tires, Campbell soups, Wrigley chewing gum) are still around in 1998 (Olsen 1995:257). And brand names are easily recognized: "Aunt Jemima," "Betty Crocker," the "Pillsbury Doughboy," and "Colonel Sanders" are well-known even though they aren't actual persons. Many consumers can recognize or recite from memory product phrases such as "Just Do It," "Snap, Crackle, Pop," "We Build Excitement," and "Breakfast of Champions." Consumers become loyal to brands and will purchase the same brand year in and year out, often passing their loyalties on to their children. In a recent study, brands were ranked by their "consumer loyalty rating," with Gerber (the baby food company) coming out on top, followed by Nike, Kodak, Tylenol, and AT&T (*Advertising Age,* October 5, 1998:3).

Firms make substantial investments in the brand images of the products they sell. In 1997, General Motors, for example, spent a total of $2.23 billion on advertising to sell its cars. Procter & Gamble, manufacturer of numerous consumer products, spent $1.7 billion on advertising (*Advertising Age*, July 13, 1998:S2). McDonald's Corporation spent $580 million in 1997 just to sell hamburgers. Taken together, the top 10 companies advertising the most (including General Motors, Procter & Gamble, Disney, Sears, Johnson & Johnson, and other well-known companies) spent over $10 billion and over $11 billion in 1996 and 1997, respectively.

Product differentiation denotes the process whereby advertisers distinguish their own products from the substitutes available in the market. Salt is salt, for example, so anyone's salt is as good as anyone else's. But the Morton Salt Company wants consumers to believe that Morton salt is different from and better than the other brands of salt that a consumer can purchase. Frequently, the differences between brands are only in the eyes of the beholders. In blind taste tests, beer drinkers often can't taste the difference between their preferred brand and those of the competition (Twitchell 1996:125). Even lifelong devotees of Budweiser, for example, have a hard time distinguishing it from other mainstream brands such as Miller, Michelob, and Old Style.[4] So what does differentiate these products from each other? Advertising and the brand images it creates. Commodities are often differentiated much more on the basis of their image and meaning than their physical or performative aspects (see Sidebar 2.3 on product differentiation).

Virtually all consumer goods have been "branded." No matter how homogeneous the actual commodity (sugar, salt, and aspirin are all pretty much undifferentiated), the creation of a brand image allows the producer to differentiate the product and give it a perceptible uniqueness. Today, even prescription drugs are branded, as drug companies try to create a distinctive image that will encourage patients to ask their doctors to prescribe a particular drug (*Advertising Age*, August 24, 1998:19). Although by law patients are not allowed to choose their own prescription drugs (that is up to the doctor, who should prescribe whatever is best given the patient's medical condition), branding can still give drug sales a valuable boost.

---

[4] So as not to pick unfairly on beer drinkers, it should be pointed out that in blind taste tests given in the 1940s to breakfast cereal salespeople, even those who sold Wheaties for a living couldn't tell the difference between it and rival whole-wheat cereals (Bruce and Crawford 1995:89). Cigarette smokers also have a hard time distinguishing their own brand from others.

SIDEBAR 2.3

Product Differentiation

Product differentiation is a strategy that companies use to reduce the level of competition they face in the market. An industry with a large number of companies that produce identical goods approximates perfect competition. In such a market, buyers need only pay attention to the price, because the goods offered for sale are perfect substitutes for each other. Firms in highly competitive markets must slash their prices and consequently don't earn high profits.

To avoid head-to-head competition with a large number of rivals, companies often introduce small changes to differentiate their product from that of the competition. Such product differentiation means that goods are only imperfect substitutes for each other, so buyers can no longer make direct price comparisons. Often, these small differences have more to do with the symbolism of a product, or its brand image, than with its physical aspects.

Chemically, aspirin is acetylsalicylic acid. In other words, all aspirin is physically the same. But drug companies coat their pills, color their pills, flavor them, shape them into caplets, add buffering elements, and so in various ways differentiate the product into Anacin, Bufferin, and all the other brand name versions of aspirin. Once differentiated, consumers have to evaluate features, flavors, and so on rather than just perform a strict price comparison.

Early advertising tended to promote products from five industries: food, chemicals (including soap and cosmetics), automobiles, tires, and tobacco. At first, the general theme of food advertising, for example, stressed the pure and unadulterated quality of the ingredients. Purity is still mentioned, but as the example of the peanut butter commercial mentioned earlier suggests, more complex messages pertaining to social relationships and motherhood get represented in contemporary food advertising. Some prepared foods are today marketed around the theme of "home cooking," and the idea that good moms cook for their families. Yet prepared foods substitute for cooking from scratch (which is why working parents purchase prepared foods in the first place), so to preserve the home-cooking image, manufacturers leave some elementary cooking steps for the consumer to perform at home (e.g., stir vegetables into the prepared sauce or add meat to the prepared mix). The image of home cooking is preserved and can be used to market the product.

More generally, ads began to focus less on the commodity itself and more on the benefits they would provide to the consumer. These included psychological benefits (you will feel better or more beautiful if you use a certain type of makeup), social benefits (you will enjoy higher status, better relationships, a happier family life if you purchase this car), and physical benefits (your health will improve with the use of vitamins). Printed ads relied less on text (written words) and more on images (either artwork or, later on, photographs) to convey their messages, and they became bigger (Pollay 1985:25, 28).

Appealing to the vanity of consumers is one way to market goods. Some goods can be enjoyed "properly" only by a "sophisticated" or "knowledgeable" consumer. For example, no one is born knowing how to properly mix and drink a dry martini or how to serve champagne. Liquor ads frequently emphasize the fact that only those who possess the requisite knowledge, training, or experience can properly consume these commodities. These commodities are not just for anyone, the ads suggest, but only for the few with rarified taste and sophistication (Appadurai 1986:41). The appearance of exclusivity can be a powerful marketing angle. Those who aspire to good taste but don't quite reach it are sanctioned. People with more money than good taste are condemned as "nouveau riche"—consumers whose financial means exceed their ability to make discerning choices in the marketplace (LaBarbera 1988).

The meanings that consumers care about evolve over time. As Americans have become more environmentally aware over the last 30 years, advertisers have discovered a new angle for promoting their products. Green marketing is now so common that how-to books have been written about it (e.g., Ottman 1993). It involves the attachment of new and valued meanings ("environmentalism," "nature-friendly") to commodities. The Body Shop is especially good at green marketing, but they aren't the only ones doing it. Plastic and paper packaging, for instance, often specifies that it is recycled or recyclable or both. Food products are touted as "100% natural" or without "artificial ingredients." In 1991, McDonald's restaurants made a well-publicized shift from polystyrene clamshell containers for its burgers to a combined paper-plastic wrap, because consumers perceived polystyrene to be environmentally unfriendly. Because McDonald's meals generate so much trash, McDonald's wisely decided to improve its image even though the new paper-plastic wraps were technically not recyclable, unlike the polystyrene. The perception of greenness mattered more than the fact of greenness.

Advertisers often displayed considerable facility in adapting their claims to the market status of the goods they promoted. Fleischmann's yeast, for instance, was used as an ingredient for cooking homemade bread. Yet more and more people in the early 20th century were buying their bread from stores or bakeries, so consumer demand for yeast declined. To boost sales, the producer of Fleischmann's yeast hired the J. Walter Thompson advertising agency to come up with a different marketing strategy. No longer the "Soul of Bread," the Thompson agency first turned yeast into an important source of vitamins with significant health benefits. Shortly thereafter, the advertising agency transformed yeast into a natural laxative (Marchand 1985:16). Repositioning yeast helped increase sales.

Similarly, when Lucky Strike cigarettes were first advertised in the 1920s, they were promoted as being good for the throat of the smoker. Celebrity endorsers recommended them for throat protection. Such a claim would seem ridiculous now and would serve only to remind the viewer of the ad that cigarette smoking is bad for the health. Cigarette advertising today says almost nothing about cigarettes per se, alluding instead to the supposed social and psychological benefits of smoking.

Many commodities were promoted as creative solutions to the problems faced by consumers. But the real creativity on the part of advertisers was in the invention of problems that their product was supposed to solve. Fear of dandruff and halitosis (bad breath) were used to promote shampoo and mouthwash. The growing list of problems for consumers to worry about included bromodosis (foot odor), homotosis (unattractive home furnishings), and acidosis (sour stomach). Advertisers were inventing problems to correspond with the manufacturers who provided "solutions" (Marchand 1985:20).

Products often acquire visibility and meaning by virtue of their connection with celebrity endorsers. Through advertising, the visibility and status of the endorser gets transferred to the commodity that he or she has endorsed. The endorser may not possess expert knowledge about the commodity and may not even use the commodity, but celebrity status nevertheless possesses value in the marketplace.

The person who today best exemplifies the marketability of celebrities is Michael Jordan. Jordan earned vast sums of money playing basketball, but he made even more off the court doing product endorsements. He has endorsed famous brand names such as Coke, Nike, Chevrolet, and McDonald's. But over the course of his career, Jordan has also endorsed, among other things, gum, cookies, erasers, tablecloths, rulers, shower curtains, soap dishes, key chains, and golf club covers (Gates 1998:48). Some of these commodities arguably have something to do with his great basketball skills (e.g., Nike athletic shoes), but others have nothing to do with what Jordan does or knows about. In such cases, the connection between the commodity and the endorser works at a purely symbolic level. Nevertheless, the large sums Jordan earns from endorsements demonstrate that purely symbolic connections can provide a powerful motivation for consumers to buy.

Diversity and Consumerism

American consumers, like consumers everywhere, are not a homogeneous group of people: They do not all want the same things, they do not all respond similarly to the same messages. At first, advertising as a profession was dominated by urban middle-class white men, who simply ignored black consumers (Marchand 1985:64). Indeed, blacks were seldom even represented in ads except in subordinate roles (e.g., as servants, cooks, railway porters, etc.). They also targeted their ads at an audience much more "middle class" than the average American (Marchand 1985:78). As advertisers became increasingly sophisticated in their understanding of consumer audiences, however, they began to target some groups more than others. They recognized the "demographics" of the U.S. population, so some ads speak more to men than to women or to African Americans than to whites. Hispanics, too, have become a demographic group recognizable to advertisers. Some advertising firms even specialize in marketing to Hispanics (*Advertising Age*, August 24, 1998:S1).

Many commodities have a gendered quality. There are clothes for men and clothes for women. There are almost no generic ungendered "clothes." There are cigarettes for men and cigarettes for women, personal grooming products for men and personal grooming products for women. The gendered quality of goods matters more to men than women, in the sense that men will generally not use "female" goods, but women will use "male" goods. That is, for example, women will smoke Marlboro cigarettes, but men won't smoke Virginia Slims, because they are too feminine. Sometimes, to get men to use or buy certain types of commodities, they have to be stripped of their feminine connotations. When a man uses an aftershave lotion or a "smoother," he is essentially using a face moisturizing cream, but to call it literally "face moisturizing cream" would seem too feminine, and men wouldn't use it. The commodity might be useful, but it would have the wrong gender meaning. Thus, the product is labeled a smoother and is explicitly associated with the masculine shaving ritual to remove the feminine connotations. Similarly, calling something an aftershave rather than a perfume makes it palatable for men, even though aftershaves and perfume are both alcohol-based olfactory cosmetics.

Male identity is something marketers have to be aware of to sell successfully. To sell boxed fruit drinks to blue-collar, working-class men, it was necessary to eliminate any suggestion that this was a kiddies' drink. The change was very simple; marketers dumped the straw and added a pull tab so that men could "gulp" their drink. Pulling the tab and gulping down the apple juice was seen as more manly than sipping the apple juice through a plastic straw. Constructing a more "macho" image for the product was largely a matter of different product packaging. The product remained the same.

Marketing to African Americans may have been limited early on, but advertisers eventually came to see the error of their ways. During the 1940s, 1950s, and 1960s, major U.S. corporations made increasing use of media with a black audience (e.g., newspapers or magazines with a predominantly black readership). To do this successfully, firms had to be sensitive to the feelings of African Americans (witness the advice offered in 1943 to white firms that wanted to sell their goods to blacks [Weems 1998:32-33]). Particularly during the 1950s and 1960s, black consumers were willing to use their purchasing dollars, or to withhold them, for political purposes. Firms that segregated customers by race or that discriminated against minorities could be subject to a boycott by African American consumers (Weems 1998:61-63). Black consumers have distinctive tastes, a fact that can be exploited by advertisers. For instance, middle-class blacks tend to consume more cognac and brandy than other consumers. Consequently, the pages of Ebony magazine have more ads for Remy Martin brandy than are found in other comparable publications. Similarly, athletic sportswear (both shoes and garments) receives heavy exposure in advertising aimed at urban minorities (Nightingale 1993:141-42).

Advertisers have perhaps performed better with respect to women. For some time, the central role played by women (as wives or mothers) in household consumption has been obvious. Women rather than men make many of the purchasing decisions, and consequently, those who wish to sell household goods, food, and so on target women as their audience. Women are also more involved in gift-giving activities such as birthdays and Christmas (just think of who keeps track of birthdays in your household or who maintains the Christmas card mailing list). Women make most of the purchasing decisions needed to meet the consumption needs of the household, but they also participate more in gift acquisition and exchange (see Caplow 1982; Fischer and Arnold 1990).

Consumerism and Globalization

We have seen that advertisers use systems of cultural meaning to sell their products. But what happens when products are sold where markets are embedded in a totally different set of cultural meanings? Given the fame of Michael Jordan around the planet, the fact that one can dine at a McDonald's restaurant in New York City, Paris, Beijing, or Moscow, and the near-universal appeal of Levi's blue jeans, it is easy to believe that product brands are being globalized along with the rest of the economy (see Chapter 7). But going from one country to another means going from one culture and language to another, and meanings and images don't always translate well. The spread of McDonald's around the world doesn't necessary mean the emergence of a single world consumer culture.

Perhaps the most obvious example of the kinds of problems faced in trying to market goods across national borders is the purely linguistic one of the meaning of names. The Chevy Nova, produced by GM, was a popular economy car with a well-established brand image. But when trying to sell it in Latin America, GM faced the problem that the name Nova sounded like "no va," Spanish for "it doesn't run." As a brand name, Nova simply wouldn't sell in Spanish.

Such linguistic difficulties are only the beginning, however. Selling goods abroad forces advertisers to confront quite profound cultural differences in the meaning of things. Even firms that have enjoyed successful international expansion have had to deal with these complexities. McDonald's, for example, had a total of 18,380 restaurants worldwide in 1995, of which 7,012 (38%) were located outside the United States (Watson 1997b:3). McDonald's possesses a very strong corporate image and prides itself on making the same food the same way all over the world. Yet its expansion overseas into places such as Asia has forced McDonald's to deal with national variations in the cultural meaning of food, dietary taboos, norms of civility, rituals of childhood, and table manners.

McDonald's has had to adjust its American-style cuisine to local preferences and food restrictions. For example, McDonald's restaurants in India substitute mutton for beef in their hamburgers because of Hindu prohibitions against the consumption of beef. They also offer Vegetable McNuggets for India's many vegetarians (Watson 1997b:23).

McDonald's has also had to adjust the interactional scripts it normally imposes on restaurant workers. In the United States, McDonald's staff members are supposed to smile at customers and be unfailingly polite in their dealings with the public (Leidner 1993). They are even supposed to follow scripts (as in "Hello, welcome to McDonald's. May I take your order?") in conversation with customers. Yet these scripts are not always culturally appropriate in other parts of the world. In East Asia, smiles are reserved for personal friends and family, not for the general public. A generic smile, perhaps the hallmark of fast food staff in the United States, gets interpreted as disrespect in Hong Kong (Watson 1997a:90-91). General smiling is not the norm, and McDonald's has had to adjust its staff training accordingly.

The birthday party is one way in which American families traditionally celebrate the growth and maturation of their children: On the yearly anniversary of a child's birth, the parents throw a party complete with guests, presents, and a birthday cake. Yet this tradition didn't exist in most parts of East Asia (Watson 1997b:19). Part of the McDonald's strategy in marketing its foreign-tasting food to Asians has been to target children (they have the fewest food prejudices and can acquire a "taste" for McDonald's hamburgers that will last a lifetime) and in particular to cultivate birthday parties as a new "tradition." In Hong Kong, for example, McDonald's offers a "party package" to parents that includes food, gifts and toys for the children, and a hostess who will lead party games and supervise entertainment (Watson 1997a:103-4). The birthday party becomes a celebratory occasion with the birthday child, and McDonald's, at the center. This marketing strategy makes even more sense in mainland China, where the government policy of one-child families means that there are many single children who have four doting grandparents who are more than happy to spoil their grandchild with trips to restaurants (Yan 1997:62).

In the United States, a typical McDonald's meal reflects the classic meat-and-potatoes model for Western food. The patty in the hamburger provides the meat, and the french fries supply the potatoes. Americans feel they can get a complete meal at McDonald's, including a main dish, a side dish, and drinks. Traditional Chinese conceptions of what constitutes a meal differ from this model, so to the Beijing clientele, McDonald's looks like a place to get snack food, not a real meal. Consequently, Chinese customers complain that McDonald's food is not very filling (Yan 1997:45-47), and customers feel obliged to get their "real" meal elsewhere. In Japan, hamburgers are considered snack food because of the absence of rice, the defining characteristic of a traditional Japanese meal (Ohnuki-Tierney 1997:168). Nevertheless, McDonald's remains an attractive place because of its fashionably "Western" image.

In a similar manner, French cooking has been fashionable in the United States for many decades, the very embodiment of high status, even though no one would ever want to make pâté de foie gras part of a regular diet (see Levenstein 1989). Dramatic changes in culinary meaning have occurred as food was introduced into the United States: What was ordinary fare for a southern Italian peasant became trendy nouvelle Italian cuisine sought out eagerly by American yuppies in the 1990s.

Conclusion

In common parlance, the term materialist is often used in a slightly derogatory fashion to refer to someone who likes to acquire and own many things. Yet, ironically, what makes commodities attractive to consumers is their symbolic rather than their material aspects. Consumers purchase meanings with their money. From the standpoint of the economy, one of the great things about symbols and meanings is that one can never be completely sated. If people purchased things only for their utilitarian value and if they didn't care about fads, fashions, and social emulation, the market would have been saturated long ago and we would face a crisis of demand (too many goods supplied and not enough demand for them). It is possible, for example, for a person to increase his or her expenditure on watches 100-fold. By switching from a Timex watch to a Rolex, the consumer acquires a higher-status good that costs a lot more but that probably doesn't tell time any better. But try increasing individual potato consumption 100-fold; no one can eat that much starch. Today, there is little symbolism or meaning associated with potatoes, and consequently, consumption reaches a maximum beyond which it is difficult to go. Without symbolism or fashion, consumption can keep pace with increased production for only so long.

The kinds of meanings that get attached to commodities draw on a small set of recurrent themes: social status, attractiveness, gender, age, social relationships, ethnicity, group membership. These core meanings get deployed in different ways as they are connected to different commodities (e.g., what makes a sports car "masculine" is very different from what makes a shaver "masculine"). Consumers easily recognize such meanings, for they are deliberately created by advertisers, marketers, and producers. But advertisers cannot devise new meanings for commodities entirely out of thin air; they have to rely on preexisting symbols, values, and cultural traditions. The situation is analogous to speech: People can say something new (utter a new sentence) but only on the basis of preexisting rules of grammar.

Today, people buy goods, either for their personal use or to give as gifts, because the associated cultural meanings are attractive or appropriate or both. The world of commodities is filled with tangible things connected to intangible meanings. Although the latter cannot be seen, smelled, or poked, they constitute an important motivation for consumer behavior. Thanks to the symbolism, buying fragrance means more than just smelling nice: It involves the adoption of a certain lifestyle, the assertion of a distinctive personality, and the public confirmation of group membership.

Physical objects have possessed meaning in all human societies and throughout history. What distinguishes the modern world is that the meaningful things people use in their lives are bought and sold on markets, and those who use the things are rarely the same people who made them. Furthermore, these meanings are shaped deliberately so that even more things get bought and sold. The rise of consumerism meant that people enacted their social identities, managed their relationships with each other, and lived their lives through the medium of commodities. The subsequent rise of an advertising industry and the advent of mass marketing meant that what these commodities represented didn't depend solely on the needs, wants, and demands of consumers but also on the desire of producers to sell more commodities.

Consumers aren't sovereign in any simple fashion; their autonomous tastes don't dictate what producers produce. But neither are producers sovereign. However much producers try to influence the desires of consumers and however clever the advertising and memorable the marketing, consumers sometimes just don't buy what producers want them to.

Two factors offset the power of advertising and marketing over consumers. First, ad campaigns seldom unfold in a vacuum. The seductive and convincing claims that Producer Z makes about her product get offset by the equally seductive claims that Producer X makes about her competing product. For example, the claim that Beck's beer best embodies sophisticated European taste confronts the contrary claim, made by a competitor, that Heineken beer is in fact the true manifestation of European sophistication. On their own, both claims, when suitably posed in a clever marketing campaign, may seem compelling. But the head-to-head confrontation of the two makes it easier for consumers to see through the hype and still make a choice.

In addition, effective advertising works only against a backdrop of preexisting and culturally specific meaning. This means that the kinds of appeals that help McDonald's sell hamburgers in the United States don't necessarily work in Taiwan or Japan. And however good advertisers are at manipulating beautiful images of their products, it is much harder to manipulate national culture.

3

Networks in the Economy

Recent college graduates are fond of saying that they have joined the "real world" after their four (or more) years of university education. Getting a job is a central part of joining this real world, and such jobs are obtained after being "on the job market." College seniors learn the art of the résumé, and scan newspapers, employment bulletins, and other publications looking for a job opening that suits them. The job market is discussed almost as if it were a distinct place where employers could meet up with unemployed college graduates whom they had never before met and hire the ones they needed and liked. Indeed, corporate employers often set up brief meetings with graduating college seniors to interview and evaluate them as prospective employees.

But how in fact do college graduates get jobs in the real world? Or more generally, how does anyone get a job? If we pay less attention to how people *talk* about the job market and focus more on the actual processes through which employers match up with employees, we find that labor markets are less anonymous and much more socially structured than one might expect. Prospective employees rarely walk into an employer's office "off the street" and get a job offer. Usually, their approach to an employer involves some combination of sponsorship, brokering, introduction, or prior connection. In other words, employees link up with employers through social networks. Job seekers might hear about a job opening through a friend or the friend of a friend. They might secure an interview because some family member has put in a good word. Or perhaps a member of their college fraternity or sorority works for a corporation, so they get access through college networks.

Labor markets are structured by various kinds of social networks: friends, kin and family, university alumni, formal organizations such as fraternities and sororities, neighbors, and informal acquaintances. Some employers, for instance, will deliberately use their current workforce to recruit new workers by asking their workers if they have any hard-working friends or relatives who need a job. The employer may never have to advertise a job opening publicly. Thus, both prospective employers and prospective employees mobilize these networks on the one hand to hire new employees and on the other to get a job.

In this chapter, we will discuss the role of **networks** and *relationships* in all kinds of markets. Such relationships exist at many different levels, ranging from personal friendships between individuals to formal joint ventures among corporations to diplomatic trade agreements between different countries. Many different kinds of relationships exist at each level, and they can vary in quality and intensity. For example, kinship and friendship are two distinct types of relationship at the individual level, and each entails a different set of expectations and obligations. Intensity varies as well. Two persons can be extremely close friends, pretty good friends, or just friends. They can be close relatives (e.g., siblings) or distant kin (second cousins twice removed).

Similarly, corporations can have a variety of relationships with each other: interlocking directorates, joint-venture agreements, equity ties, loans, research and development (R&D) partnerships, collaborative manufacturing arrangements, and so on. All of these different types of intercorporate relationships can vary in intensity. Loans can be big or small. Firms can own many or few of each other's shares. R&D partnerships can involve big budgets or little ones. Collaborative arrangements can be set up for the short term or the long run.

If one reads only introductory economics textbooks, it is tempting to conceive of markets as amorphous and anonymous places where people and firms transact. One can imagine competitive markets as involving a kind of price-cutting Hobbesian war of all against all: Everyone focuses on the bottom line and adjusts the prices and quantities of what they buy and sell to maximize profits. In fact, as we will see, markets are structured at both the individual and organizational levels by networks of relationships. Relationships introduce "stickiness" into the market: Economic transactions unfold over the long term, not just the short term. And transactions involve reciprocities, obligations, trust, and mutual understandings. What people do as individuals, and what firms do as organizations, depends very much on the kinds of networks in which they are embedded. One cannot understand economic behavior without understanding social context.

Each particular interpersonal or intercorporate relationship involves two parties (they are bilateral), but an entire network consists of the whole set of relationships among all parties. Economic networks structure a market, or an economy, in a way that is very different from the ordinary economist's meaning of market structure. The latter term is used to distinguish perfectly competitive markets from monopolies, monopsonies, or oligopolies. When economists discuss market structure, they refer to the number of buyers and sellers in the market (and the ease of entry and exit) rather than to the specific relationships between them. Market structure means something very different for a sociologist.

We will argue that the way markets are structured, in the sociological sense, affects how markets behave. To understand a particular market, one needs to know about the buyers and sellers (how many there are, etc.), the kind of commodity being sold, the way the market is regulated, and so on. But a sociologist would add to this list the social relationships between buyers and sellers.

For example, foreign firms often have a difficult time penetrating the Japanese domestic market. One reason for this has to do with how the Japanese economy is structured. Many of the largest Japanese corporations are organized into multiorganizational groupings and networks termed *keiretsu*. Member corporations are linked through loans, shareholdings, joint projects, corporate directors, and other, more informal, ties. Member firms strongly favor trading with each other rather than with outsiders. That is, if a *keiretsu*-member corporation needs additional inputs from its suppliers, it will look first to the *keiretsu*-member supplier. This kind of relationship-based favoritism makes it extremely difficult for foreign non-*keiretsu*-member firms to break into Japanese markets and sell their goods (Gerlach 1992). The obstacles faced by foreign firms can be explained only if one understands the intercorporate networks and relationships that link together Japanese firms.

Networks also matter at the individual level. People use their social networks to gather all kinds of information about job openings, market opportunities, new products, what the competition is up to, what their customers want, and so on. They also use networks to secure favors. In this second capacity, relationships are used not so much as channels of information but as clusters of reciprocal obligations and responsibilities. Someone who is a true friend usually feels obliged to assist his or her friends if they need it. More extreme forms of assistance can shade into nepotism and even corruption, but there are many ways to help out. These personal connections are not uniformly advantageous. If one is applying for a job with a firm, it helps to have a good friend "on the inside." Such friendship benefits the applicant but hurts all those without such a friend. As well, friendship imposes costs as well as providing advantages: Sometimes your friends help you, but at other times you are obliged to help them out.

Wherever networks play a role in the economy, whether at the individual or the corporate level (or somewhere in between), it becomes important to understand where such networks come from. What pattern do they follow? How do network links form? How are they sustained over time? Furthermore, individuals and corporations are usually embedded in multiple networks at the same time. For example, a person may have one network of friends, another network of kin, and yet another network of co-workers. One of these networks may have a greater effect than the others for different economic outcomes, and there may be varying degrees of overlap among them. Figuring out why some networks matter more than others is part of the puzzle.

What Is a Network?

Considered most abstractly, networks consist of sets of relationships, ties, or links between things. For our purposes, these things are economic actors of one stripe or another: individual persons, firms, formal organizations, and so on. There are many different types of relationships, which can vary in a number of different ways. Links vary in their strength (e.g., mere acquaintances vs. intimate friends), their degree of formalization (explicit contractual agreements vs. implicit understandings), and duration (short-term vs. long-term relationships). One can also distinguish between direct and indirect ties (consider the difference between friends and friends of friends). Networks exist at different levels (personal, corporate, national), and these multiple levels can affect each other (e.g., a salesperson's income depends on individual-level customer networks but also on firm-level relationships to creditors).

Whatever their characteristics, network connections matter because they involve a relationship. Relationships entail mutual obligations and expectations, a fuller sense of trust and reciprocity, greater flexibility and give-and-take, and so on. For instance, to be someone's brother isn't simply a genealogical connection; it also involves the obligations that family members have to each other. One is more likely to be able to call on a brother for help, information, and resources. You trust your brother and vice versa. People do favors for their brothers because, in the long run, they expect that their brothers will reciprocate and do favors for them.

Sociologists have been studying various kinds of social networks for many decades and have developed a number of useful analytic techniques (Wasserman and Faust 1994). Sociology offers a general vocabulary with which to speak about networks. Some of the concepts refer to the global features of entire networks whereas others characterize the position of particular persons or firms within the network. Globally, one might wish to know how centralized a network is and whether or not it is divided into subgroups. Exhibit 3.1 illustrates the difference between a centralized and a decentralized network, and Exhibit 3.2 presents a network made up of three subgroups.

Sociologists distinguish between dense networks (in which there are many links between the members) and sparse ones (in which there are few). Researchers also determine the position of particular individuals within the network. Within a friendship network, one might want to know whether a person is at the center of the group or on the periphery. (In Exhibit 3.1, Person A is more centrally positioned than Person B.) In friendship networks, central persons often have higher social status than marginal persons. It is sometimes important to be able to classify people into the different network subgroups. (In Exhibit 3.2, Persons C and D are in the same subgroup but in a different one from E. Person F occupies an intermediary position between groups.)

Why Networks Matter

Networks matter because they affect economic performance. Firms can enjoy higher profits and people can have better careers by virtue of the types of networks in which they are embedded. Brian Uzzi's (1996, 1997) research on the New York garment industry illustrates the kind of firm-level benefits that particular kinds of networks can bestow. The garment industry is populated by many small firms that perform highly specific tasks. Clothing manufacturers do very little work themselves: They mostly contract it out to specialist firms and then coordinate the specific operations. Thus, for example, fabric is sent out to a cutting contractor to be cut according to patterns created by a grading contractor. The cut fabric then goes to a sewing contractor who sews it (Uzzi 1997:39-40). In effect, the manufacturer sits at the middle of a network of contractors, coordinating and monitoring their specialized activities.

Exhibit 3.3 gives a schematic representation of the connections a typical manufacturer (also known as a "jobber") has with its contractors. With so many interconnected firms, managers in the garment industry spend a considerable amount of their time managing relationships with other firms.

Uzzi argues that firms relate to each other in two different ways: They can have "arm's-length" or "embedded" ties. **Arm's-length relationships**

EXHIBIT 3.1

Network Centralization

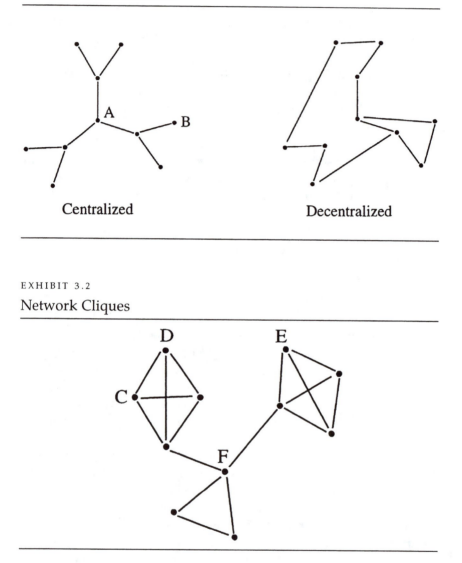

Centralized   Decentralized

EXHIBIT 3.2

Network Cliques

are akin to the proverbial business relationships: self-interested, contrac-
tually specified, highly formalized, short-term. In contrast, **embedded
ties** are much closer, special relationships. They involve repeated transactions over long periods of time. Many of the arrangements are negotiated on the basis of implicit understandings and without the need for

EXHIBIT 3.3

Typical Interfirm Network in the Apparel Industry's Better Dress Sector

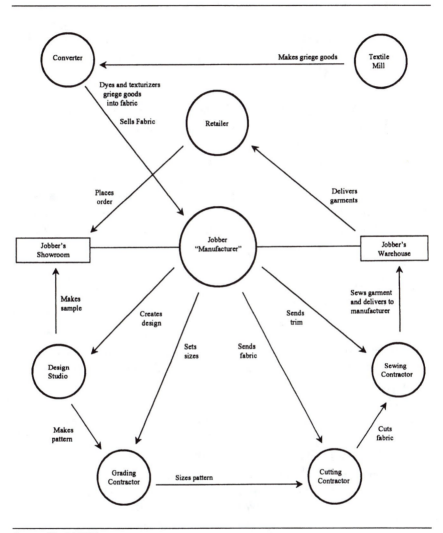

Source: Uzzi (1997).

formal contracts, and they can be easily modified if need be. Embedded ties are not just business arrangements but are also personal.

According to Uzzi, compared with arm's-length relationships, embedded ties provide three kinds of benefits: trust, information, and joint problem solving. The advantage of trust in a business relationship is that the two parties enjoy access to valuable but hard-to-specify and hard-to-price resources, and they know they will not be taken advantage of by each other. Embedded ties also facilitate the communication of rich, informal, credible, detailed, and sometimes proprietary information about each other's needs and circumstances. Such communication goes far beyond the price and quantity information normally provided as part of an arm's-length transaction. Finally, embedded ties create the basis for joint problem solving. When things don't work out, when surprises, accidents, or unforeseen contingencies occur, the two parties adapt and work things out, cooperating to make the most of a bad situation.

Uzzi shows that because of these three benefits, embedded ties can improve a firm's performance. But under some circumstances, too much embeddedness can be a liability. For instance, a subcontractor that does business with a single customer will certainly do better if the relationship is an embedded one: The customer can be trusted, information flows easily, and problems can be worked out. But if the customer gets into financial difficulty, the subcontractors' heavy reliance on it will become problematic. And having only embedded ties with other firms that themselves have only embedded ties runs the risk of the business equivalent of incest: The firm becomes trapped in a closed network cut off from new sources of information and new opportunities.

Uzzi's work focuses on the garment industry, but networks appear in many different kinds of markets. Powell et al. (forthcoming) show how firm networks affect firm performance in the biotechnology industry. Wayne Baker (1984) analyzed networks of traders in a modern stock options market. He found that as trading activity and numbers of traders increased, the market split up into subgroups or cliques. Those inside a subgroup traded more within their own group and less to people in other groups. Baker's evidence shows that this splintering of the overall market into subgroups had the effect of increasing price volatility. The network structure of the market affected how unpredictable prices would be.

The emergence of such networks shapes markets so that they do not look like the atomized, anonymous markets of economic theory. As economists conceptualize them, competitive markets are characterized by the **law of indifference** (see Jevons 1931; Landa 1981). This means that market traders really don't care about each other's personal characteristics or about social relationships. The only things that matter are the price and quantity of the good. In such a world, anyone will trade with anyone else, so long as the "money is green" or the "price is right." Issues of trust, or special relationships, simply do not arise. In network terms, traders are equally likely to trade with each other, so the network that forms is a random one. Yet in the real world, markets often display a nonrandom structure in which transactions are repeatedly built around embedded ties and social relationships. Trading partners are not selected at random.

Individual Networks

Networks exist at multiple levels, depending on who the relationships are between. One can speak of a global network that knits together nations through international trade. Or at a lower level, one can consider the network that links together persons who trade in a weekend flea market. In this section, we shall consider how personal networks operate in the economy.

Networks and Employment

One of the most important ways in which networks affect the economy is through their influence on labor markets. Social networks get used on both sides of the market, by buyers (employers) and sellers (employees) of labor power. Roberto Fernandez and Nancy Weinberg (1997) demonstrate the importance of employee social networks as a tool for businesses to recruit new employees. Frequently, an organization that needs to hire will *not* advertise its open positions in newspapers or other public media. Instead, it notifies its current employees and invites them to refer potential candidates (of course, many employers use both strategies at the same time). Fernandez and Weinberg examined the hiring practices of a large American retail bank. They found that referrals (prospective employees who were referred by current employees) were more likely to receive a job interview and much more likely to get an offer. Specifically, 30% of referrals received job offers from the bank, compared with only 3% of external nonreferral applicants (Fernandez and Weinberg 1997:892). Thus, having an inside connection made a huge difference for an applicant's chances of success.

Fernandez and Weinberg offer several explanations for the advantage that social relations conferred. Among other things, such relations give both the employer and the prospective employee accurate and detailed information about each other. They allow for quicker and more informal recruitment. In addition, new employees who have in effect been "sponsored" by a current employee often feel an obligation to perform extra well to justify their sponsor's endorsement of their character and ability. Thus, the existence of a social tie between current employee and applicant is good for both sides: The employer knows more about the applicant and can expect him or her to try to do a good job, and the applicant enjoys a better chance of getting the job he or she wants.

Recruitment networks are not, however, an unblemished social good. Those who are "networked" gain an advantage at the expense of those who are not. Because Americans' social networks are heavily structured along race, ethnic, familial, class, and neighborhood lines, by using current employees to recruit future employees an employer can inadvertently hire in a highly discriminatory manner. For example, a factory in the city of Chicago that has a predominantly Polish American workforce may wish to use its employees to hire new workers. But Polish American social networks (friendship, kinship, and so on) mostly reach out to other Polish Americans, and they are unlikely to include many African Americans, Latinos, or people from other groups. Thus, the factory will hire people of the same or similar social background as the current employees and unintentionally discriminate.

Reliance on informal networks for hiring is heaviest among small businesses. Large corporations are more likely to use the formal apparatus of official searches, public announcements, applications, and interviews. This does not mean that informal networks aren't important, however, because taken as a group, small businesses account for a significant proportion of total employment in the United States. As Tilly and Tilly (1994) note, U.S. firms with less than 50 employees numbered 5.9 million in 1993 but accounted for over 40% of the workforce (p. 302).

A very different type of recruitment occurs in "creative" industries, such as the Hollywood film industry, where people do not get permanent jobs so much as participate in shorter-term projects (e.g., making a movie, cutting a record, performing a play, and so on). Social networks again matter, but rather than firms and individuals seeking out each other to establish a long-term employment arrangement, actors, producers, directors, cinematographers, editors, and composers seek each other out to do a film project together (Faulkner and Anderson 1987). As persons build up a film career (marked out by a series of film "credits"), they establish long-term working relationships and alliances with other persons and try to work together again in future film projects. Producers, directors, and cinematographers are particularly likely to express mutual preferences for working with one another.

Faulkner and Anderson explain this peculiar network arrangement in terms of the high degree of uncertainty faced by the movie industry. No one really knows which movies will be duds and which will be block-busters. (Consider how many people predicted that the movie *Titanic* would fail.) How much the moviegoing public will like a particular film is very unpredictable, and the costs of failure are high. The overall odds of success are not good; only a handful of the many hundreds of films made each year make lots of money. And even if a particular movie proves successful, it is hard to know who truly deserves credit for the success: Hundreds of people work on a film, and they are not all abso-lutely critical for its success. Thus, filmmakers try to gain any advantage they can on the competition, and one way to do this is to use people with established track records and with whom they know they can work. Thus, networks help structure the collaborative arrangements that make movies.

In a well-known analysis of professional, technical, and managerial workers, Mark Granovetter (1974) draws an important distinction be-tween strong and weak social ties. Granovetter studied how people ob-tained the information about job opportunities that led to a new job. He found that most placements did not occur through the formal mecha-nisms of job allocation but instead happened informally, through friends and relatives. Granovetter noted that social ties vary in their strength; friends and kin can be close or distant. Connections to close kin are strong, whereas those to distant friends are weak. While one might ex-pect that strong ties are more useful (perhaps because they involve a higher level of trust or entail more obligations), Granovetter argues that when it comes to learning about new job opportunities, weak ties per-form better. Weak ties are more likely to give a job seeker access to differ-ent or more distant social circles, so he or she obtains more new informa-tion. By contrast, strong ties are more likely to provide information that one already knew.

Networks and Credit

Individual networks affect not only who acquires a job or gets the oppor-tunity to work on a project but also who enjoys access to capital. Capital is necessary for business activity, so who gets it, and who doesn't, is ab-solutely critical. Lending and the extension of credit involve transactions that pointedly raise issues of trust and information. A creditor wants to lend money only to those who can be trusted to repay their debts, and potential borrowers have an incentive to misrepresent or exaggerate their willingness and ability to repay (that way, they obtain the loan). Lenders want very much to know who can be trusted to tell the truth and to repay the money.

In the past, much lending and capital mobilization occurred through social networks. Lamoreaux's (1991, 1994) studies of early 19th-century New England banks show how lending and credit flowed through friendship and kinship networks. Banks loaned money to people closely connected to the bank's directors (relatives, personal friends and associates, and so on) to such an extent that Lamoreaux uses the term "insider lending" to characterize the pattern. Anonymous or arm's-length lending simply didn't occur. A term such as insider lending in a modern context suggests unfairness, nepotism, and favoritism. In the early 19th century, by contrast, it was a common and legitimate way for a bank to do business.

Tittler's study (1994) established the importance of social networks at an even earlier point in the history of Western capitalism (one can trace the importance of economic networks even further back, to 15th-century Florence [see McLean and Padgett 1997]). Joyce Jeffries, a mid-17th-century spinster living in England, kept a financial diary in which she recorded her lending transactions. Tittler's analysis shows the prevalence of social connections: Not only were some of her borrowers related to her, but they were often related to each other (a feature that Tittler suggests would have made it easier to determine the reputation and credibility of a potential borrower). Many of Jeffries's borrowers had preexisting relationships with her. This made it more likely that she would lend to them, and it also made her readier to forgive delinquent debts or to charge lower rates of interest. That is, Jeffries didn't simply try to maximize her profits but instead shaped her transactions in light of the relationships and social obligations in which she was embedded.

Even today, after the development of a highly rationalized financial sector, some forms of lending remain deeply embedded in social relationships. Among ethnic immigrant groups in both the United States and Britain, small businesses sometimes join **rotating credit associations** (RCAs) to obtain the start-up capital they need to operate (see Light and Karageorgis 1994; Light, Kwuon, and Zhong 1990; Sterling 1995). An RCA is an informal social group in which members agree to make periodic monetary contributions to a central fund, and the fund is then made available to each contributor in turn.

Among Jamaican immigrants in contemporary Britain, for example, members of a group of neighbors, co-workers, or friends contribute small sums every week (sometimes biweekly or even monthly) to a fund that is then given to a single member. The RCA operates at least long enough for everyone to get a turn as recipient of the fund. For people who may be unable to obtain small business or consumer loans from a regular financial institution, an RCA provides a good way to save money and generate a lump sum. The money can be used for many purposes, including buying a house, paying for weddings and funerals, or setting up or expanding a business. RCAs, unlike banks, do not have deposit insurance or any similar government guarantees. They work only on the basis of a substantial level of trust and knowledge among the participants. Among Korean immigrants to the United States, RCAs presuppose a high degree of ethnic solidarity to function (Light et al. 1990:48).

Relationships are also important in the formal financial sector. In a study of American small businesses, Petersen and Rajan (1994) found that firms that developed relationships with their banks found it easier to obtain credit and did so on better terms. Surprisingly, small firms that concentrated their borrowing from a single source were not hurt by their failure to "shop around." Cultivating a special relationship with their banker conferred advantages that more than compensated for the decline in price competition.

Networks and Sales

Personal networks matter for obtaining the capital and labor inputs necessary for business. They also influence how firms sell their products. Their effect on sales can be so substantial that some organizations build their entire marketing strategy around the social networks of their sales force. **Direct sales organizations** (DSOs) offer the best example of this pattern.

Nicole Biggart (1989) notes that well-known DSOs such as Amway, Tupperware, and Mary Kay Cosmetics depend on their salespeople to use their own personal relationships with friends, acquaintances, and family to sell the company's product. The hope is that friends and family will feel socially obliged to buy from the salesperson: After all, what kind of a brother, sister, or parent wouldn't want to help out a sibling or child by purchasing some Amway kitchen cleanser? Because sales depend so much on preexisting relationships, DSOs try especially hard to recruit women, who in modern American society perform most of the work connected with maintaining and nurturing social relationships (Biggart 1989:50). Outside of DSOs, Offer (1997:466-67) provides estimates of the substantial resources that salespeople and others devote to managing personal relationships in the pursuit of higher sales.

Networks matter on the other side of the transaction. Sellers use them, but so do buyers. DiMaggio and Louch (1998) examined American consumer purchases and found that a remarkably high proportion of them are done through network connections. People use friends and relatives not only to gather information about a commodity but also to decide who to buy from. For example, when someone in the study bought a used car from another individual, about half the transactions were between friends, relatives, or acquaintances (pp. 622-23). People also frequently used their relationships when purchasing legal services and home maintenance services.

Networks in Organizations

Interpersonal networks also unfold within organizations. Sociologists have long noted the difference between the formal structure of an organization (as reflected, for example, by the organizational chart or official chain of command) and its informal structure (who actually talks to or interacts with whom). Middle managers are at the halfway point of an official chain of command in which they receive information from subordinates and report to superiors, yet these two groups are not the only people with whom they communicate inside the firm. A manager may be personal friends with a staff member in another division and so interacts regularly with that person although there is no official communication link between the two.

Han (1996) examined how closely communication networks in the headquarters of a specialty retail chain company reflected the formal organizational structure. He focused specifically on four types of interaction between individuals: to give and receive information, to investigate or explain, to advise or consult, and to negotiate or persuade (Han 1996:50). His results showed that formal organizational structure affected who interacted with whom but did not completely determine it. Informal networks still mattered.

Individual Networks around the World

The importance of social networks is not a uniquely American, or even Western, phenomenon. Evidence from contemporary China and Taiwan suggests that social networks may matter even more in Asia than in the United States. For example, a person's connections play an important role in getting a job. These special relations are so significant that they have been given a distinctive name: *guanxi*. *Guanxi* relations involve trust, mutual obligations, and flexibility, so they are very useful in business (Kiong and Kee 1998).

Bian (1997) analyzes how people get jobs in the People's Republic of China. As in the United States, social networks and connections help a great deal. According to Bian, two kinds of resources flow through social networks: information and influence. A job seeker needs both knowledge of job opportunities and some kind of "clout" to help influence the decision makers to favor his or her application. These resources, Bian argues, flow through different kinds of networks. "**Weak ties,**" that is, distant relations, are more useful for obtaining information (a finding consistent with Granovetter's [1974] argument). "**Strong ties,**" that is, relations between people who are close kin or good friends, help to supply influence.

Even though China's economy is moving in the direction of capitalism and away from a socialist command economy, public bureaucracies and state agencies remain very important. Thus, businesspeople find it useful to cultivate clientelistic relationships with public officials who can serve as a kind of patron. According to Wank (1996:825-26), Chinese entrepreneurs think very explicitly about how to "invest" in *guanxi* capital—that is, in their relationships with officialdom. *Guanxi* capital varies (1) according to the durability of a relationship (and thus how unconditional the patron's support is), (2) by its connectivity (whether the link to the patron leads to other connections), and (3) by the extent of the obligation. Family ties, education, membership in organizations, and plain old experience help to build up *guanxi* capital. The cultivation of *guanxi* isn't motivated solely by the existence of an influential state apparatus. Jar-Der Luo (1997) argues that Taiwanese businesses are also built around *guanxi.* People often raise capital from among their own families, and even when they look to outside lenders or capital markets, personal connections and reputations are very important.

All these examples suggest that interpersonal social networks heavily influence business activity in many respects. Whether it be employment, lending, or sales, preexisting relationships structure market transactions. Of course, networks exist at several levels besides the personal one, but there, too, they have an effect.

Interorganizational Networks

If people can have relationships, so can firms. And if people have different kinds of relationships of varying intensity, so again do firms. Firms and other types of organizations can have several types of relationships with each other. The most important can be categorized roughly into three groups: exchange relations, personnel relations, and property relations. Corporations can be linked together because they exchange or transact with each other, because persons go between them, or because of formal ownership.

Perhaps the most thoroughly studied intercorporate network is the one created through boards of directors (Mizruchi 1996). Suppose two firms have a common director—that is, a person sits on the boards of both Corporation A and Corporation B. The two corporations have a link by virtue of their overlapping directorates. Such links are referred to as **board interlocks.** Because some corporate directors sit on many boards simultaneously, many corporations become "interlocked" in this fashion. Interlocks can be more or less strong (depending on the number of shared directors). The interlocks between firms create a useful connection because the mutual director can serve as a conduit for information and can facilitate negotiations and coordinate relations between the two corporations.

Through board interlocks, many corporations can become linked together into larger organizational networks. Beth Mintz and Michael Schwartz (1985) examined the networks of U.S. corporations during the 1963 to 1974 period. Taking into account all interlocking directorates, they determined which sorts of firms were at the "center" of the corporate network and which were at the periphery. Arguing that more centralized firms possessed greater importance in intercorporate affairs, they found that financial firms (banks and insurance companies) occupied the most central positions in the network (Mintz and Schwartz 1985:157). Mintz and Schwartz argue that the structure of the interlock network both reflected and reinforced the key role that financial institutions play in the allocation of capital to American business.[1] A paradigmatic example would be a situation in which a corporation puts on its board of directors the president of the bank it borrows from.

In an extension of this argument, Donald Palmer and his colleagues (Palmer et al. 1995) claim that whether or not a U.S. firm was acquired by another firm during the 1960s depended significantly on the kinds of networks into which the firm was embedded. Corporations with many interlocks to other firms were more likely to be acquired (Palmer et al. 1995:492). Their explanation for this finding was that overlapping directors served as information channels through which a firm's managers could communicate to prospective acquirers their willingness and suitability to be taken over. Corporate networks, like individual networks, can facilitate the flow of information.

---

[1] Roy (1983) shows how this network of interlocking directorates evolved in the period between 1886 and 1905 and documents the emerging centrality of banks.

Board interlocks influence who gets acquired, but they also affect how much the acquiring firm pays (Haunschild 1994). Haunschild analyzed 453 acquisitions occurring between 1986 and 1993 and measured the size of the acquisition premium paid by the buyer. (Simply put, this premium is the difference between the market price of the target company's stock before the announcement of the acquisition and the price paid per share by the acquiring company.) How much to pay for a target firm is a question that involves a lot of uncertainty, so acquiring firms try to obtain additional information on what is a reasonable price. Potential information sources include the other firms with which the acquirer is connected through board interlocks. And indeed, Haunschild found (1994:403) a positive statistical relationship between the acquisition premium paid by the firm and the premiums paid by the other firms to which it was connected for their own prior acquisitions. Apparently, in estimating what is a reasonable premium, acquiring firms are influenced by those in their corporate network.

Diffusion of Innovations

One instance of information flow through networks concerns the diffusion of innovations through organizational populations. Fads and fashions occur in business (and elsewhere), and at given moments, one can find large numbers of firms trying out the same strategy, pursuing the same idea, or applying similar innovations. Why do some firms adopt innovations before others? Why do some lead in making change while others only follow as part of the pack? Networks provide an important part of the answer.

Gerald Davis (1991) studied the adoption of the "poison pill" defense by corporations. During the 1980s, as the wave of hostile takeovers engulfed Wall Street, corporations sought ways to protect themselves from unfriendly acquirers. The poison pill was one such defensive measure. While the details vary, a typical poison pill allowed its holder to purchase additional shares in a firm at heavily discounted rates should a takeover attempt occur without the approval of the board of directors.

Among Fortune 500 firms, Crown Zellerbach was the first to adopt the device (in 1984). Very few other firms adopted poison pills until their legality was upheld by the Delaware Supreme Court in a 1985 ruling (*Moran v. Household International*). But thereafter, so many firms instituted poison pills that by 1989 over 60% of the Fortune 500 possessed them. In other words, poison pills spread like wildfire after the 1985 ruling. In explaining who adopted and when, Davis (1991) found that firms that had an interlocking director with another firm that had already adopted the poison pill were themselves more likely to adopt. Having one tie to another adopter increased the rate of adoption by about 61%, and having two ties to adopters almost doubled the rate (p. 605). With such network connections, firms were able to learn from the experiences of others and emulate what seemed to be a good strategy. This corporate innovation spread through a corporate network.

Information diffuses through many types of interorganizational networks, not just interlocking directorates. Westphal, Gulati, and Shortell (1997) studied a different diffusion process that occurred through different kinds of networks. Instead of poison pills and board interlocks, they examined Total Quality Management (TQM) programs and common membership in strategic alliances and multihospital systems.

Many hospitals introduced TQM in the late 1980s, a new management program that involved a high level of organizational commitment to the customer, as well as continuous improvement using empowered employee groups and collective problem solving. It was, in short, something of a business fad. Westphal et al. posit that some kinds of network ties are particularly important for the transfer of knowledge and information between different organizations. They focus on two in particular: (1) common membership in strategic alliances (a contractual agreement between hospitals for the provision of goods and services) and (2) common membership in multihospital systems (in which one organization owns and controls multiple hospitals). They suggest that these links help to cultivate high levels of formal and informal communication between organizations.

The first adoptions of TQM by general medical surgical hospitals occurred during the mid-1980s, and by 1993, almost 2,000 hospitals had instituted the program. Westphal et al. found that connections to hospitals that had already adopted TQM affected the likelihood that a hospital would itself adopt but in a more complex way than in the case of poison pills. After TQM became common enough to be a generally accepted management practice, network connections made adoption of TQM *more likely*. But before then, network connections made adoption *less likely*.

Managing Corporate Relationships

Given the importance of network connections for firms, it is not surprising that firms can be quite deliberate in creating or establishing such relationships. After all, strategic alliances between different hospitals, or director interlocks between two firms, do not happen due to chance. Such important relationships are carefully considered and negotiated by the two parties before they enter into them. Unlike other kinds of networks (e.g., kinship, in which a person is simply born with certain parents and siblings), interorganizational networks are a product of the organizations themselves. Firms are increasingly creating their own networks and establishing many different kinds of cooperative relations. Gulati (1995a) outlines myriad new forms of interfirm cooperation: joint ventures, joint R&D agreements, technology exchanges, direct investments, licensing arrangements, and so on. Powell, Koput, and Smith-Doerr (1996) also mention equity joint ventures, comarketing arrangements, and collaborative manufacturing as other forms of cooperation and point out that there has recently been a huge increase in corporate partnering and external collaborations (Powell et al. 1996:116).

In establishing such relationships, how do firms choose their partners? One obvious answer is that the nature of the activities that a firm wants to undertake determines partnerships. That is, a bank that wanted to develop software for Internet banking would naturally look to a computer software company with Internet expertise for a partnership. This narrows the field of potential partners but still leaves open the question of who to collaborate with. There are, for example, many software firms with Internet experience for the bank to choose from.

Gulati points out (1995a, 1995b) that preexisting relationships influence new alliances. That is, two firms with a prior history of collaboration are more likely to develop new projects together (not unlike Hollywood film people). Furthermore, even when two firms have had no prior direct contact, if they have both collaborated with a common partner (i.e., Firms A and B have never had an alliance with each other, but they have both had previous alliances with Firm C), that also increases the likelihood of a new collaboration between them (Gulati 1995b:641-42). Prior direct ties, or indirect ones, provide crucial information about a firm's potential partner. Such rich, informal, and detailed information comes only from experience, either the firm's own or that of someone the firm trusts. In industries where interfirm collaborations are very common, such as the biotech industry, firms learn how to collaborate and they develop quite distinct reputations as good (or bad) partners (Powell et al. 1996:121).

Firms manage their networks not only by deciding who, and who not, to collaborate with but also by managing the relationship itself. Sometimes specific people within firms have the particular job of cultivating and maintaining relationships with customers and clients. In a corporate law firm, for example, such a person would be called a "rainmaker," and some banks have personnel explicitly designated as "relationship managers" to deal with customers. In today's world, many large firms make regular use of the services of investment banks. A firm that wishes to borrow capital, either through selling bonds, issuing stock, or some other method, will need the help of an investment bank. Investment banks also provide advice about potential mergers and acquisitions. Because there are many investment banks, a firm requiring such services can treat each instance as a separate transaction and obtain a different bank on each occasion, or it can treat all deals as moments in a single, ongoing relationship. As Baker (1990) argues, big firms used to rely on a single bank with whom they had a long-term relationship. If the firm needed access to capital or required some advice, it would always go to its bank. Firms gave a very high proportion of their investment banking business to one investment bank, so the relationship was "monogamous." Increasingly, however, firms treat each transaction separately and do not automatically go back to the same bank each time. This means that firms spread their business among a number of investment banks.

To illustrate the difference, Baker (1990:596) contrasts Ford with GM during the 1981 to 1985 period. Both auto manufacturers made heavy use of investment banks (with 81 and 110 deals, respectively). Ford Motor Company gave 69% of its business to a single bank, Goldman Sachs. General Motors, in contrast, gave 27% of its business to First Boston, another 27% to Morgan Stanley, 12% to Salomon Brothers, 9% to Merrill Lynch, and smaller proportions to many other banks. Compared with Ford, GM spread its business around.

Building a relationship with a single bank allows for better service because of continuity, experience, and inside knowledge. But using separate transactions creates price competition and thus lower costs for the firm; it also diversifies the firm's sources of information. Each alternative therefore has both advantages and disadvantages. Baker finds that most firms pursue a hybrid strategy, giving a sizable proportion of their business to one or two investment banks (although not all of their business) but not spreading their business evenly to a maximum number of banks. The choice of strategy, according to Baker, reflects a firm's deliberate attempt to avoid becoming too dependent on any one bank and to exploit whatever power advantages it has.

Corporate Networks around the World

The existence and importance of interorganizational networks is a global phenomenon. Examples include *chaebol* in Korea and *grupos económicos* in Latin America (see Granovetter 1994). But probably the best known example comes from Japan. As mentioned earlier, large Japanese corporations are characteristically grouped together into clusters of interlinked firms called *keiretsu*. About one-half of Japan's 200 largest industrial firms maintain an affiliation with one group or another. All five of the largest commercial banks are in their own groups, as are the five leading trust banks, the top five casualty insurance companies, and four of the five largest life insurance companies (Gerlach 1992:85). These business groups are built around well-known names such as Mitsui, Fuji, Mitsubishi, and Sumitomo. A bank usually lies at the core of each *keiretsu*, and there is little duplication of industrial specialization (i.e., no more than one member firm comes from each industry so that the members do not compete with each other).

Three kinds of interorganizational ties join the member firms together (Gerlach 1992; Lincoln, Gerlach, and Takahashi 1992). Japanese companies own each other's shares, and they exchange company directors (and other lower-ranked personnel). They are also linked through loans from the core *keiretsu* bank. These multiple links constitute stable, cooperative, reciprocal, long-term relationships that encourage economic exchange with members over nonmembers. For example, if a *keiretsu* firm needs to raise capital, it will go to its *keiretsu* bank rather than to an outside bank.

The structuring of the Japanese economy around *keiretsu* networks helps to explain why foreign firms, including American ones, have had such a hard time breaking into the Japanese domestic market. Because *keiretsu* members prefer to transact with other group members, American firms always face the additional liability of being nonmembers as well as foreigners. *Keiretsu* groups have also helped to create high rates of corporate investment (profits don't have to be all paid out as dividends to shareholders) and have given Japanese firms great resilience in managing the strains associated with rapid expansion (Gerlach 1992:246).

The Importance of Networks in Markets

Why do some people get jobs and others don't? Many factors affect this outcome, but an individual's social network is one of the more important ones. Why do some firms adopt innovations before other firms? Again, the kind of networks into which a firm is embedded makes a big difference. Markets feed off information, and networks are one of the most important media through which information travels. Markets are awash in information; people and firms hear all kinds of news, rumors, and reports whose veracity may be doubtful. What they want is accurate, timely, detailed, and trustworthy information. Having a relationship with someone, or having a connection with an organization, helps to create access to reliable and credible information. Being told the truth is no good unless you can be sure that the message is true, and for this it helps to be dealing with a source you can trust.

Relationships and networks structure the flow of information, but they also structure the flow of favors and obligations. Relationships entail reciprocal expectations and mutual obligations. To get a job, it sometimes isn't sufficient simply to learn about it; you need some clout on the inside. It helps to have someone who "owes" you something, either because of some relational obligation (friends are expected to look out for each other) or because that person needs to return a previous favor (along the lines of "if you scratch my back, I'll scratch yours"). Such relational histories of reciprocal favors can develop between organizations as well as individuals (witness Uzzi's [1996] discussion of the New York garment industry).

Relationships can be used to mobilize resources needed as inputs by a company: raw materials, supplies, capital, and labor. Baker's (1990) analysis of corporate-investment bank relations shows how important it is for firms to manage their relationships well. Relationships serve as the basis for many types of interfirm collaborations (joint research, marketing, manufacturing, or whatever). They are also useful for selling a company's product. Salespeople try to cultivate good relationships with their clients or customers, and some firms (e.g., DSOs) rely almost exclusively on the preexisting social relationships of their sales force for marketing their goods. In general, strong relationships and extensive networks help to give a firm the flexibility and adaptability needed to survive in a dynamic environment. Networks allow firms to share risks with each other, pool their competencies, and exploit new opportunities (Powell and Smith-Doerr 1994:370).

Relationships vary in the extent to which they are simply given or whether they must be created. An individual person is born into a family and thereby acquires a preexisting network of kin. Persons are also born into particular ethnic groups and so gain access to ethnically based resources. People aren't born with friends, however, and so usually these relationships are created. Likewise, corporations seldom are "born" with extensive preexisting networks. (One exception is when a new corporation is formed as a joint venture of two parent companies; even at birth, the new firm has strong ties to its owners.) American corporations establish relationships with their investment banks, and Japanese firms affiliate themselves with one *keiretsu* or another. But regardless of whether individual or organizational relationships are "inherited" or are created, they must all be managed in some way if they are to be maintained. Neither firms nor individuals can afford to take their friends and allies for granted. Relationships that lie dormant for long periods of time eventually wither away and disappear.

Relationships insert economic actors into larger networks and more distant connections that extend well beyond their sphere of direct control. One can choose one's own friends, but it is much harder to manage or influence who your friend chooses as friends. Likewise, Firm A can decide to form a strategic alliance with Firm B, but it cannot decide who B forms its other alliances with. The importance of these indirect ties is most obvious in the case of information flows. Suppose Person A cultivates a particular friend because she serves as a credible source of information. By choosing that friend, rather than another, Person A clearly exerts control. Yet where the friend gets her information depends on her own relationships, which are beyond A's control. The variety and usefulness of A's information sources depend not only on how she manages her networks but also on how the people she is linked to manage theirs.

In a highly influential article, Mark Granovetter (1985) used the term *embeddedness* to denote how economic action in general was shaped by ongoing social relationships. Trust is an enormously important problem in the economy: Many kinds of economic action can be undertaken only if one can trust the other person(s). According to Granovetter, trust derives not from institutional arrangements (e.g., air-tight contracts with all the i's dotted and t's crossed) or generalized morality (e.g., a social norm that people should always keep the promises they make) but rather from the interpersonal relationships and networks that an economic actor is embedded in. The coherence and order of economic life depends less on formal contractual or bureaucratic arrangements and more on the expectations and obligations that form around social relationships. Granovetter's original argument focused especially on interpersonal relationships, but it can be, and has been, extended to encompass interorganizational or other types of relationships. Following Granovetter's more general formulation, those who wish to understand economic behavior will also have to apprehend its social context.

Ron Burt (1992) has offered a general recipe for how best to manage networks. He argues that firms will do better, and individuals will enjoy more success, if they position themselves into the **"structural holes"** of existing networks. These "holes" are where relations are absent, where links do not exist. By putting themselves into a structural hole, a firm or person can broker between different groups (playing them off against

EXHIBIT 3.4

Structural Holes

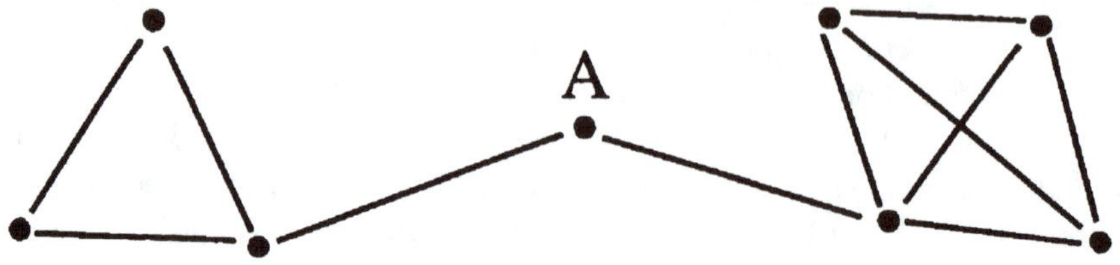

each other) and link simultaneously into multiple networks. Exhibit 3.4 identifies a structural hole in a network and shows someone (Person A) who is occupying it. Person A has positioned herself between two groups who otherwise have no contact with each other. By Burt's logic, it is better to know people who don't know each other than to know those who do.

Burt offers a general strategy that significantly recasts the meaning of competitive success in markets. Doing well is not just a matter of improving one's product or lowering prices; it also depends on the active management of networks. And to exploit all the advantages that networks and relationships offer, the network entrepreneur must comprehend the global features of networks (i.e., the existence and location of structural holes), not just the proximate features of his or her own direct network ties. For individual networks, in other words, it is not enough to maximize one's own network ties. Finding a structural hole means cultivating direct ties to others in light of the pattern of ties they have with everyone else.

Whether or not one follows Burt's advice, networks are not an infinitely pliable resource. They are built around relationships *between* people and therefore are not the property of any single individual (a husband is *in* a marriage, but he doesn't *own* the marriage). No matter how advantageous it would be to manipulate networks and relationships in a particular way, individuals and organizations cannot act unilaterally. Their networks depend not only on what they do but on what the other party does. Networks are resources, to be sure, but they are not under any single individual's control.

Conclusion

However constructed, networks shape the economy. People and firms devote substantial amounts of time, money, and other resources to the cultivation and maintenance of relationships because they matter. Networks shape information, influence opportunities, structure claims on others and obligations to them, and grant access. Consequently, networks influence a firm's performance, a person's career mobility, trading patterns, and a host of other outcomes.

4

Organizations and
the Economy

Many of us imagine that the market is a place that privileges economic efficiency above all else. Competition forces people and firms to act in a cold-blooded, profit-maximizing way. If they do not, eventually they or their firm will go bankrupt and be driven from the marketplace. And if the market embodies efficiency, then big bureaucracies seem to characterize just the opposite: ungainly, immobile, tied up in red tape, and weighed down with lots of organizational "fat." Government bureaucracies in particular have a very bad reputation for too much red tape and paperwork; for incompetence, inflexibility, and overcentralization; and for housing too many anonymous, impersonal, and inefficient bureaucrats. Politicians justify proposals to privatize state-owned companies or to relinquish government functions to the private sector, in part by appealing to the belief that the private for-profit sector does the job well, whereas the bureaucratic public sector does not.

Given the folk wisdom that associates large organizations with inefficiency, it is curious that so much of economic life in modern capitalist nations is dominated by large organizations. Even in the private sector, management consultants propose to downsize corporate bureaucracies as a way to create lean, mean, and flexible organizations. But in fact, economic development in the United States and other Western countries during the 19th and 20th centuries has been closely connected with the rise of large-scale corporations.

As the business historian Alfred Chandler (1977) has documented, big business arrived in the United States with the railroads, but as an organizational form, it soon spread to many other areas of the economy, including production, distribution, and retail. The ability of Montgomery Ward or Sears Roebuck and Co. to supplant innumerable small dry goods merchants, wholesalers, and distributors makes little sense if we assume that big organizations are always clumsy, inefficient, and slow moving. How could they have become so successful? Today, so many large organizations populate the economy that a considerable proportion of all economic activity occurs *within* the boundaries of firms rather than *between* them. Such activities do not occur in markets.

Organizations matter in the U.S. economy to such an extent that we now have an organizational economy. Large for-profit organizations dominate the U.S. economy: They make the important decisions about investment and employment that determine the overall direction of the economy. If big firms decide to invest overseas rather than domestically, the U.S. economy doesn't grow as fast. If firms decide to lay off their employees (to "downsize") unemployment rates grow higher. Large firms also dominate the economies of many other countries (e.g., Japan, Mexico, South Korea).

Organizations also matter for individuals because they provide the context for most jobs in the United States. Someone who graduates from college at the age of 22 and then works until retirement at age 65 will likely spend most of his or her work life as an employee for some kind of organization. In today's American economy, people are seldom self-employed entrepreneurs, so their work experiences are largely determined inside organizations.

Consider that in 1990, the U.S. civilian labor force numbered some 125.84 million people (U.S. Department of Commerce 1996). Some of these people (7.047 million) were unemployed and so didn't work at all. Of the approximately 118.8 million people who had jobs, most worked for someone else; 109.42 million (roughly 92%) worked as employees. An employee is someone whose pay, benefits, promotion prospects, and work experience are determined by someone else—sometimes directly by a boss, sometimes by organizational personnel procedures, and often by both. Government employees by definition work in large-scale organizations, but what about all the others? Excluding government workers (and also railroad employees), of the 93,476,000 Americans employed in 1990, 24,373,000 worked for establishments with under 20 employees; 41,689,000 workers (or about 44.5%) worked for establishments with 100 or more employees. Clearly, large-scale organizations shape the work experiences and lives of many, many people.

In this chapter, we explain some of the different ways in which organizations shape the economy. We start with that hallmark of organizational life: authority relations. To work in an organization means having a boss (unless one is at the very top of the organization). Next, we examine how organizations shape careers, conflicts, and personal life. Having documented the significance of organizations, we then consider where they all came from. Despite their ubiquity today, large organizations are a historical rarity, and the story of their appearance and spread is an instructive one.

The Power of the Boss

Although the individualist ideology of modern American society stresses the independence, autonomy, and equality of persons, in fact, only a few people are highly independent and autonomous in their work lives. This is because work in organizations entails relations of dependence and inequality. For eight hours (or more) of each day, for five days a week, an employee's actions are dictated personally by a boss and bureaucratically by the rules, regulations, and procedures of the employee's firm. One of the key facts of work in an organization is that an employees' time is not his or her own. Unlike self-employment, employment by another means having a boss to whom we are accountable. It means being a subordinate to someone else.

In large organizations, the structure of authority is highly differentiated and nuanced. There are multiple organizational layers, so most employees are simultaneously superiors (to those below them) and subordinates (to those above). A classical **bureaucratic organization** has a well-defined chain of command and an unambiguous structure of authority that depends strictly on the formal hierarchy (so that, for example, the company president has more power than a senior vice president, who has more power than a vice president, and so on down the line).[1] Thus, what an employee does in her job, how she is evaluated and rewarded, and what her future career prospects are depends very much on her direct boss. A good boss can make for a rewarding work experience. A bad boss means life at work is miserable.

Employees' dependence on their bosses cuts across the blue-collar/white-collar distinction. American assembly line factory workers, for example, have had long-standing grievances against the seemingly arbitrary control exerted over them by line foremen. One study of a GM automobile assembly plant in Linden, New Jersey, shows that factory workers welcomed workplace changes initiated in the mid-1980s as part of an attempt to emulate the successful techniques of the Japanese auto industry (Milkman 1997). An assembly line job traditionally meant

---

[1] The most influential sociological analysis of bureaucracy is that of Max Weber (1946).

highly repetitive, monotonous work while being subject to intense and even oppressive supervision.

Factory workers seldom write autobiographies, but based on his own experience, Ben Hamper (1991) offers a chilling account of life in a GM factory:

> Our jobs were identical—to install splash shields, pencil rods and assorted screws with a noisy air gun in the rear ends of Chevy Blazers and Suburbans. . . . Once the cabs were about five feet off the ground, Roy and I ducked inside the rear wheel wells and busted ass. . . . The one thing that was impossible to escape was the monotony of our new jobs. Every minute, every hour, every truck and every movement was a plodding replica of the one that had gone before. (pp. 5, 41)

In Hamper's tale, drink and drugs were one common reaction to the extreme monotony, but it is easy to see why assembly line workers would welcome changes to the workplace. Along with extreme boredom came authoritarian foremen (and other bosses), whose job it was to keep assembly line workers hard at work.

It is no accident that most factory work is so monotonous and unrewarding. **Taylorism** (also known as "scientific management") is a name given to a highly influential management philosophy originally promoted by Frederick Taylor at the end of the 19th century (Taylor 1947). Simply put, the goal of Taylorism was to analyze factory jobs into their simplest component parts and then to simplify and reorganize work to achieve maximum efficiency (Guillén 1994:41-45; Perrow 1986:57). Ever since the widespread application of Taylorism to factory work and the invention of the assembly line, the dominant pattern in American industry has been to try to simplify the tasks performed by workers so as to reduce the discretion and skill required (thus making it easier to hire cheaper labor and putting control of the workplace firmly in the hands of management). (For more on Taylorism, see Sidebar 4.1.) This pattern of work relations proved highly successful in the mass production of standardized goods and has been dubbed **Fordism** by scholars to commemorate the inventor of the first industrial assembly line, Henry Ford (Hollingsworth 1997). Hamper's description of his assembly line job reveals the worst side of Fordism.

By the 1970s, Fordist production strategies were becoming less efficient, and American auto manufacturers tried to copy their Japanese competitors. Managers of U.S. firms introduced new technologies into their factories and tried to reorganize so as to increase worker participation in production-related decision making (Milkman 1997:144-45).

SIDEBAR 4.1

Taylorism and Scientific Management

"Taylorism" was named after its inventor, the engineer Frederick Taylor. Working first in the U.S. machine tool industry, Taylor invented a method for reorganizing work that would, he argued, greatly increase efficiency and reduce the need to employ highly trained (and thus expensive) workers. Taylor conducted time-and-motion studies, complete with clipboard and stopwatch, to analyze the elementary motions used by workers to perform a particular task. Then, he redesigned the work process for greater simplicity, economy, and speed.

Suppose drill press operators in a machine shop each carry metal stock from a storage area over to their machines, put holes in the metal forms using their drill presses, and finally, place the finished pieces in a bin. Operating a drill press requires some measure of skill, so the workers in the machine shop needed to be paid more than the rate for unskilled laborers. For Taylor, such an arrangement was inefficient and wasteful. Far better to keep the drill press operators continuously at their machines and forbid them from moving or prepping their materials. The latter tasks could be given to an unskilled worker, whose wage rate would be lower. Reengineering the tasks performed by workers would raise overall productivity in the shop and allow the owners to substitute unskilled labor, or even machinery, for skilled labor. It also meant a less varied and more repetitive work process. Taylor was the management guru of his time, advocating a method that, he claimed, could improve any business.

Team-based production, quality circles, and broader (and hence more flexible) job classifications are just three of the best-known features of the new Japanese-style organization (Florida and Kenney 1991). Workers in the GM plant in Linden, New Jersey, supported such change because it had the potential to reduce the authority of foremen and supervisors over assembly line staff and could transform a highly authoritarian workplace into a more democratic one.[2]

The example of the GM Linden plant helps to illustrate three more general points: First, hierarchies of authority exemplify many large organizations and so shape employees' work experiences; second, whether a

---

[2] In the textile industry, there has been a similar turn toward more flexible production, but as Taplin (1995) points out, this hasn't resulted in much workplace democracy. Much the same holds true in Vallas and Beck's (1996) analysis of the adoption of Total Quality Management (TQM) in the pulp and paper industry.

particular workplace is rigid and authoritarian or flexible and democratic is largely up to management; last, although organizations are ubiquitous, organizational forms vary from one setting to the next.

Although we have been discussing blue-collar factory workers, these
same three points also apply to the situation of white-collar workers.
Corporate managers may claim to be interested in having subordinates
who honestly speak their minds and offer a truly independent perspective, but mostly, bosses want compliant, dependable, and supportive
people to work under them (Jackall 1988:55). White-collar subordinates
who fail to be loyal, who try to circumvent their boss, or who criticize the
boss in public run the risk of losing their jobs. Nevertheless, within the
managerial and professional ranks, superiors rarely use the kind of intru-
sive, heavy-handed methods of control that a factory foreman might employ. They must exercise their authority more subtly than that, and there
are, in fact, multiple ways to control a workforce.

In some cases, senior executives promulgate a particular kind of organizational culture to help manage a highly educated and professional-
ized white-collar workforce. Gideon Kunda (1992) studied a firm in the
computer industry (given the pseudonym "Tech") whose core workforce
consisted largely of college-educated male engineers. Tech culture was a
frequent topic of conversation in the firm and consisted of an ideology
depicting the distinctive social organization of the firm (Tech was not
only a company but also a community with a moral purpose) and articu-
lating the role of company members (ideally, Tech employees were supposed to be autonomous, hard-working, and responsible self-starters).
Tech culture created a system of normative control in which Tech employees internalized the corporate ideology. Tech culture shaped the perceptions and goals of employees in such a way that they would pursue the
company's best interests on their own, without the direct monitoring and
control that one might find on an assembly line.

In other white-collar settings, managers are evaluated using criteria
that are less tied to "objective" measures of job performance but instead
depend on more ambiguous social characteristics. Jackall (1988:49-52)
underscores the importance for managers of being perceived as a "team
player." A person may be brilliant or highly creative, but unless that person can "play ball," his or her future career prospects grow dim. A team
player is someone who works hard (and visibly so, by putting in long
hours at the office); who hasn't become too specialized; who gets along
with clients, customers, and co-workers; who is discrete and expedient;
and who expresses no strong political or moral qualms. The controls that
"team play" places on managers are no less stringent than those put on

assembly line workers, although they are informal and social rather than explicit and authoritarian.

Bosses have power, but they cannot treat their subordinates in an unrestrained and arbitrary fashion. For one thing, an employee's boss may be answerable to someone else further up the corporate ladder and so is restrained by the authority of the boss's boss. Bosses are also restrained by law (for example, the Civil Rights Act of 1964, which prohibits employment discrimination) and by the personnel policies and standard operating procedures of the organization that employs both the boss and the subordinate. Nevertheless, within these broad constraints, bosses have considerable freedom. And ultimately, it is the person at the very top of the organization, the corporate president or CEO (chief executive officer) who determines how all those underneath will fare. The top boss sets the tone for everyone, so much so that in many corporations, the CEO is a chief topic of conversation for all managers at all levels (Jackall 1988:22).

Despite these legal constraints on the power of bosses, someone who is truly unhappy with the treatment he or she has received from a boss cannot do too much to force the boss to change.[3] After all, bosses hold most of the cards. But an employee can quit and seek a different boss. Employees can, in other words, "vote with their feet." The legal doctrine of "employment at will" applies in the United States, and roughly, it means that either the employer or the employee may terminate an employment relationship at any time and without notice (Feinman 1976). Such a decision by an employee is not usually taken lightly, and an employee's willingness to endure a bad boss will depend on the availability of good alternative employment. Older workers are unlikely to quit their jobs during periods of high unemployment, even if their boss is a jerk. On the other side, "employment at will" makes it easier for bosses to fire employees, and this very real possibility is partly what gives them power over employees (in most Western European countries, by contrast, it is much harder for employers to fire workers [Tilly and Tilly 1998:132]).

The importance of bosses makes a shake-up or transition at the top of an organization an extremely uncertain time for all of a firm's employees. Robert Jackall (1988) offers two examples of corporations in which a new CEO initiated wholesale changes in the management ranks of the firm (pp. 25, 33). In one case, a new CEO reached back into his own past career

---

[3] It helps to be a member of a labor union with a collective bargaining agreement, but the proportion of the U.S. workforce that is unionized has been declining for decades (Western 1997:24).

within a particular corporate division and systematically placed and promoted his former colleagues, allies, and friends into high places. In another, the new CEO created a rule stipulating that no executives over 60 years of age could occupy a high-ranking post in the organization. At one move, an entire generation of managers was swept out of office, to be replaced by the new CEO's handpicked allies. Being the boss also gave this CEO the luxury of making rules and then changing them. As the boss and his subordinates aged, the age rule was eliminated!

Vicki Smith (1990) examined the plight of middle management in a large California bank that suffered financial difficulties in the early 1980s. Corporations that downsize their workforce frequently target middle managers for reduction. Middle management is implicated by top management for its role in corporate "waste" and "inefficiency" and for its contribution to "bloated," "overstaffed" bureaucracies. The bank's top management wanted to cut staff but also tried to get middle managers to act less "bureaucratically" and more "entrepreneurially." By putting middle managers through an extensive retraining program, top management hoped to change the corporate culture and get middle managers to think more creatively. Middle managers were also expected to rate those employees that worked under them, to take a "cold-blooded" look at worker performance, and to fire those who weren't doing well enough. Understandably, middle managers disliked having to fire any of their workers, but even so, they had no choice but to raise the productivity and performance of their units. Top management called the shots. In this bank, as in most other organizations, top management people could make wholesale changes if they wished, and there wasn't much anyone else could do to stop them.

Organizations and Internal Labor Markets

The formal hierarchies that structure authority relations in a large organization (and give some people power over others) also structure careers. Many firms are characterized by **internal labor markets.** Jacoby and Sharma (1992) offer evidence that the average duration of employment has increased over the last century in the United States. As more and more workers held quasi-permanent jobs (i.e., continued employment with the same firm), internal labor markets become increasingly important in shaping the lifetime work experiences of the labor force. By 1991, the median tenure for a 45- to 54-year-old man with his current employer was over 12 years (Tilly and Tilly 1998:216).

Within large firms, jobs get linked together into groups on the basis of a firm-specific job classification scheme. These links mean that even someone enjoying a spectacularly successful career within a firm will move up in an orderly fashion, going from one position to the next. Jobs get connected through **job ladders,** so a woman who is moving up quickly through the managerial ranks of a retail chain might get promoted from assistant manager to associate manager to senior associate manager to store manager to district manager and then to regional manager. In the engineering branch of the California Department of Transportation, employees go from junior civil engineer to assistant, associate, senior, supervising, and finally principal civil engineer (Strang and Baron 1990:479). Thus, internal labor markets determine career trajectories within the organization. Furthermore, they involve bureaucratic rules about seniority, promotion from within, standardized job descriptions, job tenure, and dismissal.

The formal organizational hierarchy determines not only the content of an employee's current job but also possible directions for future career moves. In a large organization, future upward mobility for an employee is as likely to involve job shifts inside the firm as outside. Different organizations create their own internal labor markets, and there is no canonical or standard model. But large organizations commonly rely on outside recruitment for entry-level positions at the bottom of the firm, followed by promotion-from-within for higher-level positions (Carroll and Mayer 1986:329).

Job ladders matter as much for where they don't lead as where they do. The definition of a "dead-end" job is one that doesn't lead anywhere (so someone in such a job must leave the firm to have any chance at upward mobility). To return to the retail chain example mentioned earlier, suppose instead of being hired as an assistant manager for the retail chain, the woman had been hired as a cashier, a job that typically doesn't lead to anything else. Instead of climbing through the managerial ranks, she would have languished in the same low-level position, year after year.

Job ladders help to create and reinforce inequality among workers. Goldin (1990:112-15) explains the mid-20th century wage gap between men and women partly in terms of the internal labor markets of large firms. Women employees tended to get hired as typists and stenographers, jobs that did not lead anywhere within the firm (i.e., they were *not* the "bottom rung" of a tall job ladder). Men would also start out at the very bottom (e.g., in the mail room). But if they showed promise, in contrast to women, they would get moved into the accounting division (as an accountant, teller, collector, cost controller, etc.), which often served as a kind of way station for those on the move into the higher ranks of the firm. Thus, long-time female employees tended to end up in much lower positions in the firm than did male employees of comparable seniority and, consequently, got paid much less. Workers of comparable ability, starting out in roughly similar entry-level positions, could experience highly divergent careers depending on the job ladders into which they were placed.

In a similar fashion, southern railroads in the late 19th and early 20th centuries had explicit rules about which racial groups could perform which jobs (Sundstrom 1990). On trains, black employees could rise no higher than middle positions such as brakeman or fireman. Top positions, such as conductor or engineer, were reserved for white employees only. Thus, job ladders for blacks were much shorter than job ladders for whites. Furthermore, the wage systems set by southern railroads paid different incomes to whites and blacks, even when they performed the same work. White firemen and brakemen made 10% to 30% more than black employees doing the exact same job (Sundstrom 1990:429).

The structure of internal labor markets, like much else in large organizations, is ultimately determined by top management. If the CEO wants to revise personnel policies and reorganize job ladders and job classifications, change will occur. DiPrete and Soule (1986) discuss one such instance of organizational change. In response to political pressure, the U.S. federal government during the 1970s deliberately tried to increase promotion from the lower ranks of the federal civil service into the higher ranks. Until then, white-collar jobs within the civil service had been divided into two distinct groups: lower-level clerical and technical jobs and upper-level managerial and professional jobs. Promotion from one group to the other was rare, so two distinct career patterns existed, with separate points of entry and different destinations. Because women and minorities employed by the federal government were concentrated in the lower-level jobs, starting in the 1960s, the government came under considerable political pressure to equalize its own treatment of male and female, white and minority employees. Upward-mobility programs to increase promotion between the two groups were instituted in the early and mid-1970s, with some measure of success (DiPrete and Soule 1986:300).

Private corporations have also felt the need to respond to the political events of the 1960s and in their employment policies to comply with the Civil Rights Act of 1964. Edelman (1990, 1992) shows how organizations adopted various internal labor market features to help manage job-related disputes and ensure fairness in employment. Specifically, firms set up formal grievance procedures to deal with disputes involving their nonunionized workers (unions usually have a grievance procedure as part of their collective bargaining agreement), and many also instituted equal employment opportunity and affirmative action offices and rules. The mere existence of such procedures and institutions helps corporations to signal to the outside world that they are committed to fairness.

Firms restructure their internal labor markets in response to market pressures as well as to political pressures. In the 1970s and 1980s, many American firms suffered at the hands of foreign competition. U.S. manufacturers, in particular, that had perfected the art of mass production, seemed to have been eclipsed by their Japanese counterparts. Numerous management advice books and gurus touted the superiority of Japanese modes of organization and enjoined American managers to reshape their firms along Japanese lines.

According to Smith (1997), adoption of elements of Japanese-style work relations is one of the major changes occurring today with U.S. corporations (recall the spread of TQM among health care organizations discussed in Chapter 3). Various institutional features are being implemented to encourage more employee involvement by modifying the internal labor market rules that govern who does what job. These features include quality circles, teamwork, job rotations, and self-management. Some of these measures seem attractive when contrasted with monotonous assembly line work. Expanding job descriptions and rotating people through different jobs helps to save employees from falling into "mindless ruts," but it also makes more demands on them and requires them to be expert in a larger number of distinct tasks (Smith 1997:322). Team-based production, by contrast, really does represent an attractive change for many employees because it alters workplace authority relationships. Power in the workplace becomes more decentralized and shifts out of the hands of foremen. Employees acquire more say in how to perform their own jobs.

Organizations also determine how their employees will be paid and how much. Only rarely are wage rates set by the outside labor market alone. In the early years of the 20th century, the sums paid to many factory workers depended essentially on the personal whims of the factory foreman (Jacoby 1984). With the spread of internal labor markets during the 20th century (we will say more about this process later on), wages became more systematic. Workers can be paid in many different ways. Some employees might be paid monthly salaries that depend neither on their personal productivity nor on how much time they spend on the job.

Others might be paid on an hourly basis, so their compensation would be a strict function of time spent at work. Still others might be paid on a "piecework" basis, with their wages depending on some direct measure of productivity. Of course, combinations of these various methods of compensation are also possible, but it is generally up to the organization itself to determine its system of employee compensation.

In his study of department store salespeople, Petersen (1992) found differences both in how such workers were paid and in how much they were paid. Petersen discusses three different pay systems, one in which the worker receives a straight salary (a flat wage, no matter what the level of productivity), another in which salary is based on a straight commission (i.e., wages depend on sales or productivity and nothing else), and a combination salary plus commission system (a base salary plus additional funds that depend on productivity). Generally, a straight salary or salary plus commission system gives the worker more income security. Employers, however, usually regard the commission system as better for themselves because unproductive workers get nothing (i.e., the risk of low productivity is borne entirely by the worker, not the employer). Straight commission may be attractive to employers, but without some wage security, it becomes harder to hire good people, so firms often must compromise. Petersen found that among department store salespeople, those paid on an incentive system generally made more money than those paid a straight salary (p. 83). How much money they made depended on their personal performance but, more fundamentally, on the compensation scheme instituted by the organization they worked for. (See Sidebar 4.2 for examples from the textile industry.)

Our discussion thus far has focused on the way organizations determine the wages they pay to their employees, but today, many firms also offer nonwage forms of compensation. Health care, dental plans, life insurance, child care, and retirement benefits are some of those most commonly offered to employees. Using 1993 data, Bassett et al. (1998) studied employer-sponsored, defined-contribution pension plans, typically known as 401(k) plans. The employer contributes a sum to a participating employee's individual account. The employee decides how that sum is to be invested, and the money is usually deducted from the employee's pay (and sometimes matched by a proportional contribution from the employer). When the employee retires, whatever amount has accumulated over the years is then made available to support the retiree. The total sum going into 401(k) plans is considerable ($69 billion in 1993), but in fact, only about 42% of workers have employers who offer such a plan (Bassett et al. 1998:1). Many Americans work for employers who do not offer pen-

SIDEBAR 4.2

Culture and Pay

Some believe that technological requirements combine with the imperatives of economic efficiency to dictate how employee effort and output are measured and rewarded. There is, in other words, one best way to measure and reward what workers do. But in fact, Richard Biernacki (1995) shows in an insightful comparison of the German and British wool textile industries that even direct competitors do not necessarily converge on a single "one best way" to do such things.

Biernacki focuses on two contemporaneous national competitors in the same industry, producing the same product, using the same technology, organized in a similar fashion, and employing a similar workforce. In both countries, workers were paid on a piece rate system—that is, in terms of "how much" they produced. But how worker productivity was measured in the two countries differed sharply and in ways that cannot be explained in terms of technology or efficiency.

In English textile mills, weavers were paid on the basis of the length of cloth woven, holding constant the density of the cloth (weft threads per inch). In Germany, weavers were paid by the number of times the shuttle in their loom shot back and forth, again holding constant the cloth density. Biernacki argues that these differences are inexplicable in terms of efficiency or technology (indeed there were no technological differences between the two industries, and both methods worked equally well). Rather, these two systems of remuneration reflected fundamentally different cultural conceptions of labor: "In Germany, workers were remunerated for the conversion of labor power into a product; in Britain, they sold their labor as it was concretized in a product" (Biernacki 1995:73).

---

sion plans at all. More generally in the United States, many nonwage benefits (such as health insurance, dental plans, child care, etc.) come only from employers (the government doesn't offer them to U.S. citizens). People who do not have the good fortune to work for the right employer must provide for themselves and are consequently often left in a situation in which they do not receive adequate care.

The situation in the United States contrasts quite dramatically with that in other advanced industrialized countries. In Western Europe, for example, access to health care and pensions doesn't depend on employers because the government provides them to everyone. Consequently, U.S. private employers pay a much higher proportion of total health insurance and pension benefits than do employers in Western Europe (Dobbin 1992:1416-17). Furthermore, because they are not tied to employment, access to health care and pensions is more general and more evenly distributed in Western Europe than in the United States.

The Organizational
Context for Conflict

An individual's workplace experience varies depending on the organization. So far, we have touched on some of the most obvious aspects of jobs: wages, nonwage compensation, promotions, and so on. But workplace experiences involve other things as well. How do organizational differences affect the people who work in them? How are social interactions influenced by organizational context? We answer these questions by focusing here on one specific feature of organizational life: conflict.

Calvin Morrill (1995) studied the effects of organizational context on conflict among top executives in 13 different corporations (which ranged from a large communications firm with 60,000 employees to a much smaller packaging firm with "only" 500 employees). Conflict is ubiquitous in organizations and is an unfortunate aspect of virtually everyone's work life. But it varies from explicit to covert, from confrontational to nonconfrontational, from concentrated to diffuse. Conflict also varies depending on who it occurs between (executives of the same rank vs. superiors and subordinates), how it is resolved (e.g., one aggrieved party acts unilaterally, the two sides resolve the issue together, or a third party is brought into the picture), and what it is about.

Morrill found that conflict among business executives often possessed a surprisingly personal quality. The five most common issues about which people fought were promotion and compensation, management style, personal life, personalities, and individual performance (Morrill 1995:69). Important corporate issues (such as organizational strategy, resource allocation, and administrative jurisdiction) mattered less. He also found that executives used a variety of strategies to deal with conflict, including temporary avoidance (simply staying away from the person who was the source of the problem), endurance (putting up with the problem), confrontation, challenge, and authoritative command. Not all conflicts resulted in explicit fights.

Morrill discovered that executive conflict varied systematically from one organizational context to the next. Three cases in particular illuminated the pattern. Morrill identified one company, "Old Financial" (a profitable savings and loan with about 10,000 employees) as a "mechanistic bureaucracy." At Old Financial, formal rank mattered a great deal and people generally did things "by the book." Communication among executives occurred through official channels (memos, reports, meetings, etc.), and those executives who obeyed their superiors and complied with the official chain of command did best (Morrill 1995:98). The formal hierarchy at Old Financial had a big effect on conflict, and authoritative commands (verbal or written) were the most common conflict management action taken in response to fights between superiors and subordinates. Subordinates often simply tolerated superiors who caused problems or combined avoidance with exit strategies. If a subordinate did confront a superior about a grievance, he or she followed up with conciliatory gestures (Morrill 1995:121).

In contrast with Old Financial, "Independent Accounting" was a regional office of a big accounting firm. This firm's core business involved commercial auditing and tax services, but it had branched into business consulting as well. The accountants were sharply divided between the senior members of the firm who had "made partner" (and who owned the firm) and those who had not (the "associates"). Morrill terms this an "atomized organization" because of the high degree of independence among the partners. Almost no partner had much power over other partners, although they all obviously had considerable power over the associates. Furthermore, the partners worked autonomously, performing services for clients in engagements that could last anywhere from a few weeks to several months in length.

The absence of formal authority differences among the executives, all of whom were partners, had a big effect on conflict. According to Morrill (1995:158), the two most common conflict management strategies were avoidance and toleration. With so much independence among the partners, it was easy for them to avoid each other or to tolerate problems if need be. Authoritative commands were simply not an option because so few partners had any formal authority over the others.

Morrill's third case involved "Playco," an entertainment company with some 20,000 employees. Playco's executive ranks had been deliberately reorganized in the 1970s along matrix lines. This meant that executives were organized along two dimensions simultaneously: functional groups (e.g., sales, finance, operations, engineering, etc.) and product groups (cross-classifying the two dimensions created a product by function matrix, hence the term "matrix organization"). Because new products were introduced constantly and old products phased out, product groups changed often. Executives fit into two authority structures simultaneously, one of which was in constant turmoil. This dual structure complicated and blurred lines of authority.

Unlike the partners in Independent Accounting, Playco executives worked closely together. Indeed, there was intense interaction among them (Playco executives both socialized and worked together). Consequently, they couldn't resolve conflicts either through authoritative commands or by ignoring each other and sticking to their own clients. Without clear formal hierarchies, Playco executives created reputational hierarchies. They put enormous weight on their own personal honor and public reputation, and the intense interactions they had with each other helped to create and diffuse such reputations. Conflict at Playco was both explicit and confrontational, and executives spent a lot of time fighting among themselves. The three main forms of conflict management were vengeance, challenges, and public insults. Executives with a good reputation were better able to mobilize allies in support of their own position on a matter, whereas those with bad reputations couldn't muster much support.

The point of Morrill's analysis is that organizational structure and culture affect how executives manage their conflict with each other. Conflict within any group of individuals is inevitable, but the organization sets the terrain on which the combat unfolds. The deliberate institutionalization of a matrix system among Playco top executives during the 1970s had a huge impact on the dynamics of conflict and conflict management. The professional organization among partners at Independent Accounting had a similarly profound effect on conflict. Organizations determine not only the career patterns, remuneration, and formal working conditions of those who work in them, they also shape to a large degree the kind of social interactions that occur among employees.

Workplace and Personal Life

Organizations influence the experiences that workers and managers have on the job, whether they concern formal issues such as pay and promotion or informal matters such as social interaction. But organizations can also reach outside the workplace and shape aspects of people's lives that we ordinarily consider to be more "private" and "personal." Their impact, in other words, is more than just 9 to 5.

Some organizations involve a fairly clear separation between the personal life and the work life of an employee. For example, consider a steelworker. So long as the worker shows up on time and performs the job well, it really doesn't matter what sort of family life or personality the worker has. How the steelworker dresses or cuts his or her hair is irrelevant to the job. In the steel industry, the person of the individual producer and the qualities of the product are distinct from one another.

Other kinds of organizations sometime reach into what we ordinarily consider to be the more private and personal affairs of the people who work for them. This can happen particularly in those kinds of work in which there is no sharp distinction between the commodity or service being produced and the producer. **Interactive service work** offers one example of this pattern. The personality, comportment, and appearance of a waiter, hairstylist, flight attendant, or personal trainer are all an integral part of what a customer pays for when dining at a restaurant, getting a haircut, traveling by air, or working out at a gym.

Firms in the interactive service sector will often dictate to their employees how they will dress and interact with customers. Robin Leidner (1993) shows how the fast-food restaurant McDonald's scripts and routinizes the ways that members of its counter staff interact with customers. Conversations with customers are not left to extemporaneous chance or to the spontaneous moods of workers. Rather, McDonald's trains its staff, and teaches them scripts that they are expected to follow closely, to ensure that each interaction is polite, predictable, and expeditious. Thus, comportment and appearance, which we often suppose to be a genuine expression of one's individual personality, is shaped by the employer to conform with what it wants. Many firms in the service sector are like McDonald's in dictating norms of appearance, style, and interaction for their workers.

Nicole Biggart (1989) analyzes a situation in which firms do not try to control personality and appearance so much as appropriate the social and personal networks of their sales force. Direct sales organizations (DSOs) are in the business of selling various consumer goods without using a fixed retail location. They include firms such as Amway and Mary Kay Cosmetics, which produce personal care and grooming products, household cleaning products, and so on, and sell them in people's private homes. DSOs typically do not employ their salespeople directly and so have little formal legal authority over them. Rather, members of the sales force operate as independent contractors. Thus, the main form of coercion available to employers—namely, the threat of job termination—is not open to DSOs.

Without formal legal authority over its salespeople, DSOs cannot dictate interactive scripts, personal appearance, hair length, and other aspects of comportment. But according to Biggart, DSOs find other ways to influence their sales force and get them to sell the firm's products. In particular, they instill in their sales force a positive, entrepreneurial ideology that celebrates the firm's products. For example, selling vitamins isn't just about pills but involves the affirmation of a positive, healthy lifestyle. The formally independent status of the sales force is upheld as a virtue because it means, according to the entrepreneurial ideology, that the success of each salesperson is in his or her own hands: Opportunity is theirs for the taking. In this manner, DSO corporate headquarters serves as a fount of ideology as well as a source for the product.

With such personal commitment to the product by the sales force, selling is interpreted less as an instance of simple market exchange and more as an occasion for sharing or gift giving (Biggart 1989:116). The purveyor of vitamins is "sharing" with his or her friends the opportunity to live a healthier, happier lifestyle, not just selling them a commodity. Recasting sales into the idiom of gift giving makes good sense given how much DSOs use the social networks and familial connections of the sales force. DSOs strongly encourage their salespeople to sell to their friends and families and in general to exploit the social and normative obligations that others have to them. In fact, without a store or fixed retail location to use, people often sell out of their homes, so marketing to friends and family seems only natural. Flexibility of hours and the compatibility of work with child care only reinforce the "family-friendly" orientation of many DSOs. (It also makes the job especially attractive to women, who constitute approximately 80% of the DSO sales force.)

If corporate ideology helps compensate for the absence of formal legal controls in the case of direct sales, it can also complement and bolster such controls in the case of the high-tech computer company studied by Gideon Kunda (1992). As mentioned earlier, the core "Tech" workforce was composed mostly of young college-educated engineers. Practically the entire workforce, from top management on down, recognized that Tech possessed a distinctive organizational culture. This culture was promulgated by top management (who often made public presentations to employees about what sort of a corporation Tech was) and used as a system of normative control. As "good" members of Tech, employees were expected to live up to the expectations articulated in Tech culture. Tech workers were supposed to be extremely hard-working, perfectionistic, and autonomous individualists who were motivated by their own initiative (so much so that becoming "burnt out" was a public sign of one's commitment).

The tenets of Tech culture were articulated and reinforced both formally and informally and by both managers and employees alike. Even work group meetings whose ostensible purpose was to accomplish a specific work-related task ended up being occasions for the invocation of Tech culture (Kunda 1992:153). Tech's system of normative control encouraged employees to drive themselves and each other much harder than would be necessary as part of a regular 9 to 5 job, and doubtless, this undermined the quality of Tech employees' personal lives.

Through the use of formal and informal controls, by means of explicit hierarchical authority and tacit organizational culture, organizations have come to shape many aspects of the work and personal life of the people who work for them. Working conditions, promotion prospects, pay and other forms of compensation, social status, interpersonal relations on the job, personal appearance and demeanor, familial relations, and social life have all, in some way or other, been affected by the demands that organizations make on their members. Yet organizations have not been always been a common feature in the economy. If large-scale organizations seem ubiquitous today, 150 years ago they were anything but commonplace. Thus, one way to understand the importance of organizations for economic life is to follow the growth and development of the organizational economy. Why did big organizations come to dominate the modern American economy?

The Formation of an Organizational Economy

To economists and social scientists who believe in the efficiency of competitive markets, the emergence of large-scale organizations was for a long time something of a mystery. For Adam Smith ([1776] 1900), author of *The Wealth of Nations*, the East India Company, the corporate giant of his era, grew and flourished thanks to a government-granted monopoly on trade with the East Indies: Protected from competitive market forces, the company could grow in size. For many of Smith's disciples, large firms couldn't survive in truly competitive situations, given that markets were assumed to be the most efficient social mechanisms available for the allocation and pricing of goods. One explanation for the existence of large firms was offered in 1937 by Ronald Coase, who was later to win the Nobel Prize in economics. Coase pointed out that the kind of economic coordination performed by the market (Adam Smith's famous "invisible hand") was performed inside firms by the entrepreneur/boss. The price mechanism didn't operate inside firms.

A firm that requires something always faces a "make-or-buy" decision: Should the firm purchase the commodity on the market, or should it provide the commodity itself? For instance, a company that needs legal advice can provide its own through in-house counsel (the "make" alternative), or it can outsource legal services and hire an independent law firm (the "buy" alternative). For some kinds of commodities or services, the cost of negotiating, monitoring, and enforcing a market agreement could be quite high. Market transactions entailed what Coase called "marketing costs" (Coase 1937:403), a set of costs that firms did not have to bear for their own internal transactions. When transaction costs were high, it could be cheaper for a firm to supply the commodity itself rather than purchase it. For firms that had to acquire many such commodities repeatedly, the boundaries of the firm would in effect expand to encompass multiple transactions.

In his theory of **transaction costs,** Oliver Williamson (1975, 1981, 1985) updated and elaborated Coase's idea that certain costs were associated with coordinating transactions inside and outside of markets. Some kinds of transactions generated transaction costs that could be handled better inside a firm than on a market. In other words, under some circumstances, a large organization could be more efficient than a market: The prevalence of such circumstances explains the prevalence of organizations.

Alfred Chandler's Analysis

These abstract arguments by themselves do not explain the historical rise of large corporations and their dominating role in the modern economy. For historical evidence, we can look to Alfred Chandler's influential discussion of American corporations in the 19th and 20th centuries. Chandler (1977) argues that "modern business enterprise took the place of market mechanisms in coordinating the activities of the economy and allocating its resources" (p. 1). Instead of markets and the small firms that traditionally inhabited them, large firms coordinated the flow of goods through production and distribution and also allocated funds and personnel. **Administrative coordination** replaced **market coordination,** and the spread of administrative coordination necessitated the growth of managerial hierarchies. In Chandler's analysis, middle managers performed the work of administrative planning and coordination. As firms got larger, they had to hire more and more middle managers.

In the early part of the 19th century, small traditionally organized businesses produced commodities and distributed goods. They were owned and operated by a single proprietor, or a partnership, and had only a few employees at most. Management information systems consisted of double-entry bookkeeping, a simple method for tracking debits and credits used by merchants since the 15th century. These numerous small firms populated the American economy and built up commercial networks that could efficiently manufacture and import or distribute goods throughout the nation. The networks that spanned the country consisted of small firms connected through arm's-length market transactions. As Chandler (1977) puts it, "This quickly created continental commercial network was coordinated almost entirely by market mechanisms" (p. 27). Both trade and production expanded during the first part of the 19th century, but such growth did not produce any institutional innovation. Firms became more numerous and specialized, but they did not alter their basic organizational features.

For technological and organizational reasons, the first large-scale businesses emerged among railways and telegraphs (Chandler 1977:81). As they grew during the 1850s, railways and telegraphs began to develop the organizational structures and accounting procedures central to the operation of the modern large firm. To run a railroad, for instance, a firm needed to acquire and maintain new and complex forms of equipment and fixed assets. Geographically dispersed activities performed by numerous employees had to be coordinated exactly so that trains would run safely and according to schedule. All this required the creation of a sizable administrative apparatus to plan, manage, and monitor what the firm's employees did. Chandler claims that "without the building of a managerial staff, without the design of internal administrative structures and procedures, and without communicating internal information, a high volume of traffic could not be carried safely and efficiently" (p. 94). As railroads grew, so did their administrative hierarchies and the number of middle-level managers they employed.

The development of railroads influenced the rest of the economy in two ways. First, railroads made long-distance overland trade much cheaper. More bulk goods could be shipped all over the United States than ever before. This helped to integrate regional markets and create a national market for producers and distributors, thus allowing them to take advantage of economies of scale and grow larger. Second, railroads served as an administrative model for subsequent businesses. The organizational methods and administrative procedures developed by railroads to manage their own internal activities were copied by other corporations (Chandler 1977:188). Thus, changes in transportation and communications begat the emergence of large corporations in production and distribution.

In explaining these changes, Chandler argues that administrative coordination was simply more efficient than market coordination when dealing with geographically dispersed, highly complex tasks involving large numbers of persons whose efforts had to be carefully meshed together. Rather than viewing large bureaucracies staffed with middle managers as the embodiment of unresponsive inefficiency, Chandler claims that they appeared and grew in the middle of the 19th century for a very simple reason: They outperformed the competition. Managers relied on newly developed accounting procedures and information systems to help them manage.[4] As firms grew, cost accounting replaced double-entry bookkeeping.

Responses to Chandler

Several sociologists have taken issue with Chandler's analysis of the rise of large firms, and in particular, they disagree with the singular importance he attributes to economic efficiency as the arbiter among organizational alternatives. Railroads were driven as much by government policy as by market efficiency. Frank Dobbin (1994), for example, shows how important the actions of state and local governments were in the early decades of railroads. To encourage railroad construction, state and local governments often offered substantial financial aid to entrepreneurs. Up to 1861, these governments invested in railroad bonds, gave away free land, lowered taxes, and in various ways provided about 30% of the total capital invested in railways (Dobbin 1994:41). Later, governments were as influential for what they didn't do as for what they did. Unlike European governments, the U.S. government played no role in setting technical standards for the industry (the most important being track gauge, the standard distance between tracks).

After a period of intense activity, state and local governments became less involved in railways, and eventually, only the federal government played a continuing role. This role, however, was confined largely to issues of pricing and competition. With the establishment of the Interstate Commerce Commission and passage of the Sherman Anti-Trust Act, the federal government regulated the railroads to encourage market compe-

---

[4] For an interesting discussion of 19th-century information technology and how it was used by large firms, see Yates (1989).

tition and discourage discriminatory pricing. Dobbin shows that economic efficiency was not the only thing affecting the railroads and that at different times, state, local, and federal government had an important influence (Fligstein 1990). The growth of American railroads was as much a political as an economic process and so was deeply embedded in the institutionally and culturally distinctive quality of American politics.

William Roy (1997) agrees with Chandler that the railroads were very important but differs over how they became so. He argues that the rise of large firms represented more than just the appearance of a new organizational form; it marked the emergence of a fundamentally new kind of property. Small firms owned by single proprietors or partners embodied traditional forms of property; business assets were tangible forms of wealth over which the owner had complete control. Large publicly traded corporations, in contrast, were "socialized property" (Roy 1997:10). They were owned by many shareholders, not just one or two. And individuals often owned small pieces of many corporations.

The people who owned large publicly traded corporations seldom ran them, so ownership became separate from control. If formal ownership reposed among the shareholders, actual control was usually in the hands of company managers and directors (Berle and Means 1968). These changes in property fundamentally altered relationships between managers, owners, employees, and creditors (Roy 1997:6). As the first large-scale corporations whose shares were widely held and publicly traded on financial markets such as the New York Stock Exchange, railroads exemplified the new type of property (Navin and Sears 1955).

Corporations are very much the creation of law (and not just the market), and therefore have no independent existence apart from government and politics. The law defines what "unitary, singular organizations can exist and act with legal sanction" (Roy 1997:148). Like real living persons, corporations are allowed to own property, to sign contracts, employ people, and so on—but only because the law allows them to do so. Because legislatures make laws, political conflict invariably shapes what corporations are allowed to do. Roy discusses three particular features of corporate law to illustrate his point: (1) intercorporate stock ownership (can corporations own other corporations?), (2) the powers of boards of directors (how independent should they be with respect to shareholders?), and (3) limited liability (should shareholders be liable for the debts of the corporation beyond the amount they invested in the shares?). The ability of corporations to own other corporations, the spread of limited liability, and the increasing autonomy of directors all contributed to the socialization of property (Roy 1997:148-64).

One of the distinctive characteristics of American corporations (unlike those in other countries) is that the legal framework within which they operate is set at the state level, not by the federal government (Grandy 1989:677). Corporate headquarters are quite mobile, so they can easily shift from one state to another. Thus, many of the rights and powers enjoyed by corporations were acquired as part of a legal "race to the bottom." To attract corporations to their jurisdiction, state governments get into a legal competition with each other, trying to "outbid" other states by offering the most appealing corporate law and thus encourage the most incorporations.[5] During the late 1890s, New Jersey offered legal features most attractive to large businesses, so many firms incorporated there. Delaware emulated New Jersey's statutes and went even further by lowering tax rates, to get corporations to shift further south (Grandy 1989:685).

Roy (1997) directly criticizes Chandler's efficiency explanation for the rise of large corporations. If corporations appeared because they were more efficient, Roy argues, then they should have developed first in those industries characterized by high capital intensity, high productivity, and rapid growth (p. 38). Yet this was not the case. Instead, Roy emphasizes two other factors, the control over capital and the power of the state, to explain how and why large corporations appeared (p. 262).

Neil Fligstein (1990) offers some other significant modifications to Chandler's version of the story. In addition to public policy, which both Dobbin and Roy recognize, Fligstein underscores the importance of cultural factors. In particular, Fligstein discusses the role of the cognitive frameworks that managers use to interpret their situations and decide what to do. These "conceptions of control" help managers figure out an appropriate and rational organizational strategy, and they influence how managers respond to their competitors and allies in other markets. These conceptions are not idiosyncratic or personal. Rather, at a given point in time, one or another conception is the dominant perspective.

Fligstein traces the history of American big business as a succession of conceptions of control. Since the 1880s, there have been four: direct control of competitors, manufacturing control, sales and marketing control, and finance control (Fligstein 1990:12). The first engendered strate-

---

[5] The ability of corporations to influence government policy by "voting with their feet," has a parallel at the international level. In a globalized economy, the threat of capital flight can force national governments to lower taxes, remove objectionable regulations, and otherwise make public policy more hospitable to corporations. See Chapter 7 on globalization.

gies such as predatory competition, cartelization, and the creation of monopolies. The second led to strategies such as backward and forward integration of production, mergers to increase market share, and the establishment of oligopolistic product markets.

With the third conception of control, firms were led to focus on sales and to pursue the strategy of product differentiation and market expansion. Finally, the last and most recent conception of control, dominant since the mid-1960s, led to a focus on short-term financial measures of performance, diversified mergers, and a "portfolio" conception of the firm (Fligstein 1990:251). These different conceptions of control, and the transition from one to the next, resulted from the combined effects of public policy, market dynamics, and the internal structure of large corporations.

The Emergence of Internal Labor Markets

A number of the distinctive organizational features we discussed earlier in this chapter came with the growth of the largest firms. Larger firms meant that a greater proportion of productive activities occurred within firms than between them. It also meant a larger number of workers to manage. Jacoby (1985:40) points out that the average iron and steel plant employed 65 workers in 1860, 103 in 1870, and 333 in 1900. The growth of large corporations was associated with the development of internal labor markets, so administrative decisions replaced market decisions as a determinant of labor force dynamics. The formation of internal labor markets was highly discontinuous, with periods of accelerated development followed by times of quiescence and even retrenchment.

According to Jacoby (1984, 1985), internal labor markets were adopted by American industrial firms mostly during two periods of crisis: World War I and the Great Depression (Jacoby 1984:23).[6] Under the traditional system used by industrial firms in the late 19th century, top management had little interest in employment issues, choosing instead to leave such matters in the hands of foremen. The latter wielded considerable power and had almost total control over hiring, employee supervision, and pay. The system of employment at will meant that, legally,

---

[6] Of course, some firms adopted internal labor market features even before World War I. Carter and Carter (1985) show how a number of New York City department stores instituted wage and promotion systems to cultivate greater commitment to the firm from low-wage workers. Furthermore, Sundstrom (1988) shows that internal promotion and worker training was practiced widely before World War I.

foremen could do pretty much what they wanted. (Remember, this period preceded the labor legislation of the 1930s and the antidiscrimination legislation of the 1960s, so few laws constrained what employers did.) Employees could be hired or fired at a moment's notice. And although this freedom to terminate the employment relationship applied equally to employees (i.e., they could quit at a moment's notice), in practice, the balance of power fell heavily on the side of employers.

Foremen were anything but fair or systematic in how they hired and paid workers. Different workers doing exactly the same job could be paid very different wages. Different foremen in the same firm might pay different wages for the same job performed in different departments. Thus, compensation was very unsystematic. Employees also suffered from highly unstable employment: They could be fired or laid off with virtually no notice, and there was no guarantee that they would be rehired if the firm needed to expand its workforce in the future (Jacoby 1984:27). Foremen used the "drive" system, a combination of close supervision, threats, and abuse, to get their employees to work harder.

Starting in the early 20th century, labor unions and personnel managers combined to criticize the traditional system and to try to change it. Representing the interests of workers, unions opposed the arbitrary and unconstrained power of foremen in the workplace. Workers wanted more stable employment and more systematic compensation. Thus, unions pushed for the classification of jobs into consistent categories and the standardization of pay received by persons working similar jobs.

Personnel managers, who were trying to become more of a profession, also criticized the drive system on the grounds that it led to labor unrest and unstable working conditions. They proposed to take employment decisions out of the hands of foremen and centralize them in the personnel department (i.e., to take over those decisions themselves), which would promulgate systematic worker evaluation, training, promotion, and compensation. Yet unions and personnel managers could not easily supplant foremen until the conditions were right. In the United States, World War I helped to create those conditions because between 1916 and 1920 unemployment fell to its lowest levels in decades. War mobilization meant more jobs (and fewer immigrant workers) than before, and the threat of termination, a foreman's most effective weapon, essentially disappeared. Unionization and strike activity increased substantially during the war (Jacoby 1985:136) and helped to shift the balance of power away from foremen.

The number of large firms with personnel departments increased from less than 7% in 1915 to 25% in 1920 (Jacoby 1984:36). These departments took away from foremen the function of selecting and assigning new employees. They also restricted the ability of foremen to discharge workers. Personnel managers set about rating and classifying jobs in the belief that internal promotion systems engendered greater commitment from employees because they could expect, in the long run, to remain with the firm (e.g., an employee might stick with a relatively low-paying, entry-level job if it would eventually lead to a better job with the same employer). High turnover among workers was regarded as a serious problem.

During the 1920s, as labor markets loosened again and unemployment rates climbed, power shifted back to foremen, and many personnel departments were weakened or abolished altogether. Union membership declined and strike activity fell (Jacoby 1985:172). The tide turned again during the Great Depression, when new government labor regulations and resurgent unions stimulated the growth of formalized internal labor markets (Jacoby 1984:53). Firms needed personnel experts to be able to document their compliance with new government rules, and consequently, the proportion of large firms with personnel departments increased dramatically between 1929 and 1935-36 from 55% to 81% (Jacoby 1985:233).

Labor market conditions tightened again during World War II, but with widespread unionization and the increased involvement of the federal government in labor relations, after the war there was no retrenchment akin to the early 1920s. Companies with a unionized workforce faced pressure to systematize pay, institute seniority provisions, and regularize promotions. But companies without unions found adoption of these features a useful strategy to prevent unionization. Internal labor markets became an enduring feature of large corporations.

Although the institutionalization of internal labor markets earlier in the 20th century was advantageous to firms (internal labor markets helped to ameliorate labor militancy, facilitated compliance with legal regulations, and gave workers a long-term interest in their employer), more recently, firms have found them increasingly onerous. Internal labor markets make a firm's workforce less flexible because they make the hiring, training, promotion, and dismissal of employees subject to bureaucratic rules. Furthermore, permanent full-time workers are eligible for various expensive nonwage benefits (health, retirement, etc.).

To recapture some flexibility and cut labor costs, firms have resorted to two strategies: dismantle internal labor markets outright and rely increasingly on temporary workers or subcontractors whose jobs are not subject to internal labor market rules (Parker 1994). As such strategies spread, the labor force becomes increasingly split between a small number of core workers who enjoy stable, well-paid employment with benefits and a larger number of peripheral workers whose jobs are less secure and offer worse compensation (Tilly and Tilly 1998:217).

Complex combinations of employment status are now in evidence: Smith (1994:298) analyzes situations in which companies have contracted out their photocopying and duplication services to an independent subcontractor (dubbed "Reproco"). Because both Reproco and its corporate clients use temp workers, one can find the client's permanent and temp workers, and the permanent and temp workers of Reproco, all working together in the same workplace. The ability of employers to monitor and control their employees diminishes in such situations. Reproco employees, for example, are physically dispersed to the client's offices and not under the watchful eye of the Reproco management. And because they do not work directly for the client, clients cannot treat them like employees (see Gottfried 1991).

The change in organizational size and structure studied by Chandler and others was extremely important, but small firms didn't disappear from the U.S. economy (Atack 1986). And today, new organizational forms are emerging all the time. In some industries, firms follow neither the pattern of large bureaucratic organizations nor that of small proprietorships. Instead, in the Silicon Valley computer industry, in American biotechnology, and in northern Italian textiles, one finds a dense network of small interconnected organizations (see the discussion of interorganizational networks in Chapter 3).

Much of the economic activity of such firms doesn't occur internally or through arm's-length market relationships (i.e., given the choice between "make" or "buy," firms choose neither). Rather, activity occurs through recurrent collaborative relationships that firms cultivate among themselves. Firms do joint ventures together or they codevelop and comarket new products. Whichever external relationships they create, their internal structure doesn't resemble the large bureaucratic structure of the railways, mass distributors, and mass producers that Chandler examined. Individual careers involve much more lateral mobility (e.g., a computer programmer will shift from one firm to another) than occurs in the classic internal labor market.

Conclusion

Large firms developed over the course of the 19th and 20th centuries. Their growth was driven by a number of different factors, including economic efficiency, politics, culture, and law. Small firms have never disappeared; indeed they remain numerous. But today, they exist in an economy that contains many large firms. In 1992, 15,495,000 proprietorships operated in the United States (measured by the number that filed tax returns), compared with 3,869,000 corporations. Those proprietorships received $737 billion in receipts, whereas the much smaller number of corporations received $11,272 billion (U.S. Department of Commerce 1996:533). Although they are less numerous, corporations nevertheless dominate proprietorships in terms of their economic impact.

Large firms affect a national economy differently than do small ones. For instance, in market economies, inefficient firms lose money and eventually go bankrupt and close down. Closure of a small firm—for instance, a mom-and-pop grocery store—may be inconvenient for customers (who now have to drive further to get milk) and an unfortunate event for a handful of employees, but there are seldom any long-lasting economic or social consequences. Closure of a very large firm, in contrast, can throw tens of thousands of people out of work on a single day, devastate the local economy of a town or city, and pull down other firms with it (e.g., suppliers and creditors). Thus, the decisions made by managers of large firms (to invest here or there, to close down, to expand production, to retool, etc.) are extremely fateful for the economic well-being of entire communities. The emergence of large corporations centralizes economic decision making into private hands.

One cannot focus on economic efficiency alone to explain the existence of large firms. Other political, legal, cultural, and institutional factors also have affected the rise and shape of big corporations. One of the clearest demonstrations of the importance of government for business is the extent to which business tries to influence government. Were public policy simply irrelevant to business, corporations could safely ignore it. But in fact, business interests are active in areas such as trade, environmental policy, labor policy, health and safety regulation, taxes, and energy policy (Vogel 1996:7). Business lobbyists and political action committees (PACs) recognize that how well their clients will do depends critically on the decisions that politicians make, the laws they pass, and the policies that the government pursues.

The consequences of large organizations are as varied as the causes. Corporations now have a huge impact on the working and personal lives of millions of people and their families. Formal employment procedures, informal organizational culture, job ladders, and compensation are all determined by employers. But so are dress, personal appearance, and how an employee interacts with customers and clients. Few areas of life are unaffected by the rise of large firms.

5

Economic Inequality

All over the world today, free markets are spreading, bringing new opportunities and new challenges to previously regulated economies. In Russia, once the cradle of world socialism, managers of formerly state-owned enterprises have been hard put to apply their skills to the much more rigorous environment of market competition in a global economy. As one Russian manager remarked,

> The pace of change is beyond description and the only constant in our enterprise is continuous change. . . . Everyone is groping to solve problems and to acquire the skills necessary to compete as we move to privatize our industry. . . . Russians have a history of being able to adapt to difficult situations, but our move to a market-driven economy is a dire test. (Longenecker and Popovski 1994:35)

Since the late 1980s, many nations have experienced similar rigors in their transitions from socialism to capitalism. Even among nonsocialist nations, governments have been privatizing their nationally owned industries and deregulating industries previously subject to government supervision and control. As markets increase in importance on a global scale, their consequences become more significant. One of the most important of these effects is economic inequality. Even the most vocal advocates of free markets admit that they produce winners and losers. Some people earn high salaries, while others earn low salaries; some people amass large fortunes, while others do not; some people receive loans, while others are denied them; some people are quickly promoted inside corporations, while others are not.

If unfettered markets are associated with such divergent outcomes, why are governments around the world so eager to promote them? In the United States—widely considered to be the most advanced free market, industrialized country in the world—a common answer to this question is that a system in which people can pursue their own individual self-interest will ultimately be beneficial to society as a whole. This is not a new idea, for Adam Smith's ([1776] 1900) *The Wealth of Nations* laid out the notion that the private pursuit of gain would lead to public benefits for all. In this view, Microsoft CEO Bill Gates may have amassed more wealth than the 20 million Americans at the bottom of the heap, but his ideas have made all Americans wealthier; his fortune serves as an incentive for other enterprising Americans to develop more good business ideas. On the other hand, the plight of the American poor provides an incentive for lower-class Americans to work hard and do better for themselves and their families.

Free market advocates justify the economic inequalities associated with markets in terms of efficiency: By providing a greater incentive for individual hard work and initiative, freer markets are supposed to lead to more competitive national economies and a bigger economic pie for everybody. Interestingly, these same advocates claim that markets will eventually make other forms of inequality disappear—namely, inequalities based on pure discrimination rather than on differences in productivity and ability.

In this view, discrimination on the basis of race, gender, religion, or any other extraneous characteristic is eliminated by market incentives. For example, a firm that refuses to sell its goods to African American consumers (perhaps because of racial bias on the part of the owner) will simply lose market share to its competitors. In the long run, the argument goes, the rigors of free market competition will eliminate the evils of discrimination and lead to pure meritocracy. This argument is frequently cited as a reason for abolishing affirmative action.

In this chapter, we document the patterns and magnitude of different kinds of economic inequality in market economies, particularly that of the United States. We examine the connection between economic differences and other social distinctions, primarily race and gender. What explains economic inequality? How has it changed over time? Do economic advantages and disadvantages get reproduced over time and across generations, or does meritocracy prevail? Does market competition truly lessen the extent of discrimination? Can government intervention help to resolve the extremes of inequality or at least alleviate the sufferings of the disadvantaged?

Throughout this chapter, we present evidence that markets lead to inequality. We also take issue with the idea that the inequality generated by markets necessarily leads to the most efficient economic outcomes. At the same time, we examine how the inequalities generated by markets are not always based on merit. Markets are always and everywhere embedded in nonmarket social relations. As a consequence of these underlying systems of embeddedness, markets do not necessarily eliminate discrimination against women, minorities, or individuals from lower-class backgrounds. Rather, markets can often reproduce patterns of discrimination.

Inequality in Perspective

One of the fundamental topics of sociological and economic research is **economic inequality,** or differences between the economic circumstances of individuals in a given society. Two of the topics most discussed by social scientists are monetary income and wealth. **Income** is a flow of resources that you receive over a period of time, such as the weekly paycheck you get from your job, the monthly interest you earn on your savings account, or the annual pension you receive after you retire. **Wealth,** on the other hand, is something that you already possess rather than a flow you receive over a time period. Examples of wealth include household items such as cars and VCRs but also more substantial forms of wealth such as real estate, savings accounts, stocks, and bonds. Modern industrial societies are all characterized by inequalities in both income and wealth: Some people have more, and other people have less.

Although income and wealth are the economic resources most commonly studied by social scientists, there are other important resources, such as access to credit and competitive prices. Some people are able to get loans so they can buy things that they could not otherwise afford (such as houses), and others are not. Similarly, some people are able to purchase the things they need at more affordable prices than other people. Access to these two sorts of socioeconomic resources often varies by race and gender—an issue we will return to in the section on race, gender, and inequality.

Income Inequality

Inequalities of income are not static and unchanging but, rather, change a great deal across time and space. To look at how inequality differs in different countries or how it has changed over time, we need a way to measure it. One simple method to measure income inequality is to divide the population of income earners into fifths (or quintiles) and then calculate what proportion of total income each fifth gets. Thus, we consider how much income the top (or richest) fifth receives compared with the second fifth or with the bottom (poorest) fifth. In a society with absolute income equality, every fifth would receive exactly one-fifth of the total income. In a society with extreme inequality, the top fifth would get all the income, and the bottom four-fifths would get nothing. Real societies, of course, fall somewhere between these two extremes.

How have Americans been doing overall? Are their incomes rising or falling? If there is such a thing as progress, then presumably the average person earns more as the decades go by. Some data over time can answer these questions.

Exhibit 5.1 illustrates a pattern of historical income growth that many others have noted and discussed (e.g., Krugman 1990; Levy 1995). From the end of World War II until the early 1970s, Americans enjoyed a long period of economic growth that resulted in higher overall incomes. Thus, median family income rose from $16,345 to $32,490 between 1947 and 1974. The figures in the table are all in constant 1990 dollars, so the rise is not due to inflation but reflects an almost doubling of real family incomes over the 27-year period. Since the early 1970s, however, income growth has slowed down and even stagnated. From 1974 until 1991, a 17-year period, median family incomes went from $32,490 to $34,488, only a 6% increase.

The post-World War II era is therefore divided into two distinct periods: One went from the end of the war until the early 1970s and generated considerable income growth; the second period started in the early 1970s and goes up until the present. In this period, incomes have stagnated and have increased hardly at all. To be sure, the U.S. economy (as measured by gross national product, gross domestic product, or whatever) has grown a lot since 1972, but the income of the typical American family hasn't improved much at all.

On the question of how income is distributed across different groups, let us begin by considering household income. If we divide all households into the richest fifth, second-richest fifth, and so on, what share does each fifth have of the total income earned by all households? Remember that in a situation of perfect equality, each fifth of the households would receive a fifth of the income. Exhibit 5.2 shows how income is distributed in the United States and how this distribution has changed over time.

As this table shows, the top fifth makes a lot more money (48.7% of total income in 1995) than does the bottom fifth (only 3.7% in 1995). In 1995, the top fifth earned more than 13 times as much income as the bottom fifth. Twenty years earlier, this ratio was less than 10. The postwar period of economic growth that led to rising household incomes for Americans in general also resulted in declining income inequality through the 1950s and 1960s. America became a more equal society dur-

EXHIBIT 5.1

Median Family Income, Selected Years (1990 dollars)

1947	$16,345
1949	$15,699
1954	$18,629
1959	$22,386
1964	$25,483
1969	$31,292
1974	$32,490
1979	$34,595
1984	$33,251
1989	$36,062
1991	$34,488

Source: Danziger and Gottschalk (1995:42).

EXHIBIT 5.2

Proportion of Total Household Income Received, by Household Quintiles, Selected Years (in percentages)

	1935	1955	1975	1995
Top fifth	51.7	44.3	43.2	48.7
Second fifth	20.9	24.5	24.8	23.3
Third fifth	14.1	17.4	17.1	15.2
Fourth fifth	9.2	10.5	10.5	9.1
Bottom fifth	4.1	3.3	4.4	3.7

Source: Hacker (1997:49).

ing those decades. But afterward, inequality began to grow again, especially during the 1980s. Even as overall incomes stagnated, income inequality expanded.

The same pattern is reflected in the changing relationship between economic growth and poverty. For most of the postwar period, poverty rates declined when the U.S. economy grew quickly. As the economy expanded, everyone became generally better off, including those at the very bottom of the income distribution. But starting in the 1980s, this happy link between economic growth and poverty disappeared. Even though the American economy grew substantially over the decade, poverty did not shrink as it once did (Blank 1997:55-56). And during the recession of 1990-1991, poverty increased as usual: People lost their jobs and incomes declined. But afterward, as the economy rebounded strongly in 1992 and 1993, poverty continued to grow! Economic growth was no longer a sure cure for poverty.

The extent of income inequality in the United States is best gauged by comparison with other advanced industrialized nations. Is the United States a country with a high or low degree of inequality? Data gathered as part of the Luxembourg Income Study allow for some cross-national comparisons. Here, the relevant measure of inequality is the ratio of percentile to median income. How do top income earners compare with the typical (in this case, median) income? How do bottom income earners compare? How big is the distance from the top to the bottom? Exhibit 5.3 answers these questions for six different countries in the mid-1980s.

In Australia in 1985, the income level that separated the poorest 10% from all those people earning more was just 46.0% as much as the median income, whereas the income that divided the top 10% earners from the rest was 186.5% of the median income. This means that if you were poor enough to be in the bottom tenth, you earned less than half as much as the "average" wage earner. The ratio of these two numbers measures the distance between the highest and lowest income earners, and in Australia the former was about four times as much as the latter (186.5/46 = 4.01). Similar ratios are presented for all the other countries in the table. What is striking about the results is that the U.S. ratio is largest (5.94, compared with 4.02 in Canada, the next largest). Income inequality was highest among Americans and lowest among Swedes.

This table also helps to pinpoint the source of the inequality. It is not so much that the rich in America earn much, much more than the median income as that the poor earn much, much less. The ninetieth percentile in the U.S. is 206% of the median, which is higher than the other countries but still in the same ballpark (Great Britain followed closely with 194.1%). But the tenth percentile in the United States is only 34.7% of the median, substantially below that in any other country. What seems to make income so unequally distributed in the United States is that relatively speaking, the bottom of the income distribution is much lower in the United States than elsewhere (Gottschalk and Smeeding 1997:661). Thus, to account for the growth in inequality over the last two decades, we should focus on what has happened to poor people in America and why they haven't done well.

EXHIBIT 5.3

Ratio of Ninetieth to Tenth Percentile of Income, Mid-1980s, Selected Countries

Country	Year	10th Percentile as % of Median (P10)	90th Percentile as % of Median (P90)	Ratio of P90 to P10
Australia	1985	46.0	186.5	4.01
Canada	1987	45.8	184.2	4.02
France	1984	55.4	192.8	3.48
Sweden	1987	55.6	151.5	2.72
United Kingdom	1986	51.1	194.1	3.79
Unites States	1986	34.7	206.1	5.94

Source: Wolff (1996:448).

Wealth Inequality

If income concerns how much money a person acquires during a particular time period (say, a year), then wealth has to do with the total value of what her or she already possesses. A person's estate will usually include both assets (home, car, savings, pension fund, etc.) and liabilities (home mortgage, car loan, and other debts), and the combination of these two determines his or her overall wealth. If total liabilities exceed total assets, a person could even have negative net worth.

Since the 1980s, the wealth of the typical American has stagnated and even declined somewhat. The median net worth of an American household went from $51,051 in 1983 to $45,630 in 1995 (Wolff 1998:135). At the same time, the percentage of households with zero or negative net worth increased from 15.5% to 18.5%. Both the wealth and the incomes of Americans have stagnated in recent decades.

As with income, we shall describe the distribution of wealth and how uneven it is. To begin, we shall use the same method as with income: dividing the population into fifths and then comparing them. If wealth were equally shared among all Americans, each fifth would own one-fifth of the total wealth. But this is far from the truth. In 1983 and 1995, total household net worth was distributed as shown in Exhibit 5.4.

This table reveals that the top one-fifth wealthiest households owned over four-fifths of total wealth. And the bottom two-fifths had a very small share of the wealth, which got even smaller during the 1980s,

EXHIBIT 5.4

Percentage of Total Household Net Worth Owned, by Household Quintiles, 1983, 1995

	1983	1995
Top fifth	81.3	83.9
Second fifth	12.6	11.4
Third fifth	5.2	4.5
Bottom two-fifths	0.9	0.2

Source: Wolff (1998:136).

declining from 0.9% to 0.2%. If we examine the very upper regions of the wealth distribution, the top tenth richest households controlled 68.2% of the wealth in 1983 and 71.8% in 1995 (Wolff 1998:136). The distribution of wealth in the United States is even more lopsided than the distribution of income.

It is hard to know if the distribution of wealth today in America is unusual or just typical unless we make comparisons, either over time or across different countries. To do this, we will focus simply on the percentage of total household wealth owned by the richest 1% of households. When this percentage is high, it means that inequality is high too. First consider how this percentage has changed over time. Exhibit 5.5 shows how the share of total household wealth owned by the richest 1% has changed between 1922 and 1992.

Between 1922 and 1992, the proportion of total wealth owned by the extremely rich, the top 1% of American households, has varied quite a bit. Over the years for which there are data, inequality peaked in 1929, at the end of the "Roaring Twenties" and just before the start of the Great Depression. Inequality was at its lowest level in 1976, when the richest households owned "only" 19.9% of total wealth. Since the late 1970s, wealth inequality has been growing and in 1989 reached its highest level in 60 years. Since then, it has leveled off somewhat but remains at a high level by historical standards.

International comparisons are difficult because of the lack of systematic data on wealth, but some contrasts can be made. In the United States in 1983, the top 1% of households owned 33% of the total gross household assets. At roughly the same time in France (1986), by comparison, the top 1% owned 26% of the total assets. In 1986, the top 1% of Australian households held only 19.7% of the wealth, the top 1% of Canadians owned 17%

EXHIBIT 5.5

Share of Household Wealth Held by Richest 1% of American Households, Selected Years

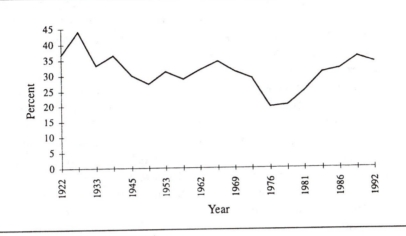

Source: Wolff (1995:62-63; 1996:436).

of the wealth in 1984, and the top 1% of Swedes owned 16.5% in 1985-1986. In the mid-1980s, wealth inequality was less in France, Canada, Sweden, and Australia than in America (Wolff 1996:446; 1998:149). These international differences with respect to wealth mirror the differences we previously saw with respect to income. In both cases, the United States has a higher level of inequality than do other advanced industrial nations, and in the United States, income and wealth inequality grew substantially during the 1980s.

Inequality and Efficiency

The evidence shows that when compared with other nations, economic inequality is relatively high in the United States. Furthermore, inequality in the United States has grown in the recent past and now is at a historically high level. But is inequality a good or a bad thing? And what happens when it becomes extreme?

American democracy was founded on a fundamental belief in equality: Each adult citizen has an equal voice in the political process (one person, one vote). Does this affirmation of equality extend from the political to the economic sphere? Apparently not. Even as people recognize the principle of one person, one vote, nobody is seriously proposing that wealth or incomes be equalized too. Inequality is legitimate in the market but not the polity.

Some economists and politicians assert that economic inequality serves a useful purpose: The possibility of wealth provides the *carrot* and the threat of poverty offers the *stick* that motivates ordinary people to work hard and strive for success. By this argument, inequality leads to economic efficiency. Without extremes of economic well-being, people wouldn't have a good enough reason to work.

This argument may sound plausible at first, but the motivational effects of inequality are greatly exaggerated. First consider that economic inequality is much lower in countries such as Japan and Germany, which have enjoyed greater economic success in the post–World War II period (having gone from ruins to riches) and which are filled with hard-working people. As measured by the distance between rich and poor, both the carrots and the sticks are smaller in Japan and Germany compared with the United States, but this didn't undercut economic growth in either country.

Second, for the motive argument to work, income and wealth would have to go to those who work hardest or who are the most deserving (in terms of talent, productivity, etc.). Much of the wealth that people possess is inherited and so isn't distributed meritocratically (Kotlikoff 1988). People can be very wealthy because they happened to have rich parents, not because they are themselves especially talented, productive, and so on.

Finally, consider that organizations that demand the very most from their personnel often rely the least on economic incentives. The armed forces, for example, ask of their personnel that they risk their very lives and perhaps make the ultimate sacrifice. Such demands require highly motivated personnel. But compared with a large corporation, for instance, the level of income inequality in the armed services is very low. In the 1990s, a typical corporate CEO earned about 200 times as much as the average worker (compared with only 30 times as much in the 1960s). By contrast, a U.S. Army four-star general with 26 years experience will earn in 1999 $129,600 a year, or about nine times as much as a private first-class with two years of experience. Success in the army is not rewarded with large bonuses or big increases in income. Yet the people working for the army are called on to make far greater sacrifices than those who work for large corporations. Something besides money is motivating them.

Under some circumstances, economic inequality can actually make people work *less* rather than *more*. One study of wage differences in corporations noted that people tend to view exorbitant wage differences as unfair (Cowherd and Levine 1992). If the difference between what a corporate CEO earned and the wages paid to the factory workforce got too great, widespread perceptions of unfairness made it harder to maintain the morale of the workforce. Many recent corporate strategies involve a renewed emphasis on product quality and customer service satisfaction. For these strategies to work, top management needs to get the involvement and cooperation of service workers and factory workers (who are the people who actually interact with customers or build the firm's products). Highly motivated workers are more likely to go along with such quality programs than are demoralized, unmotivated workers. And one of the key determinants of worker motivation is whether they believe they are being treated, and paid, fairly. This sense of fairness comes out of a series of comparisons: How do they fare compared with similar workers employed by the competition? How do their wages compare with those earned by other people in the same organization?

Suppose a corporate CEO slashes the wages of the firm's assembly line workers to cut production costs and is rewarded with a big annual bonus. Under such circumstances, income inequality within the firm would increase dramatically. Such a change does not, however, typically motivate low-ranking workers to work harder. Rather, employees who look at their own shrinking paychecks in comparison with the windfall earned by the CEO tend to become dissatisfied with their lot. Their enthusiasm for the job, their morale, and their willingness to "go the extra mile" and ensure high product quality all tend to diminish. Product quality may actually be hurt rather than helped by workers' perceptions of unfair wage differences.

If enormous inequalities are unnecessary or even detrimental to worker motivation, what other consequences might they have? Some have studied the effects of inequality on economic growth and have concluded that extreme economic inequality actually hurts growth (Persson and Tabellini 1994). Looking at 9 countries (including the United States) since the early 19th century and using cross-national data on 56 different countries, their results show that higher inequality leads to lower economic growth. According to their explanation, extreme inequality unleashes the kind of political fights that undercut investment. For example, in countries where a privileged few control most of the wealth, the bulk of the population (who are poor) will agitate for government policies that tax or even confiscate the wealth of the few and redistribute it to the poor. Such policies threaten property rights, discourage investment, and ultimately mean lower growth. The famous 19th-century commentator Alexis de Tocqueville viewed the relatively equal distribution of property in America (compared with Europe) to be a stabilizing force for democracy (Tocqueville 1969:637).

On the other hand, extreme inequality seems less pernicious if accompanied by a high degree of mobility. Mobility means that those who are disadvantaged today have a good chance of being privileged tomorrow or that their children will enjoy this chance. It is easier to live with economic deprivation if the future prospects of a better life seem good, even when the difference between deprivation and privilege is large. Suppose you go to a class in which the professor every day rewards half of the students with $1,000 each and punishes the other half with extreme public humiliation. These two experiences are highly unequal, and class members experiencing humiliation wouldn't be very happy. However, if they thought that at the next class they still had a 50-50 chance to get the $1,000, they might continue to attend. But if the same group of students were rewarded, or punished, over and over again, the unhappiness would soon boil over.

The economy rewards some people with high wages and "punishes" others with low wages. When the difference between high and low is large, unhappiness and envy increase. But feelings of envy are more easily assuaged if the people earning low wages have a good chance of enjoying high wages later on. Mobility makes inequality easier to live with.

In the U.S. economy, just how much mobility is there in earnings? Gottschalk (1997:37) divided up wage earners into quintiles (top fifth, second fifth, etc.) and calculated the extent of income mobility among the quintiles over a 17-year period. A person in the bottom earnings quintile in 1974 had a 42% chance of still being at the bottom 17 years later and only a 7% chance of making it into the top quintile. Those in the second-to-the-bottom earnings group had a similarly small chance of making it to the top; only 6.7% of them rose to the top between 1974 and 1991. Over this period, there were few rags-to-riches stories to be told. The only group with a more than 50% chance of being in the top quintile in 1991 were those who were already there in 1974! Apparently, the best way to get rich is to start out that way. This lack of mobility makes economic inequality more difficult to tolerate—at least for the people at the bottom.

Recent Trends in Inequality

Whether extremes of inequality are good or bad for a democratic country, it is important to understand why inequality has grown in the United States to such a high level. Recall that what distinguished American income inequality from the other countries was that in the United States, poor people had relatively lower incomes compared with the typical American income. So the explanation will focus more on why poor people in American are relatively worse off than poor people elsewhere. But it will also have to consider how economic inequality relates to other important social differences.

The distribution of income has been influenced by a combination of changes in the American economy (some in response to global developments), in American families, and in American public policy. Economic growth used to be the simple answer to poverty and incomes: Making the economy grow would raise incomes and lower poverty. But for a variety of reasons, this simple policy answer doesn't work anymore.

The stagnation of wages hasn't occurred equally to all working Americans or in all jobs. Rather, some people are better off, some are worse off, and the overall picture is one of no great improvement during the 1980s and 1990s even though the U.S. economy has grown substantially during these two decades. In particular, the wages paid for less skilled work (jobs that require only a high school diploma or less) have declined substantially. Even though unemployment is currently low and many people have jobs, for unskilled workers, the kinds of jobs they can obtain pay poorly and offer few benefits. Consider Exhibit 5.6, which shows the wages of men who are in the prime of their working lives but who differ in terms of their level of education.

The wages of highly educated men haven't changed much since the late 1960s; they were pretty much at the same level in 1989 as 20 years earlier. Comparing the heights of the two kinds of bars, it is also clear that education has always paid off: Higher education leads to higher wages. Higher education also reduces the chances of unemployment. (In 1989, the unemployment rate for men with less than a high school education was 9.4%, whereas for men with more than four years of college it was only 2.3%.) But the 1970s and 1980s weren't good decades for unskilled or uneducated workers, whose wages declined over the period by almost 25%. Wages similarly declined for men with a high school education. Stable wages among highly educated workers combined with lower wages for uneducated workers to produce growing income inequality, and the wage difference between college-educated and high school-educated workers has been growing since the late 1970s (Murphy and Welch 1993:106).

Four reasons have been offered to account for the sorry fate of unskilled American workers (Danziger and Gottschalk 1995:149). First of all, technological change in the workplace has lessened the demand for

EXHIBIT 5.6

Median Annual Earnings of Men Aged 35 to 44, by Education (in 1989 dollars)

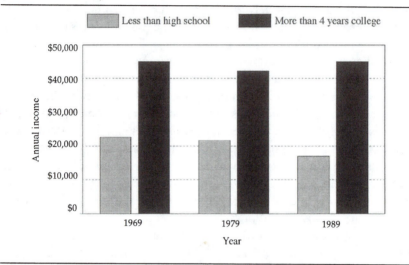

Source: Levy (1995:56).

unskilled workers (and lower demand has led to lower wages). Widespread computerization, for example, has changed the nature of both blue-collar and white-collar work. Manually operated lathes in machine tool shops have been replaced with computer-controlled lathes; lathe operators need less skill than before and fewer of them are needed, so their wages decline. Office work now requires the ability to operate a personal computer, so the demand for unskilled clerks has simply disappeared. In 1993, 45.8% of all workers used computers on their job, so computer literacy has become an increasingly necessary job skill (U.S. Department of Commerce 1996:423).

In addition to technology, the world environment for American workers has changed. The international economy is now a global one in which unskilled American workers have to compete with unskilled workers from overseas, who usually work for much less money (Feenstra 1998:41). This puts a strong downward pressure on the wages paid to domestic unskilled workers (Blank 1997:66-67). Third, the strength of American unions has declined substantially. In 1969, 29% of nonagricultural workers were unionized, but by 1989, this was down to just 16% (Freeman 1993:137). Through their collective bargaining agreements, industrial unions tend not only to raise the wages of those they represent (who traditionally had below-average education) but also to equalize wages. In 1983, for example, unionized American workers had median weekly earnings of $388, compared with earnings of $288 for nonunionized workers (U.S. Department of Commerce 1996:438). But as unionization rates decline, fewer workers are able to use collective bargaining agreements to boost their wages.

Finally, unskilled workers often work for minimum wages. The law sets a minimum standard below which it is illegal to go. Congress determines the minimum wage and periodically adjusts it upward. Given political differences between Republicans and Democrats about how often, and how much, to raise the minimum wage, it has in fact failed to keep pace with inflation. During most of the 1980s, the minimum wage remained fixed at $3.35 per hour. With inflation, its real value declined about 30% (Fortin and Lemieux 1997:79). Unskilled workers making minimum wages thus became worse off as inflation eroded the value of their earnings.

Whatever the reasons, low-skill male workers have been hard hit. Even during good times when unemployment is low, the kinds of jobs that low-skill workers can obtain pay increasingly lower wages. Their declining wages have offset the gains enjoyed by highly educated workers to create an overall picture of stagnation and have contributed to the growth in income inequality.

Overall economic inequality has also been influenced by changes in American families and the connection between gender and work. One dramatic change has been the increasing participation of women, including married women, in the workforce. With traditional gender roles, a woman might work for a few years while she was single, but after marrying, she would quit her job to stay at home and raise her children. The workforce participation rate refers to the percentage of people who are either working or trying to get a job. In 1980, the participation rate for men was 77.4%, meaning that over three-quarters of American men were either working or looking for work. In 1990, the rate for men was 76.4% and in 1995 it was 75.0%. Over this period, male participation rates changed very little.

Among women the story is very different. Female participation rates in 1980 were 51.5%, 57.5% in 1990, and 58.9% in 1995. They were substantially lower than the rates for men but rising quickly. If we distinguish single from married women and examine a longer time period, the changes become even more dramatic. Consider Exhibit 5.7.

In 1960, the workforce participation rate for single women was 58.6%, rising to 66.8% in 1995. In 1960, the participation rate for married women

EXHIBIT 5.7

Female Workforce Participation Rates, by Marital Status,
Selected Years (in percentages)

	1960	1990	1995
Single	58.6	66.7	66.8
Married	31.9	58.4	61.0

Source: U.S. Department of Commerce (1996:399).

was only 31.9%, growing to 61.0% in 1995. The rate has grown for all women, but the change has been especially dramatic for married women. In fact, the difference between single and married women has steadily shrunk over time, and now marital status has little effect on whether or not a woman works in the labor force. (It remains true that women with higher education are more likely to be in the labor force.) Of course, one has to be careful to understand the difference between work and work-force participation. Much of the work women do is unpaid (e.g., domestic labor, cooking, child rearing, etc.), so that a woman who isn't in the work-force may nevertheless still be working. It just means she isn't working for wages.

One reason that more married women work for pay may be that their husbands' wages can no longer adequately support a family, so two in-comes become necessary. Indeed, the share of family income provided by wives has increased from 8.5% in 1959 to 21.5% in 1991 (Danziger and Gottschalk 1995:77). Another reason is that married women are delaying having children and are having fewer children (Bianchi 1995:112-14). This makes it easier for them to stay longer in the labor force. Finally, higher education leads to more paid work, and women's educational attainment has been rising steadily (Blau 1998:125).

If men's overall wages have stagnated and have even declined among less educated male workers, what has been happening to women? Ex-hibit 5.8 shows the situation for American women.

As with men, education pays off for women; everyone earns more with a higher level of education. The experience of women over time, however, differed markedly from men. Highly educated women enjoyed a 15% increase in their real earnings between 1969 and 1989, and unlike male workers with low education, poorly educated women did not suffer a big decline in their wages. In fact, the earnings of women with less than a high school education rose a little. Poorly educated women, unlike

EXHIBIT 5.8

Median Annual Earnings of Women Aged 35 to 44, by Education (in 1989 dollars)

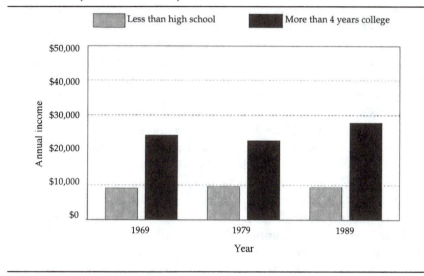

Source: Levy (1995:56).

poorly educated men, tended not to have the kinds of jobs hit hardest by de-unionization of the workforce and globalization of the economy. Thus, over the 1970s and 1980s, as men's wages stagnated and women's wages rose, the male-female earnings gap continued to close (although it remains substantial).

Finally, changes in public policy have affected overall inequality. Two policy changes, in taxes and social welfare programs, have had the biggest influence. Although federal welfare programs have come under considerable criticism in the last decade and, consequently, have been radically altered, they enjoyed some success. The divergent fates of children and old people illustrate the strengths and failings of the American welfare state.

A typical life unfolds like this: A person is born and in the early part of life is supported by his or her parents (or some other adult) until finished with formal education and joining the workforce. Then for many decades a person works (and perhaps raises a family). At around the age of 65, the person retires and is supported through some combination of savings, pension fund, Social Security, or family contributions. Thus, life begins and ends with periods of economic dependence.

People who are economically dependent do not support themselves through their own earnings and so experience a greater risk of living in poverty. But dependent children are today generally much worse off than dependent retirees, and public policy has made the difference. In 1966, poverty rates for the elderly were 28.5% versus 17.4% for children. Proportionately more old people lived in poverty than did young people. By 1989, the situation was *completely reversed*: 19.0% of children lived in poverty, and only 11.4% of the elderly were impoverished (Gottschalk and Danziger 1993:167). Even more recently, 20.8% of children under 18 lived below the poverty line in 1995, whereas only 10.5% of people aged 65 or older did so (Hacker 1997:63). Historically, the elderly were worse off than children, but poverty among the old began to decline and dropped below the poverty level for children in 1973-1974 and has stayed lower since then.

Social welfare policies that target the elderly have been very successful in reducing poverty (Blank 1997:20). Together, Social Security and Medicare expenditures support the standard of living and meet the health care needs of the elderly. These programs are expensive, but they do the job they were intended to do. Furthermore, since Congress adopted indexing in 1972, Social Security payments have automatically risen along with the cost of living. Inflation hasn't undercut the value of the public support the elderly receive. In 1950, the average retired male worker and his wife received public financial support equal to one-third of the poverty level. By 1989, that average had risen to 1.5 times the poverty level (Danziger and Gottschalk 1995:83-84). Public support for the elderly is one example of an American welfare program that works.

Other persons have been able to claim support from the government. Until welfare reform in 1996, one of the chief programs was Aid to Families with Dependent Children (AFDC), which provided cash assistance to poor families with young children. The predecessor to AFDC, Aid to Dependent Children, had been established during the New Deal along with Social Security (Amenta 1998:81). But unlike Social Security, AFDC was never indexed to increase automatically along with inflation, and the level of benefits varied from one state to the next (also unlike Social Security). AFDC benefits increased only intermittently, so in real terms their value declined very considerably. In 1970, the median state paid $792 per month to help support a single mother and her three children. By 1993, the median amount in real dollars was down to $435 per month (Blank 1997:100). Even when combined with other forms of public support, such as food stamps, the benefits were not generous. For a single mom with two children, the poverty line in 1994 was $11,940. Such a family receiving the typical level of AFDC support and getting food stamps obtained $7,086 worth of public assistance—about 59% of the poverty level (Blank 1997:96). At the same time that public support for the elderly was increasing, support for children declined. No wonder poverty is now lower among the elderly than among the very young!

The latest set of changes in welfare policy (e.g., the replacement of AFDC by block grants to the states) is likely to mean even less generous benefits and more poor people and children living in poverty. One of the more unfortunate aspects of childhood poverty is that it often leads to other undesirable consequences later on in life: Poor children are more likely to experience health problems later in life and are less likely to finish high school or go on to higher education (Lichter 1997:122). And given how much spatial segregation combined with racial segregation concentrates poverty among African Americans, the effects could be dramatic (Massey and Denton 1993:149).

The other public policy that has had a noticeable impact on inequality lies in the area of taxation. Even as social welfare support for the poor was declining in the 1980s (with the important exception of programs for the elderly), federal tax changes occurred that had considerable distributional consequences. In the early Reagan administration, the Economic Recovery Tax Act (ERTA) of 1981 cut corporate taxes, reduced the marginal tax rates in the highest personal income bracket from 70% to 50%, and lowered tax rates in all the other income brackets. The Tax Reform Act (TRA) of 1986 simplified personal income taxes by establishing just three tax brackets (15%, 28%, and 33%). Thus, the marginal tax rate in the highest income bracket declined from 70%, to 50%, to 38% and finally down to 33% after 1988 (Fullerton 1994:168). As personal income taxes went down, however, other taxes rose. Social Security payroll taxes increased 25% between 1980 and 1990, in large part to help cover the growing cost of Social Security.

The decrease in income taxes and the increase in Social Security taxes did not exactly offset one another. Neither the benefits of the income tax cut nor the burdens of the Social Security tax increase were evenly distributed among income earners. Put simply, high-income earners benefited the most from tax cuts, whereas low-income workers bore more of the burden of tax increases. The net effect of these tax changes was to increase inequality.

The key to understanding how taxes influenced inequality lies in the difference between these two kinds of taxes. Income taxes were progressive, whereas Social Security taxes were regressive. With increasing marginal tax rates, personal income taxes took a higher proportion of income as income rose. With regressive taxes, taxes decline as a proportion of income as income goes higher. The reduction in personal income tax made it less progressive and so disproportionately benefited higher-income earners. The increase in Social Security taxes, however, disproportionately hurt lower-income earners. When put together, the two changes reinforced each other. For example, the average marginal tax rates of the bottom one-tenth of income earners increased from 11.5% to 14.6% between 1980 and 1990, whereas the tax rates of the richest one-tenth decreased from 44.3% to 32.6% over the same period (Gramlich, Kasten, and Sammartino 1993:242). In tandem, these two sets of tax changes increased income inequality. And when combined with changes in welfare policy, changes in taxation further amplified the level of inequality in America (Gramlich et al. 1993).

Looking at economic inequality in the recent period reveals several important lessons. First, the level and extent of inequality isn't a timeless fact of nature: Inequality changes over time, sometimes growing, sometimes shrinking. Second, although inequality is fundamentally influenced by developments in the economy, various social and political factors also play an important role. How open a country's domestic economy is to international economic forces depends on government decisions about trade and tariff policy. Public policy determines the progressivity or regressivity of a nation's tax structure and the level of public financial support to poor or dependent populations. And changes in gender norms and family life affect the proportion of men and women in the labor force.

Race, Gender, and Inequality

Most Americans believe that a certain amount of economic inequality is fair. After all, some people have more important jobs than others; some people work harder than others; some people are smarter. As a result, in the United States, most people believe that a measure of inequality is fair and legitimate (just *how much* inequality is fair and legitimate is a different issue). However, in contrast to their beliefs about economic inequality (i.e., inequality in economic resources), most Americans today also believe that *inequality of opportunity* is wrong. We tend to believe that everybody should have a fair shot to succeed and fulfill the "American Dream," regardless of irrelevant factors such as race or gender.

Are markets the best way to guarantee equality of opportunity? Today, there are many policymakers, economists, and journalists who say that markets guarantee equality of opportunity better than government regulation. Economists such as Gary Becker (the 1992 Nobel Prize winner in economics) have argued that discrimination is economically irrational and will in the long run be punished in competitive markets. According to Becker (1968, 1971), a discriminator is someone who, for example, prefers not to hire women workers even if they are as productive as men. Discriminators have a kind of distaste for particular groups of people and avoid dealing with them. But nondiscriminating employers can take advantage of the irrationality of discriminating employers by hiring women at lower wages and enjoying their cheaper but equally productive labor.

If markets are competitive, nondiscriminating employers will outperform the discriminators, and if they do not mend their ways, the latter will eventually be driven out of the market. Thus, while discriminators hurt those they discriminate against, in competitive markets they also hurt themselves. One can easily extend the argument to discriminating sellers, lenders, and so on. For instance, a shoe store that refuses to sell to African Americans will simply reduce its own market share and allow other shoe stores to profit by serving African American customers.

Others have followed Becker's line of reasoning (e.g., Epstein 1992; Friedman 1962) and have come to the conclusion that the best remedy for discrimination is simply to unleash market forces. By making markets as free and as competitive as possible, discriminators will be punished for their irrational distastes and be bankrupted by nondiscriminators. In a strong version of this argument, Epstein (1992) even claims that antidiscrimination legislation, such as the Civil Rights Act of 1964 (which, among other things, prohibited discrimination in employment on the basis of sex, race, religion, and ethnicity), has the perverse effect of making labor markets less competitive and so allows discrimination to flourish. Epstein argues that labor markets should be completely deregulated so as to make them as competitive as possible and recommends that antidiscriminatory legislation be repealed (see also Sunstein 1991).

If these arguments are true, people can take genuine moral comfort from recent trends around the globe: As markets spread and get deregulated and as privatization occurs, the overall effect will be to make markets more competitive. And market competition favors nondiscriminators over discriminators. If true, these arguments lay the groundwork for a seemingly improbable political coalition between social liberals who oppose discrimination and economic conservatives who favor free markets. In this view, government programs that try to create more opportunities for women and minorities do more harm than good; rather than having laws and government programs, markets should be left alone to work their magic.

In contrast, we take issue with the claim that markets stop discrimination. Throughout this book, we have seen that markets are embedded in nonmarket social relations. This means that when people go to the market to hire an employee or to purchase a commodity, they may not be as indifferent to factors such as race, gender, and ethnicity as the economic "law of indifference" would suggest (Jevons 1931). Consider, for example, that problems of information in markets are often resolved through informal rather than formal means. Finding employees through social networks may help the employer find somebody reliable to work in his or her firm, but it may also result in a racially homogeneous workforce. If the employer is a white male, it is likely that most members of his social network are also white males; the common practice of hiring through social networks is likely to reproduce patterns of discrimination.

The embeddedness of markets in systems of cultural meaning can also reproduce discrimination. Markets do not exist separately from cultural values and meanings—some of which include racial and gender stereotypes. For example, the Aunt Jemima brand of breakfast foods once depicted as its logo the face of a black "mammy" wearing a kerchief on her head. Nowadays, the romanticization of the subservient "Auntie" is considered offensive to most Americans, and the company has updated its label to depict a modern, kerchiefless Aunt Jemima.

The Aunt Jemima example illustrates the tendency of markets to use preexisting cultural meanings and stereotypes: When stereotypes of the "happy slave" were considered acceptable to most white Americans, they were used to market products. This tendency of markets to reinforce existing cultural values is particularly important in the labor market, which determines the earnings and standards of living of most Americans. For example, race stereotypes prevalent in American culture may mean that some Americans would be uncomfortable dealing with African American investment bankers. If this is the case, it is economically rational for investment firms to hire only whites as investment bankers rather than risk losing their clientele. Kirschenman and Neckerman (1991) illustrate how much use employers make of ethnic and racial stereotypes—using a job applicant's race as an indicator of work ethic.

A somewhat less obvious but still important way that cultural values influence economic outcomes is through the social and cultural construction of family responsibilities. Today, we tend to think of work and family as separate spheres. In reality, however, what happens in the family can have an enormous impact on what happens in the labor market and vice versa. In particular, culturally determined notions of women's and men's appropriate roles have important consequences for the jobs that men and women get and how much they get paid for those jobs.

Legalized Inequality

Until recently, certain kinds of economic inequality in the United States were not only tolerated but actually enforced by legislation. These differences did not result from the mysterious operations of the market, the discriminatory preferences of private individuals, or the misguided attempts of government to regulate markets. Rather, they sprang from the deliberate intent to enshrine inequality in the law. The net effect of these legal inequalities was to create inequalities in economic opportunity.

Men and women used to be treated very differently by the law in the United States. One important discrepancy concerned the property rights of married women (which were enshrined at the state, not the federal, level). A single woman could own her own property, as could a man of any marital status. But when a woman married, by law, her property automatically became her husband's (Salmon 1986:41). She could no longer freely use, control, or dispose of it as she saw fit (after marrying, a woman became a *feme covert*, literally a *kept woman*). This legal distinction created huge economic differences between men and women, because only some women (but not all) could own property. Married women possessed some claim over the property of their husband but only as a surviving widow. *Dower* was the term for the rights a widow had over her deceased husband's estate. Traditionally, a widow was entitled to one-third of the real property (i.e., land) that belonged to her husband (Staves 1990:27), and when she died that third reverted to the other heirs.

Such ideas about married women's property rights changed only slowly in the United States. In early 19th-century Pennsylvania, for example, married women could inherit property, receive it as a gift, or earn income. But so long as they were married, this wealth automatically became the property of their husbands. Not until the middle of the 19th century did individual states revise their laws so that married women enjoyed the same rights as single women. Pennsylvania passed legislation in 1848 allowing wives the right to own the property they had inherited or been given. Then in 1872, legislation was passed that allowed married women to keep the money they earned (Shammas, Salmon, and

Dahlin 1987:88-89). All along, of course, marital status made no difference to the economic rights of men.

Even though marital status did not matter among men, not all men
were legally equal in pre-Civil War America. Slaves did not enjoy the
same property rights as freemen because slaves were themselves a form
of property. Slaves couldn't own things in the same way as the general
free population. Even after slavery ended, laws restricted property rights
in a way that maintained racial boundaries separating blacks from
whites. In 1911, the city of Richmond, Virginia, passed an ordinance that
established separate white and black neighborhoods within the city
boundaries. Many southern cities followed this example, and such laws
in effect prohibited homeowners in one racially designated neighborhood from selling their homes to people from the "wrong" race (Rice
1968). They were not free to sell their homes to whomever they wished.
This tradition carried on after World War I with the spread of "restrictive
covenants"—legally sanctioned agreements entered into by white homeowners of both North and South that prevented blacks and other minorities from buying homes in white neighborhoods.

Legal inequality affected public as well as private facilities. In the late
19th century, the U.S. Supreme Court ruled that blacks were not legally
entitled to use the same public facilities as whites—the famous "separate
but equal" doctrine. As a result, blacks were legally forced to use segregated and inferior public schools, hospitals, public transportation, and
other facilities. Not until the 1950s and 1960s, due to the strenuous efforts
of the Civil Rights movement, was legal inequality among the races finally ended in the United States.

Such legally mandated forms of inequality are much rarer in today's
world. Married and unmarried American women now possess the same
legal rights over property as men. Legal equality among the races in the
United States is a more recent achievement, occurring in the 1950s and
1960s with the demands of the Civil Rights movement. Title VII of the
Civil Rights Act of 1964 prohibited discrimination in employment and
established the Equal Employment Opportunity Commission (EEOC) as
an enforcement mechanism of the federal government. (The act also out-
lawed segregated public accommodations and prohibited racial discrimination by any institution receiving federal funds.)

Despite the abolition of legal inequality, however, various forms of
economic inequalities between the sexes and among different racial
groups have persisted. The following sections discuss these different
forms of economic inequality and suggest some sociological explana-

tions for the persistence of economic inequality by race and gender. First, we will discuss race and gender discrimination in labor markets. Second, we will look at racial discrimination in access to credit. Finally, we will discuss the influence of race and gender in determining prices.

Inequalities in U.S. Labor Markets

U.S. labor markets are among the most competitive and unregulated in the world. If competitive markets on their own reduce discrimination, the effect ought to be strongest in the United States. Yet racial and gender-based discrimination remains a problem in the United States, despite laws that explicitly prohibit it. Neither competitive markets nor federal law have ended discriminatory practices in the market. We shall not here consider the failings of the law but concentrate rather on the issue of why markets don't stop discrimination (Sunstein 1991).

One way to think about **employment discrimination** is as a kind of preference on the part of employers not to work with or hire certain kinds of people. Conceived this way, discriminatory behavior seems likely to be punished in competitive markets as nondiscriminators take advantage of the opportunities that discriminators forego. But suppose it isn't the employers who want to discriminate but instead someone else, a third party. Perhaps a shoe store doesn't employ black salesmen and women because racially biased customers won't patronize a store with a nonwhite salesforce. Or maybe airline passengers get nervous at the sight of a female airline pilot, so airlines don't hire women into that job. In such cases, the discriminatory actions of employers simply reflect the discriminatory preferences of people (in this case, customers) who are in a position to impose their preferences on the employer. In such circumstances, market competition need not reduce discrimination. In fact, it may even reinforce it.

It is also possible that discriminators make employment decisions on the basis of general stereotypes that have some basis in reality. If it is hard to measure performance-relevant characteristics at an individual level, employers may sometimes rely on general group differences to make their decisions. This is what economists term *statistical discrimination*. For example, suppose employers care about the work commitment of their employees—the willingness of workers to set aside their personal and family lives and devote themselves to their jobs. The work commitment of a specific individual is very hard to measure, but employers may know that men are generally more willing to sacrifice their personal and family lives than are women, so it is rational for the employer to favor hiring men over women. In this instance, employers are using gender as a crude signal, or proxy, for work commitment.

Discrimination may also continue in markets because of its enduring effects on human capital. Among other things, worker productivity depends on the education and experience of the worker. More training and experience generally make people better at what they do. Wages reward productivity, so workers with better education and more experience will earn more money. But education and experience don't happen just by accident. And if certain people are favored over others when it comes to educational opportunities or experience on the job, such discrimination can have lasting effects. For instance, a corporation might put more men than women through on-the-job training programs, or the educational system might give higher-quality schooling to whites than to blacks.

Gender in the Labor Market

It is commonly known that men generally receive higher incomes than do women—even when we compare women and men who work similar hours. In this section, we shall try to figure out how big the difference is and what causes it to occur. Many factors could explain the difference. Perhaps women get different kinds of jobs (presumably lower paying) than do men. Occupational segregation by gender, as it is called, might be due to differences in what people want (e.g., men want to be firemen and women want to be nurses), in their qualifications (e.g., more men go to law school, so there are more male lawyers), or in employer preferences (e.g., corporations prefer to have female rather than male receptionists). Or perhaps women get paid less even when they hold exactly the same job as a man.

To appreciate the difference between men's and women's earnings, consider that in 1993 median annual earnings for full-time male workers equaled $31,077, whereas for full-time women workers it was $22,469, or about 72 cents on the dollar (U.S. Department of Commerce 1995:477). Although still far short of equality, this represents substantial progress. In 1969, women working full-time made about 56% of what their male counterparts earned. As discussed earlier, one reason women were able to close the gap with men over the last 25 years was that men's wages stagnated, whereas women's wages continued to climb (Blau 1998:131).

Sometimes people earn differing wages because they hold different jobs. Doctors, for example, earn more that dental hygienists, so if more men become doctors than hygienists, and women the reverse, men will generally earn more than women. **Occupational sex segregation,** in other words, may help to explain male-female wage differences. Some occupations are so closely linked with one sex or the other as to become sex identified. In 1995, for example, 99.4% of all dental hygienists and 98.5% of all secretaries were women (Hacker 1997:197). On the other hand, only 7.5% of sheet metal workers were female, even though women constituted 46.1% of the workforce in 1995. An even lower proportion of women were automobile mechanics (Reskin and Roos 1990:19). Secretarial work is woman's work, whereas being a car mechanic is a quintessentially male job.

Women are dramatically over or underrepresented in certain occupations. In the United States, there are currently very few female mechanical engineers or airplane pilots, and very few men work as kindergarten teachers, nurses, or child care workers. This kind of occupational segregation has played an important role in creating gender inequality because women were often kept from good jobs and confined to lower-paying jobs. Sometimes explicit rules dictated the exclusion of women from certain kinds of work. A survey done in 1940 found that many large corporations had personnel rules that deliberately prohibited women from holding jobs as executives, department heads, engineers, mail clerks, or accountants. Instead, the rules reserved jobs such as typist, stenographer, or telephone operator for women only (Goldin 1990:112). Needless to say, male executives made a lot more money, and had much better career prospects, than female typists!

Such blatant discrimination did not occur only in the private sector. The 1930 personnel rules of the California Civil Service were explicit in taking gender into account for wages paid. Even when the qualifications needed were the same, jobs occupied mostly by women were to be paid less than jobs occupied mostly by men (Kim 1989:42). When asked to justify these differences, personnel executives explained that working men had families to support, whereas working women did not. Sometimes these personnel rules focused not only on the gender of the worker but also on marital status (in the case of women). Marriage bars were adopted by many American public school systems during the 1920s and 1930s (Goldin 1990:170-71). They stipulated that only single women could work as teachers and that a female teacher who got married would be fired. Marriage bars did not apply to men. Part of the justification was that married women were supported by their husbands and so did not really need their jobs. Married women took jobs from married men, who had families to support, or from single women, who had to support themselves (Pedersen 1987).

After the Civil Rights Act of 1964, explicitly discriminatory personnel rules became strictly illegal. It is still possible, however, to achieve a high level of occupational segregation through informal steering and implicit normative rules. Consider that there are today almost no male secretaries or female auto mechanics even though no explicit rule stops anyone from holding such a job. And jobs matter not only because of present income but also because of future prospects.

A dead-end job is one that doesn't lead anywhere. As we saw in Chapter 4, many large firms organize themselves internally around job ladders. This means that typical careers inside the firm involve progression up an ordered series of jobs (e.g., entry-level employees start out as junior sales associates and then move up to sales associate, assistant sales manager, associate sales manager, sales manager, regional sales manager, assistant vice president for sales, etc.). People don't just get promoted from any position in an organization to any other one; they proceed through an orderly sequence of jobs. Unfortunately, some kinds of jobs in firms don't lead anywhere; they aren't at the bottom of a job ladder. And often, those are the kinds of jobs that women tend to get.

The 1940 survey mentioned earlier also revealed that the jobs reserved for women (e.g., typist) were dead-end jobs, whereas those reserved for men (e.g., accountant) could lead to further advancement within the firm, if the man proved to be energetic and talented (Goldin 1990:113). Thus, a man and woman with high school educations who were hired by the same firm into junior positions (typist for the woman, and mail clerk for the man) would begin their careers looking quite similar. A smart man starting in the mail room could find himself at a much higher, and better paid, position in the firm in 10 years. But a smart woman, starting in the typing pool, could expect only to be promoted to senior typist, or some similar position, after 10 years of hard work. Being a typist was a dead-end job.

As we saw in Chapter 3, social networks can play an important role in providing a person with useful information and resources. A lot of people hear about job openings, for example, from their friends, relatives, and acquaintances. But such networks do not form at random. One study found that women's social networks tended to include more kin and fewer co-workers and advisers than men's networks (Moore 1990). In career settings, women are often excluded from the old boy's networks that can offer the sponsorship, inside information, and political intelligence needed for a successful career. These informal networks never exist on paper and are a part of no organizational chart, but they can greatly influence someone's prospects for promotion.

At any given time, some jobs have strong gender associations. But because these are socially constructed qualities, they can change over time. Secretarial work, for example, now seems like a truly female kind of job. Yet it was not always so. In fact, before the Civil War, office work was a male preserve. It was only at the end of the 19th century, with the invention and widespread adoption of the typewriter, that women started to perform these kinds of tasks. In a relatively short period, secretarial work became heavily feminized and was performed mostly by single women (Davies 1982). The occupation of bank teller underwent a similarly dramatic transformation from male to female.

Historically, American women have tended to be less qualified than men for professional jobs and so were less likely to hold them. But recently, the situation has been changing. Whereas in 1964, only 4.0% of architecture degrees were granted to women, in 1994 36.6% were. In law, the figures jumped from 3.1% to 43.0%, and in medicine from 6.5% to 37.9% (Hacker 1997:190). An increasing number of women are acquiring the specialized training needed to launch a professional career. Women may not yet have caught up to men, but they are getting close.

For general education, women are as likely to graduate from high school as are men, but women still lag when it comes to completion of college. In 1994, for example, 81.0% of men and 80.7% of women had completed four years or more of high school. That same year, 25.1% of men and 19.6% of women had finished four years or more of college (U.S. Department of Commerce 1995:157). Nevertheless, women have been catching up to men in their general educational attainment, so education differences have become less and less a factor in accounting for income differences across gender.

Women, Jobs, and Family Responsibilities. One difference that hasn't gone away concerns the special responsibility that women have for raising children. Whether married or single, mothers generally shoulder much more of the responsibility for child care and rearing than do fathers. These special responsibilities have a big impact on a woman's ability to pursue a career in the workforce.

Single parenthood is probably the toughest family situation to be in, but it mostly involves single moms with their kids rather than single dads. It means that a woman has to care for some number of children without the help and economic support of a husband. If the children are young, she has to juggle paid employment with full-time child care. Combining these two activities is especially difficult in the United States (compared with other countries) because of the lack of publicly funded child care and weaker laws supporting parental leave. Compared with working single mothers in Sweden, Canada, France, or Germany, a working single mother in the United States has a much harder time combining maternal work with regular paid labor (Waldfogel 1998:140-41).

Even with a husband present, working women tend to perform more of the domestic work than men. Data from 1987 show married working women spending an average of about 33 hours a week doing housework (especially cooking and cleaning), whereas their working husbands performed about 20 hours a week of housework (Reskin and Padavic 1994:151). Even when both husbands and wives were working full-time, the women did a lot more of the domestic work. This may explain why, when other things are equal (level of education, experience, occupation, etc.), women with children still tend to earn less than other women (Waldfogel 1998). Whether she is married or not, a working mother faces additional demands and bears nonwork responsibilities that make it harder for her to devote her time and energies to her career. Married men with children suffer no such penalty, because the division of domestic labor means that their wives will do most of the child-related work, so the man's career doesn't suffer. In fact, married men earn more than single men, other things being equal (Waite 1995:495).

The clearest test of gender differences comes from a study of men and women graduating from the University of Michigan law school (Wood, Corcoran, and Courant 1993). These are all people with the same advanced educational credentials: a J.D. from an elite law school. To acquire a professional degree requires lots of motivation and hard work. The graduates all begin their legal careers with the same level of inexperience, and at least at the outset, they all receive similarly high incomes. But the study follows what happens to them over time, and gradually significant gender differences appear.

In their first year on the job, the men in the classes of 1972 to 1975 earned a median salary of $39,428 (remember, this was a high salary in the early 1970s). The women weren't far behind, earning a median salary of $36,851 (93% of the men's salary). Fifteen years later, however, a big gap had opened up. The median for the same group of men was now $114,588, whereas the median for women was $70,963, only 62% as much (Wood et al. 1993:423). The study found that responsibility for child care explained much of the difference between men and women because it reduced the hours and experience of working lawyer-mothers. More recent cohorts of law school graduates appear to be following the same trajectory, although the male-female wage gap isn't quite as large.

Women undergraduates in college today frequently profess a desire to have both a career and a family and thus to combine paid work in the labor force with mothering at home. Evidence from the past suggests how hard it has been to do both of these things successfully. Goldin (1997) studied five cohorts of U.S. female college graduates to see how they reconciled work and family. Mostly, they didn't. Of the first cohort (graduating between 1900 to 1919), half either did not marry or, if they did marry, did not have children. In those days, college women were much less likely to get married or have kids than less educated women.

The second cohort of women, graduating between 1920 and 1945, married at a higher rate but usually had very short careers that began immediately after graduation and ended in just a couple of years. The third cohort, who finished college between 1946 and 1965, generally combined work and family by having their family first and then reentering the labor force after the children were sufficiently old (teenagers at least). Such a strategy severely restricted the kinds of careers they could pursue. The fourth cohort, graduating between 1966 and 1979, also tried to combine work and family but followed the opposite strategy from the previous cohort. This cohort postponed having children to have their careers first. Then, when in their 30s and 40s, they would start to have kids. But postponing children that long also led to high levels of unintended childlessness.

It is still too soon to know what will happen to the most recent cohort of women, graduating between 1980 and 1995, but their aspirations usually include having both a career and a family. Over the course of the 20th century, such a combination has been hard for college-educated women to achieve, because one side or the other usually has to give way. But perhaps the chances of success are best for the most recent cohort.

For various reasons, the incidence of single-parent families headed by women has climbed in the last several decades. The proportion of American women who are single parents has almost doubled, climbing from 6.1% in 1970 to 11.6% in 1995. The increase was particularly pronounced among less educated women who were unlikely to be able to obtain good jobs (Blau 1998:142). Given how hard it is to be both a single mother and a wage earner, incomes tend to be lower and the poverty rate higher. In 1993, for instance, the median income for all U.S. families with children was $36,200. The median income for families headed by single women was only $13,472 (U.S. Department of Commerce 1995:476). The same pattern shows up on poverty rates. Among all the family types, race groups, or age groups in the United States, single mothers with children experience the highest poverty rates: In 1993, the rate was 48% (Blank 1997:147). Not surprisingly, a high proportion of female-headed families are on some form of public assistance (AFDC and its successors, food stamps, etc.). As single parents, it is very hard for such women to hold full-time jobs, and often, the only kind of work they can obtain (low skill, low wage) means that their earnings still keep them and their families below the poverty line (Blank 1997:96). Furthermore, such jobs typically have few benefits (either health, dental, or retirement).

As mentioned earlier, the welfare benefits given to a single mom to support herself and her family are inadequate to achieve even a poverty-level standard of living. And the magnitude of the shortfall has increased substantially over the last two decades (Blank 1997:101). So how do these women take care of their families? In their study of welfare-dependent single mothers, Edin and Lein (1997) found that people responded to the inadequacy of public assistance by supplementing their incomes in three ways: (1) Working in the formal, informal, or underground economies; (2) obtaining cash assistance from boyfriends, family members, or absent fathers; or (3) getting community groups and charities to help pay over-due bills (Edin and Lein 1997:17). They found that the shortfall (welfare minus expenses) ranged between $189 and $519 per month, depending on where the family lived. Clearly, extra money had to come from some-where, and single mothers usually (and unsurprisingly) chose to break the rules that apply to welfare recipients rather than see their children starve.

Although they have been slowly shrinking, significant income differ-ences remain between American men and women. Some of the discrep-ancy is explained by women's lower labor force participation rates, but women have been catching up to men in this respect. Historically, the difference partly depended on female workers' generally having lower levels of education and experience, but there too, the male-female differ-ence is shrinking. Occupational segregation also played a role as certain jobs became sex typed and men and women were funneled into different kinds of work. Generally, women's work was less remunerative and of-fered fewer long-range opportunities than men's work. Paid work and parental work are hard to reconcile, so while women retain primary re-sponsibility for domestic and child-rearing duties, some income differ-ences will likely remain. Where these differences hit hardest is among poorly educated single mothers, who must simultaneously be primary parents and primary wage earners and whose wages tend to be very low.

Race in the Labor Market

In the United States, race is centrally linked to inequality. Historically, of course, slavery was defined in terms of race, but even 140 years after the

EXHIBIT 5.9

Median Household Income, 1967 to 1997, by Race (in 1997 dollars)

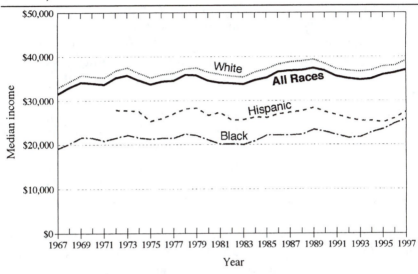

Source: U.S. Department of Commerce (http://www.census.gov/hhes/income/histinc/h05.html).

abolition of legal slavery, large differences still exist between different racial groups. These are surely some of the most important instances of what Charles Tilly (1998) calls "durable inequality."

We shall begin by considering income differences over time. Exhibit 5.9 shows the median household income for white, black and Hispanic Americans between 1967 and 1997, as well as for all races.

This figure reveals the magnitude of the difference between white and minority households and shows also that the gap isn't shrinking. In 1970, black households earned about 60.9% of what white households earned. In 1993, the proportion of black to white income was 59.3%. The situation for Hispanic households is somewhat better: The ratio to white income was 69.4% in 1993. But that difference too has been relatively stable over time. A similar contrast can be found for poverty and unemployment rates, both of which are higher for minorities than for whites.

Perhaps this income difference can be explained in terms of education. Some minority groups do not achieve the same level of education as whites and, consequently, will not be as well qualified for higher-paying jobs. The evidence suggests that education indeed plays a role. Having a college degree really boosts an individual's income, and in 1994, 22.9% of all white Americans aged 25 or older had graduated from college. By comparison, only 12.9% of African Americans and 9.1% of Hispanics were college graduates (U.S. Department of Commerce 1995:157). Given how hard hit unskilled workers' salaries have been, those with lower levels of education have particularly felt the brunt. Racial differences in education undoubtedly explain at least part of the racial differences in income.

Education doesn't explain everything, however. Even among people with similar educational credentials, racial differences still remain. In 1993, a white adult with a Ph.D. earned on average $4,449 per month, or about $53,000 per year. That same year, the average black person with a doctorate degree earned $3,778 per month, or about $45,000 per year (U.S. Department of Commerce 1995:158). Racial income differences emerged among those with the highest possible educational credentials. A similar pattern existed for those with bachelor's degrees: Whites averaged $2,682 and blacks averaged $2,333, or 87% as much. Something besides education explains the black-white income gap.

Occupational segregation in the United States worked at the level of race as well as gender. Through a variety of means, minorities were both under- and overrepresented in certain kinds of jobs. As recently as 1995, only 1.5% of aerospace engineers and 1.2% of airplane pilots were black, and only 1.2% of chemical engineers were Hispanic. Conversely, blacks are strongly overrepresented in occupations such as postal clerk, nursing aides, hospital orderlies, and telephone operators. In the past, employers were sometimes quite explicit about their racial preferences. A 1960 sample of help-wanted ads taken from major newspapers such as the *New York Times, Chicago Tribune,* and *L.A. Times* showed that employers did not want just cooks, waitresses, or housekeepers; they wanted white cooks, white waitresses, or black (then termed "colored" or "Negro") housekeepers (Darity and Mason 1998:66). Occupational segregation affected more than just wage differences between racial groups. Working conditions could also vary systematically. One study of a pipe manufacturer in Pittsburgh found that black employees were segregated into the most hazardous jobs, and consequently, they experienced more health problems than white workers (Maloney 1998).

Even today, more than three decades after the passage of the Civil Rights Act of 1964 outlawing racially discriminatory employment practices, minorities face discrimination. A steady stream of successful lawsuits suggests that even large well-known corporations can discriminate.

In 1996, for instance, Texaco settled a class action suit charging racial discrimination and paid out $176 million in damages (Darity and Mason 1998:78).

Although the Civil Rights Act has clearly given those who feel they have been subject to employment discrimination the legal basis on which to file a lawsuit, has this legislation helped to reduce discrimination? This may sound like a silly question (and one might conclude that the answer is obviously yes) except that this law represents a kind of government intervention in the labor market. Some (e.g., Epstein 1992) have argued that any form of government regulation, however well-intentioned, makes markets less competitive, and so allows discrimination to flourish.

To evaluate the impact of the Civil Rights Act, Heckman and Payner (1989) studied black employment in South Carolina's manufacturing industry (mostly textiles) between 1940 and 1970. They found that the number of black men and women employed in the industry began to increase sharply in 1965, coincidentally just after enactment of the Civil Rights Act. They considered a variety of alternative explanations that might account for the sudden shift but rejected them all. They concluded that federal antidiscriminatory legislation did significantly improve black employment.

Social networks operate along racial as well as gender lines. Such informal networks can be very important as sources of information about job opportunities, market information, career advice, and so on. Just as women tend to be excluded from old boy networks, social networks fall along racial lines with more connections within racial groups than between them. Feagin and Imani (1994) examined the construction industry in a southern U.S. metropolitan area and found that black contractors tend to be on the periphery of the social, friendship, and collaborative networks that contribute so much to business success. The discrimination need not be deliberate or malicious: Indeed, often, firms simply want to deal with those they already knew, have worked with in the past, or with whom they had some kind of working or social relationship. But use of informal social networks reinforces racial divisions. Such discrimination is harder to prevent using the law because legislating friendships, acquaintanceships, or other informal social relations is both impractical and undesirable.

Race, Mortgage Discrimination, and Wealth Inequality

Thus far, we have been discussing inequalities in labor markets and how these lead to income inequality by race and gender. Another form of economic inequality can be found in the possession of wealth of different groups (Oliver and Shapiro 1995). In 1993, the median net worth of white American households was $45,740; the median worth of black and Hispanic households was $4,418 and $4,656, respectively. Black incomes may have equaled 59% of white incomes in 1993, but black household wealth equaled only 9.7% of white household wealth. The racial disparity in wealth is much greater than the disparity in income.

Unlike income, which for most people depends primarily on employment, the accumulation of wealth by ordinary people often depends on access to credit. For example, most Americans do not have the cash available to buy a new automobile; they must purchase their car on credit and make monthly car payments. For many Americans, the single most valuable asset they possess is their home. In 1995, homes constituted over 30% of total household wealth (Wolff 1998:139). Homeownership enables many Americans to build up equity in a possession that increases in value over time (rather than throwing their income away in rent) and to end their working lives with a valuable possession that can be an important source of security in their old age or left to their children after they die. Homeownership is a central feature of the "American Dream."

Because so much personal wealth resides in the family home, racial differences in homeownership partly explain racial differences in overall wealth. In 1995, the homeownership rate among blacks was 42.2%; for Hispanics it was 42.4%. Among whites that same year, the rate was 70.8% (U.S. Department of Housing and Urban Development 1996:79). The connection between race and homeownership is surprisingly complex. Only the wealthiest buyers are able to pay for their homes in cash, so most have to borrow money by getting a home mortgage. Housing markets depend directly on credit markets. Thus, homeownership depends on mortgage lending and how easily people from different racial groups can borrow money.

In addition, where people live affects educational and job opportunities for themselves and their families (Massey and Denton 1993). People typically work within commuting distance of their homes, their children go to school within an even shorter distance, and social networks depend on residence. Where people live is enormously consequential.

The mortgage market has provided a test case for ideas about discrimination in markets. A bank that refuses to lend to a qualified borrower because of race or gender (or some other characteristic) is deliberately forgoing a profitable opportunity. Banks that operate this way, so the argument goes, won't survive for long in a competitive market. Thus, discrimination should disappear, because it is economically unsustainable. For many years, banks and other home mortgage lenders were accused of discriminating against minorities. For many years, banks have responded to such accusations by claiming that their decisions were based on hard economic facts, not on race or ethnicity. If minorities were denied mortgages at a higher rate than whites, it was because minorities tended to have lower incomes and were more likely to default on their loans. What looked like a racial decision was in fact a rational decision.

In 1992, the Federal Reserve Bank of Boston published a report that addressed these questions in a detailed study of mortgage lending in the Boston area (Munnell et al. 1992). The study compared mortgage denial rates for whites and minorities, taking into account all the economic characteristics that banks said they used as the basis for approving or rejecting a mortgage application. As anyone who has applied for a mortgage can tell you, lenders want to know a lot about borrowers: income, total debts, credit history, prior bankruptcy, the appraised value of the home, net wealth, occupation, size of the down payment, age, marital status, and the number of dependents, among other things. Many of these are characteristics relevant to the risk of borrower default, so it makes good sense that a lender would want to know this information about a potential borrower. For example, someone who earns a high income is more likely to repay a $150,000 mortgage than someone who earns a low income. And because we know that whites and minorities differ significantly when it comes to wealth and income, perhaps this explains why lenders deny minority applicants at a higher rate than whites.

In the Federal Reserve Bank of Boston study, minority applicants were 2.7 times more likely to have their mortgage applications denied than whites (Munnell et al. 1992:21). The study found that some of this discrepancy was explained by economic differences between white and minority applicants. Black and Hispanic applicants tended, for example, to have less wealth, lower incomes, and poorer credit histories than their white counterparts. *But these economic differences did not account for all the difference in rejection rates.* After taking into account economic differences, minority rejection rates were still 1.8 times higher than the rate for whites (Munnell et al. 1992:42). Because 1.8 is less than 2.7, some of the difference between whites and minorities is explained by underlying economic differences. But if economic differences explained everything, the ratio should have dropped down to 1.0, not 1.8.

According to the study, white and minority applicants who unambiguously met lenders' criteria for creditworthiness were granted loans. And applicants who completely failed to meet lenders' criteria were denied mortgages, whether they were white or not. But many people have mixed financial histories; maybe they bounced a few checks when they were still in college, or perhaps their debt-to-income ratios are just slightly above the acceptable threshold. When the merits of the application were somewhat ambiguous (i.e., neither clearly an accept or a reject), white applicants tended much more than minority applicants to get the benefit of the doubt. Lenders recognize that lending rules cannot always be applied in a cut-and-dried, hard-and-fast fashion. But it seems that this necessary flexibility and discretion was used to benefit some racial groups more than others.

The Federal Reserve Bank of Boston study unleashed a storm of controversy, with some people criticizing the research (Becker 1993a; Berkovec et al. 1994) and others confirming its general findings (Carr and Megbolugbe 1993; Kim and Squires 1995; Ladd 1998; Tootell 1993; Yinger 1995). The results are not easily dismissed, however, particularly because of their consistency with evidence on other forms of discrimination affecting housing and credit markets. Mortgage lenders require borrowers to insure their homes, something that is harder for minorities to do than whites, given the relative unavailability of insurance in inner-cities relative to suburbs (Squires, Velez, and Taeuber 1991). Furthermore, poor minority neighborhoods are often underserved by the banking industry (Caskey 1994).

Discrimination in mortgage markets, housing markets, insurance, and financial services has played a key role in creating a residentially segregated society. There are no more municipal laws such as Richmond, Virginia had in 1911 explicitly mandating racially segregated neighborhoods. But the effect is much the same. Racially, American cities in both the North and the South are highly segregated (Massey and Denton 1993:47). And no ethnic or racial minority group has experienced more segregation than African Americans (Massey and Denton 1993:26-33). Despite 30 years of antidiscrimination policy, there was no dramatic change toward integration in the major metropolitan areas of the United States. Rather, racial residential segregation has proved to be a remarkably stable, even intractable, situation.

Residential segregation has the effect of so concentrating poverty into neighborhoods that joblessness, low incomes, and welfare dependency become the norm. Poor inner-city communities become increasingly isolated from the outside world (Wilson 1996). Few formal or informal social networks lead out of the ghetto. But the effects of this pattern do not apply only to poor blacks, for middle-class and higher-income blacks are themselves highly segregated (Massey and Denton 1993:86).

Race, Gender, and Price

Thus far, we have focused on racial and gender differences in income, wealth, and access to credit. At least one other important market feature varies depending on race and gender. Some prices, whether fixed or negotiated, vary depending on whether the buyer is male or female or on what racial group the buyer belongs to. Such variation occurs even for similar or identical goods. If prices are determined by supply and demand, then one and only one price ought to prevail within a market. Economists refer to this as the "law of one price."

First consider fixed-price goods. These are the kinds of services or commodities that have a publicly posted nonnegotiable price: Buyers don't haggle. At an upscale hair salon in Evanston, Illinois, women are charged $7 to $8 (or about 20-25%) more for a shampoo and haircut than men, even when it takes just as long (35-45 minutes), and even when performed by the same hairstylist. At a dry cleaner around the corner, a woman's cotton blouse costs $3.50 to clean and a man's cotton shirt costs only $1.50. These examples reflect a more general pattern in which women are charged more. Even the price of generic clothing, such as a dark-colored wool turtle neck sweater from the same designer, varies depending on whether it is for sale in the men's or the women's department of a department store. For men, the sweater costs $97.50, whereas for women it was $145.00 (Whittelsey and Carroll 1995:13). Such price differences mean that women must pay more than men, although the rationale for the difference isn't obvious. Perhaps once upon a time, when men all had short unstyled hair and women wore elaborate hairdos, it made sense to charge women more because it took more work to fix their hair. But today hair length varies more from person to person than from man to woman, and both sexes are equally prone to vanity.

Buyers mostly face fixed posted prices when they purchase goods, but occasionally, they must bargain over the price of a commodity. Americans typically bargain for houses and cars (in the latter case, Saturn is an exception). Bargaining over a price makes it likely that two people buying the same item will not pay the same price. Some people may be better at driving a hard bargain than others. Do gender or race make a difference in bargaining?

One study done of car purchases found significant differences between men and women both in terms of the initial and the final price negotiated for the purchase of a car (Ayres and Siegelman 1995). Multiple testers were trained to bargain in the same way and then were sent off to purchase new cars at Chicago-area dealerships. Each time, they at-

EXHIBIT 5.10

Average Markup over Dealer Cost, by Race and Gender of Tester (in percentages)

	Initial Markup	*Final Markup*
White males	9.20	5.18
White females	10.32	6.04
Black females	12.23	7.20
Black males	17.32	14.61

Source: Ayres and Siegelman (1995:308).

tempted to buy the same car with the same options and followed the same bargaining strategy. Yet male testers came away with lower prices than female testers did. And white testers received lower prices than black testers. Exhibit 5.10 shows the average percentage markup (over the dealer cost) achieved by white male, white female, black male, and black female testers in bargaining for the identical car. Markups are given for both the initial offer and the final price.

As the table shows, no one fares as well as white males in the car market. White males obtained an average final price that represented a 5.18% markup over the dealer cost. The other three groups had to pay a higher markup, especially black females and males. What makes this result truly puzzling is that it did not depend on the sex or race of the car salesperson or the owner of the dealership. The price differences emerged whether the salesperson or the dealer was male or female, black or white.

Conclusion

Markets are associated with substantial and enduring forms of economic inequality. Whether on the basis of income, employment, wealth, or the prices they pay, some people are better off than others. The extent of inequality varies from one country to the next and over time. And some important social distinctions figure prominently in these varied forms of economic inequality, especially race and gender.

As markets spread and come increasingly to govern more and more of the world's economy, their consequences for inequality will also become more common. We are likely to witness an overall increase in economic inequality. And although industrial deregulation and the decline of the public sector may make markets more competitive, they need not reduce discrimination. Some telling changes have already occurred in the countries of Eastern Europe as they undergo the transition from socialist-style command economies to free market economies. Whatever their faults, socialist economies were designed to prevent widespread income differentials. As Kornai shows (1992:318-19), income inequality was lower in socialist countries than in capitalist countries. Their success at reducing income differences can be seen by the growth in differentials as socialist economies shift over to capitalism. One study of the Baltic countries (Estonia, Latvia, and Lithuania) documented very considerable increases in income inequality in only four years (Cornelius and Weder 1996). Similarly, income inequality grew dramatically in Russia during its transition to a market economy (Brainerd 1998).

Like a magic genie let out of a bottle, economic change has unleashed forces pushing in the direction of more inequality than before. This chapter has challenged two of the most common assertions about the virtues of free markets. The first is that the extreme economic inequalities arising from the operation of markets are a good thing and increase efficiency. The second is that discrimination on the basis of extraneous characteristics such as race and gender will disappear as markets become more prevalent. Free markets are indeed spreading around the world, but they bring with them various warts and shortcomings. They aren't going to solve the problems of discrimination and inequality by themselves, and under some circumstances, they may even make these problems worse.

6

Economic Development

What is the first thing that comes to mind when you think of economic underdevelopment? Californians probably have a better understanding of the term than many other Americans, because as one of the richest states in the United States, California shares a border with the poor Mexican state of Baja California Norte. Many Californians have had the unforgettable experience of crossing the border between the Californian city of San Diego and the Mexican city of Tijuana, which essentially takes the U.S. visitor from an orderly and prosperous urban area to a much poorer one—a striking contrast for people on both sides of the border. At the same time, thousands of Mexicans can be seen crossing the Tijuana-San Diego border, drawn by the substantially higher wages that even low-level jobs in the United States can provide. Miles of corrugated iron fencing stretch along the border to prevent job-seeking Mexicans from crossing the border illegally.

The contrast between San Diego and Tijuana is merely one highly visible example of the gap between the rich and poor countries of the world. This gap has enormous consequences for the lives of the people who live in these different countries. Exhibit 6.1 illustrates how economic resources provide opportunities not only to live better in material terms but to live longer because of better nutrition and health care—particularly important for young children, who are more likely to die of curable diseases in Mexico than in the United States.

Why are some countries rich and other countries poor? Is it possible for poor countries to become better off? And if this is possible, what is the best strategy that underdeveloped countries can employ? These are the central questions in the study of economic development and the ones we will address in this chapter. Many different theories can be advanced to explain why some countries became rich and others stayed poor—and how the latter might hope to "catch up." Today, many economists and policymakers see free markets as the best way of helping poor nations to

EXHIBIT 6.1

Mexico and United States, Gross National Product per Capita, Average Life Expectancy, Percentage of People Living on Less Than $1 per Day, 1995

	GNP per Capita ($US 1995)	Average Life Expectancy	Percentage of Population Living on Less than $1/Day
Mexico	$ 3,320	72 years	14.9
United States	$26,980	77 years	< 1

Source: World Bank (1997).

improve their national incomes, thereby enabling their citizens to enjoy the kind of living standard we take for granted in a rich country such as the United States.

For example, the North American Free Trade Agreement (NAFTA) has been promoted by economists and policymakers not only as a way of creating new markets for American products but also a way to gradually erase economic differences between the United States and Mexico. NAFTA's removal of government regulations inhibiting foreign investment and trade is supposed to create economic incentives that will help Mexico grow and develop. Because of NAFTA and previous free trade agreements, the San Diego-Tijuana border is marked not only by miles of fences to prevent illegal migration but also by numerous foreign-owned factories that have been established on the Mexican side of the border.

This chapter takes a critical look at this widespread faith in free markets as the key to development success. In its extreme form, this popular idea holds that the only thing preventing poor countries from becoming rich are their barriers to free trade and excessive government regulation: If the "invisible hand" of the market were only allowed free reign, economic development would follow as a natural consequence, and all citizens of the world would live in similar conditions of prosperity. A more sociological approach, in contrast, views economic development as arising from markets that are socially, politically, and culturally constructed: Like all other economic phenomena, economic development is embedded in social relations that must be taken into account in any development recipe.

Economic Development Defined

Mexico belongs to a group of countries conventionally known as "underdeveloped" (or more recently, "less developed" or "developing"). In contrast, the United States belongs to an elite group of countries considered to be "developed," which also include most Western European countries, Australia, New Zealand, Canada, and Japan. Developed countries have higher national incomes and tend to have both higher levels of industrialization and more equitable income distribution than underdeveloped countries.

While we who live in the wealthy countries tend to take our comfortable lifestyles for granted, in fact, about four-fifths of the world's population lives in less developed countries. Although Mexico seems like a poor country by U.S. standards, it actually belongs to the group known as the "middle-income countries," which are relatively better off compared with truly poor countries such as Haiti or Bangladesh. Of the three least developed continents on the globe, Africa is the poorest; in 1995, the African nation of Mali had a gross national product (GNP) per capita of $250 (compared with Mexico's $3,320) and an average life expectancy of 50 years (compared with 72 years in Mexico) (World Bank 1995).

What exactly do we mean when we use terms such as development or underdeveloped? Although some authors have distinguished between economic, social, and political development (Handelman 1996), economic development is often abbreviated as just plain "development"—a convention we will follow in this chapter. Economic development is a *normative* concept—that is, it makes sense only in the context of people's notions of right and wrong or good and bad. The idea is based on the assumption that it is better for human beings to live longer, more materially comfortable lives. It is also a fundamentally *relative* concept, in the sense that what counts as "developed" changes over time. The standard of living and life expectancy that people in the United States had in the year 1900 would have made it an underdeveloped country by today's standards; but by the standards of its day, the United States of 1900 was a developed country. Part of the problem of underdeveloped countries is that there is no fixed point of development to catch up to: As countries such as the United States and Japan continue to grow and become more technologically sophisticated, countries such as Mexico are in danger of falling increasingly far behind.

Although they have mostly agreed on the fundamentals, economists have often disagreed on the details of what causes economic development—and on distinguishing causes from effects (Hirschman 1958:1).

For example, even during the heyday of "development" economics in the 1950s and 1960s, there was still disagreement among economists about the role of different economic variables in development, such as manufacturing, agriculture, population, or capital. Did economic development begin with an industrial revolution, with increased agricultural productivity, or with capital accumulation and investment? Should underdeveloped countries invest in making farming more productive, or should they try to encourage investment in factories?

In this chapter, we will not attempt to settle these debates, but we will generally assume that industrial manufacturing is the best development path for most Third World countries. Some land- and resource-rich countries such as Australia and New Zealand managed to provide high standards of living for their people based on the export of agricultural products; others, such as Kuwait and Saudi Arabia, have built their economies on exporting oil and petroleum products. However, the majority of the countries considered to be developed today—such as the United States, Germany, Japan, and Great Britain—became wealthy by expanding the proportion of the national economy devoted to manufacturing (as opposed to agriculture).

Most inhabitants of the Third World live in countries that lack sufficient land and natural resources relative to their populations (more than two-thirds of the developing world lives in China and India). Common sense suggests that industry is a more efficient way to provide jobs for an expanding population than agriculture, which requires a lot of land and less manpower as it becomes increasingly mechanized. A question we will focus on in this chapter, therefore, is not whether or not industrialization is good for development but, rather, how best to industrialize.

One thing all economists agree on is that economic development requires sustained and rapid growth, as measured by the increase in national income per inhabitant—or real per capita gross domestic product (GDP, defined as the total value of all final goods and services produced in a given national economy, divided by the number of people in that nation, and adjusted for inflation—hence the "real"). However, real per capita GDP growth alone does not sufficiently capture what we mean by economic development, which is much easier to identify in hindsight—that is, after it has become clear that growth has led to development. In an effort to clarify this distinction, an economist named Joseph Schumpeter distinguished between growth and economic development, asserting that development occurred only when there were technical innovations and new production techniques (Martinussen 1997:24).

Another economist, Albert Hirschman, defined development more abstractly as a process stemming from "calling forth and enlisting for development purposes resources and abilities that are hidden, scattered, or badly utilized" (Hirschman 1958:5). Development, according to Hirschman, does not result from the mobilization of an entire economy at once but, rather, from the mobilization of key, strategic sectors that could pull the rest of the economy along with them. Thus, for example, a dynamic textile industry can create demand for cotton in the countryside, for transportation, for fashion designers, for mechanical engineers, and so on. This "pushing" and "pulling" process was something Hirschman called the creation of "forward-and-backward linkages."

Another aspect of economic development not captured by GDP growth is the social transformation that improves the welfare of the society in general, not just for a few people at the top. One famous theory developed by Simon Kuznets postulated development as initially increasing inequality, as entrepreneurs reaped returns on their investments (and wages continued to be low); later in the process, inequality would stabilize and then decrease (Martinussen 1997:60). Apparently, Kuznets's theory holds true only for some countries; for example, it doesn't seem to work in the recently developing East Asian countries such as South Korea and Taiwan, which "combined rapid growth with relatively equal, and even improving, income distribution" (Haggard 1990b:224). In any case, different countries have historically made different choices regarding the twin priorities of economic growth on the one hand and social welfare and equality on the other. Exhibit 6.2 shows that many countries with similar levels of wealth have very different "human development indexes" (which aggregate the dimensions of life expectancy, educational attainment, and household income).

Thus far, we have defined the concept of economic development according to some of its most salient characteristics, such as growth in national income, industrialization, increased social welfare, and more equitable income distribution. The most interesting debates about development today, however, are not about what *defines* economic development but, rather, what makes development *happen*. What has been the key to the development success of countries such as the United States, Germany, and Japan? And what should a country such as Mexico do to become richer and provide a better standard of living for its people? The answers offered by many economists to these sorts of questions will be discussed in the following section.

EXHIBIT 6.2

Similar Human Development Index (HDI), Different Income, 1993

Country	HDI Value	GNP per Capita (US$)
New Zealand	0.927	12,600
Switzerland	0.926	35,760
Argentina	0.885	7,220
Costa Rica	0.884	2,150
Vietnam	0.523	170
Congo	0.517	950

Source: United Nations Development Programme (UNDP) (1996).

From *The Wealth of Nations* to Neoliberalism

In a recent interview, the well-known economist (and later Treasury Secretary for the Clinton Administration) Lawrence Summers summarized the view that has become prevalent among economists in recent decades about the key to economic success in any country, whether rich or poor. "What's the single most important thing to learn from an economics course today? What I try to leave my students with is the view that the invisible hand is more powerful than the [hand of the government]. Things will happen in well-organized efforts without direction, controls, plans. That's the consensus among economists" (Summers quoted in Yergin and Stanislaw 1998:150-51).

Summers's reference to the invisible hand is significant, because it provides a good example of the recent revival of old ideas among economists and policymakers. The idea that market forces left alone can bring economic growth and prosperity can be traced back to the classical economic thinkers of the late 18th and early 19th centuries, a time when many European countries were embarking on the road to economic development. The two early thinkers whose ideas have the most influence in the late 20th century are Adam Smith, popularly known for his notion of the invisible hand of the market, and David Ricardo, whose ideas form the basis of contemporary economic thinking about international trade.

The Classical Economists

Economic development in Europe did not occur simultaneously in all countries but rather was uneven, and advanced faster in some countries than in others. By the time of Smith and Ricardo, England was ahead of its neighbors in many respects, thanks to an industrial revolution that was making mass-produced goods available for popular consumption, turning peasants into workers, and making capitalists enormously wealthy.

As less developed European nations struggled to catch up to their neighbors, and more developed ones fought to maintain their advantage, a political-economic system known as mercantilism emerged. The idea behind mercantilism was to protect domestic industry from foreign competition by imposing **tariffs** (taxes on imports) and other barriers to inhibit the sale of foreign products at home. Mercantilism also gave the firms of a given country a monopoly on the sale of goods to the colonies of that country—an enormous boon to these firms at a time when colonies were extremely important. For example, only British firms were allowed to sell goods in the 13 American colonies, whereas the French colony of St. Domingue (later Haiti) was exclusively serviced by French merchants. The mercantilist system was a form of what is more commonly known today as **protectionism**—basically, the protection of domestic producers from foreign competition through tariffs and other import barriers.

Adam Smith was both a critic of mercantilism and a keen observer of the emerging capitalist system. Although much of what Smith ([1776] 1900) said in his masterwork, *The Wealth of Nations*, seems quite matter-of-fact today, it seemed revolutionary at the time that it was written. This was because Europe was emerging from a system of social relations based on tradition and religious faith rather than free markets. Lacking the guidance of tradition to ensure proper behavior, many wondered if people in the marketplace would degenerate into anarchic behavior, stealing and murdering in pursuit of their own individual gain.

Smith's contribution to this debate was his contention that the marketplace would not degenerate into anarchy and chaos but, rather, could help make everybody better off by harnessing the power of individual greed. In the marketplace, each selfishly motivated individual is confronted by a host of similarly motivated individuals; as a result, each actor is forced to meet the prices offered by competitors. Among the beneficial effects of competitive markets are lower prices to consumers, the elimination of the production of unwanted goods and the expanded production of wanted ones, and incentives for technical innovation to lower production costs. In such a system, the investor is "led by an invisible hand to promote an end which was no part of his intention. . . . By pursuing his own interest he frequently promotes that of the society more effectually than when he really intends to promote it" (Smith [1776] 1900:345).

Smith also observed that the power of the invisible hand was often stymied through the sometimes well-intended efforts of people to create desirable moral outcomes through government intervention. The artificial fixing of food prices to help protect consumers, for example, often had the unintended effect of creating food shortages (and black markets), because farmers refused to sell their goods at the low official prices. The mercantilist system made a few traders extremely wealthy but impoverished thousands of consumers who had no choice but to purchase the overpriced products sold by the merchants of a single nation. In a system in which every nation tried to "beggar its neighbor" through restrictions on imports from other nations, Smith believed that all nations became worse off.

Smith's critique of mercantilism was taken up further and systematized by David Ricardo, an English economist born around the time of the publication of *The Wealth of Nations*. Ricardo's theory of "comparative advantage" is now standard fare in any introductory economics course. In brief, it shows how every country is better off specializing in whatever it produces most efficiently and exchanging goods in a system of free international trade. For example, Washington State has a cool climate congenial for growing apples, whereas Florida is a hot state where oranges flourish. Great greenhouses could be built to sustain the orange industry in Washington State; conversely, air-conditioned indoor orchards could be used to grow apples in Florida. To make these domestically grown fruits competitive, the governments of Washington and Florida could charge high tariffs on imported fruit. But would this really make the inhabitants of Washington and Florida better off? The idea of comparative advantage is simply that it is much more efficient for Florida to specialize in oranges, for Washington to specialize in apples, and for each to trade freely with the other.

Although neither Smith nor Ricardo wrote specifically about the issue of economic development (the term had not been coined yet), the implications of their writings for less developed countries were immediately apparent. In the late 18th century, England was a leader in the production of industrial goods. Other countries, such as the newly independent United States of America, had little industry and specialized in the export of raw materials such as cotton and timber. The classical economists' recommendations for an underdeveloped country such as the United States were that it should continue to specialize in the export of raw materials and continue to import industrial products from England. This recommendation was, of course, very much in the national interest of England, which wanted to continue to sell its industrial products in America and which urged the new government of the United States to engage in practices of free trade.

Smith and Ricardo Ignored

Did the leaders of the newly independent United States see the wisdom of the classical economists' advice and follow it? Mostly not. Alexander Hamilton, one of the founding fathers, thought that it was a bad strategy for the United States to continue in this economic role and that the only way to ensure prosperity for the emerging United States was to protect domestic manufacturers from foreign competition (Hamilton 1791). Abraham Lincoln also supported protectionism, adhering to the view that "the abandonment of the protective policy . . . must result in the increase of both useless labour, and idleness; and so, in pro[por]tion, must produce want and ruin among our people" (Lincoln quoted in Eckes 1995:32).

In the United States, protectionism was particularly important in the post-Civil War period, when the United States made the transition from an agrarian to an industrial economy (Krooss 1974:406-7; Levy and Sampson 1962:236-37). Exhibit 6.3 shows an early 20th century political cartoon supporting protectionism in the United States. Not until later in the 20th century, when U.S. industries had become internationally competitive, did the U.S. government became an advocate for international free trade. Other countries that ignored Smith's recommendations were Germany and France, which both industrialized under protectionist systems during the 19th century.

Why were nations such as the United States, France, and Germany able to develop in the 19th century despite their interference with the invisible hand and comparative advantage? One possible answer is that comparative advantage in some goods is more conducive to economic development than others. By systematically *creating* a comparative advantage in industrial goods rather than the export of raw materials, the United States became better off than it would have been if it had continued to specialize in cotton and timber.

This was essentially the argument put forward by many intellectuals and policymakers in countries that were still underdeveloped by the 20th century, such as the nations of Asia and Latin America (and those of Africa after decolonization). By the 1940s, the idea that underdeveloped countries needed to industrialize through protectionism had become par-

EXHIBIT 6.3

"Standing Pat." Uncle Sam, the Protectionist, Triumphs over John Bull, the Free Trader

Source: Judge, November 14, 1903. Special Collections, Alden Library, Ohio University.

ticularly popular among the officials of the U.N. Economic Commission on Latin America (ECLA), which promoted a set of policies similar to those espoused by Alexander Hamilton and Abraham Lincoln in the previous century.

Toward the beginning of the 20th century, Latin American countries specialized in the production and export of raw materials and agricultural products, such as coffee, cotton, minerals, and petroleum—just as the United States had scarcely 100 years before. The ECLA economists argued that if Latin American countries continued to specialize in these goods, they would face intractable economic, social, and political problems that would prevent development from occurring. In other words, pursuing comparative advantage did not necessarily lead to economic development.

In keeping with their focus on the goal of using government policy to help promote economic development, the ideas of the ECLA are often referred to as **developmentalism.** The ECLA economists observed that most Latin American countries depended heavily on the export of one or two primary commodities (such as cotton and bananas). One of the problems with a commodity such as cotton, argued the ECLA, was that its price was liable to fluctuate greatly on international markets. Moreover, for two reasons, there was always a general downward pressure on the price of cotton. First, many underdeveloped countries were producing cotton and attempting to undersell one another on international markets. Second, technological advances often replaced products such as cotton with synthetic substitutes (such as nylon and polyester). As a result, as the prices of primary commodities such as cotton and bananas went down, underdeveloped countries would have increasingly limited revenues to purchase imported industrial goods.

The specialization of countries such as Mexico and Colombia in primary commodities also had *social* consequences harmful to the goal of economic development. Industrial revolutions, such as those that had already occurred in England and the United States, created industrial jobs for people who had formerly worked on the land; people who got jobs as factory workers received paychecks that enabled them to buy industrial products, leading to increased production, in turn leading to more jobs, and so on, in a virtuous cycle. In contrast, the international competitiveness of the production of a primary commodity such as cotton depended either on low wages or on increasing mechanization that put farm laborers out of work: neither option was likely to provide higher wages and a better standard of living for the population. As droves of Latin Americans began to flock to cities from the countryside in search of work, the idea of government-sponsored industrialization became extremely compelling.

To become industrialized, the developmentalists argued, Latin American countries needed to protect domestic business from imports originating in developed countries. Why? Because foreign imports drove potentially industrializing domestic entrepreneurs out of business. For example, a Mexican entrepreneur starting a bicycle factory faced overwhelming disadvantages with respect to Schwinn and other bicycle manufacturers located in the United States. Not only did Schwinn have the advantage of decades of experience in the industry, and immediate access to raw and intermediate materials that came with being located in an industrialized country, but Schwinn also had easy access to the U.S. capital market. Mexican consumers might be better off in the short run under a free trade regime, but their interests needed to be sacrificed to pursue the long-term development of the Mexican economy.

In keeping with these sorts of ideas, from the 1940s until the 1970s or 1980s many underdeveloped countries adopted developmentalist policies in which the visible hand of government intervention guided the invisible hand of the market. One way that governments intervened was by passing protectionist legislation that imposed tariffs and other barriers on foreign imports. Other developmentalist policies included low-interest loans and subsidies to industries, outright government ownership of some strategic industries (especially petroleum), and special tax incentives. In some countries, this development strategy led to relatively high rates of growth. In Mexico, for example, annual growth rates averaged over 6% between 1945 and 1970, leading many observers to speak of a "Mexican miracle."

While Latin American and other countries experimented with forms of government intervention that led toward *capitalist* development, another group of underdeveloped countries undertook a more radical form of government intervention: socialism. Karl Marx conceived of **socialism** as a temporary stage that countries would go through *en route* to the utopian social order of communism, a radically democratic society in which social rewards would be distributed according to the principle of "from each according to his ability, to each according to his need" and in which governments would become unnecessary and disappear.

The real-world application of Marx's ideas turned out somewhat differently than expected. First, communism as Marx conceived of it was never reached, and a new popular meaning of the term came into circulation: "Communist" lost its utopian meaning, and came instead to describe a group of countries with totalitarian political systems and centrally planned economies.

Second, socialism was imposed in countries that Marx would have said weren't ready for it. Marx believed that countries had to pass through successive stages of economic development to achieve socialism and then communism. Socialism was appropriate only for countries that were already industrialized, such as Germany or England. But as it turned out, the first country to have a socialist revolution—Russia—was underdeveloped and agrarian. Soviet military occupation subsequently imposed socialist economies on the countries of Eastern Europe, but in many Third World countries, these models were adopted voluntarily by revolutionary nationalist governments, including those of China, Algeria, North Vietnam, and Cuba (Kornai 1992:22-26). Exhibit 6.4 illustrates how widespread these systems had become in the world by the late 1980s. We will refer to the "really existing socialism" of these countries as "state socialism" to distinguish it from the utopian socialism conceived of by Marx (Konrád and Szelényi 1979). The fundamental difference between state socialism and capitalism is that productive assets are owned by the government in the former and by private agents in the latter. For example, in Cuba in 1988, public sector production accounted for 95.9% of national income, compared with West Germany (around 10%) and the United States (less than 2%) (Kornai 1992:62-90).

Although Cold War-era politicians in the United States correctly identified many of the ways in which state socialism was economically inferior to U.S.-style capitalism, their comparisons often failed to acknowledge that most of the state-socialist countries were much poorer than the United States at the time that they became socialist. While it was reasonable to compare among developed countries (such as East and West Germany) or underdeveloped countries (such as North and South Korea), it was unfair to compare the economic performance of the United States and the Soviet Union. In fact, the economic achievements of many state-socialist countries appeared substantial if they were compared with where these countries had started out.

For example, at the time of the Russian revolution in 1917, the United States was on the verge of becoming one of the world's most powerful and advanced economies, whereas Russia was a backward, weak, and underdeveloped country. In contrast, after World War II, the Soviet economy was strong enough to make the Soviet Union a military superpower—and the number-one rival of the United States. Some of the most consistent benefits following state-socialist revolutions in underdeveloped countries were in the areas of health and education. In Cuba, for example, illiteracy was virtually eliminated from the island after the revolution in 1959; average life expectancy on the island by the late 1980s was 75 years—only a year lower than the United States (Pérez-Stable 1993:92; World Bank 1997).

Of course, a valid and frequent criticism of state socialism during the Cold War was the absence of democracy: The economic and social

EXHIBIT 6.4

The State Socialist Countries, 1987

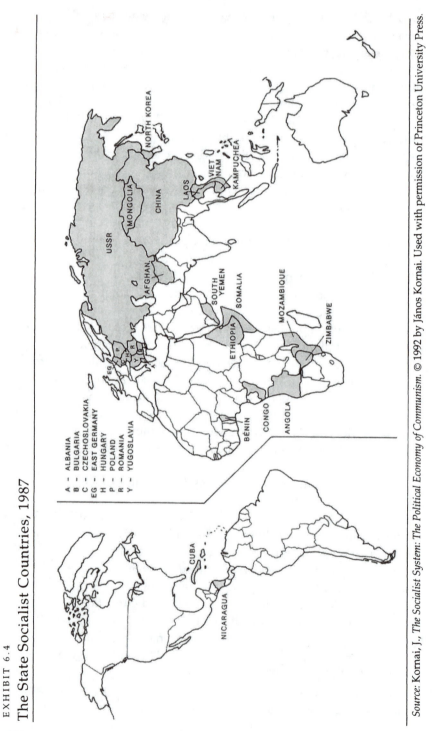

A – ALBANIA
B – BULGARIA
C – CZECHOSLOVAKIA
EG – EAST GERMANY
H – HUNGARY
P – POLAND
R – ROMANIA
Y – YUGOSLAVIA

Source: Kornai, J., *The Socialist System: The Political Economy of Communism.* © 1992 by János Kornai. Used with permission of Princeton University Press.

achievements of state-socialist countries occurred under totalitarian political regimes. Nevertheless, it is also true that during the Cold War the United States supported many nondemocratic *capitalist* countries as allies, including (at different times) almost all of Central and South America, South Vietnam, South Korea, Taiwan, the Philippines, Indonesia, Zaire, and Haiti. As far as economic development was concerned, some of these nondemocratic capitalist countries were wild successes (e.g., South Korea and Taiwan); and others were dismal failures (e.g., Haiti and Zaire). In the capitalist as well as in the state-socialist world, the relationship between democracy and development has always been complicated and ambiguous.

Smith and Ricardo Revived

We have seen that during the initial phases of European economic development in the 18th century, the classical economists Smith and Ricardo offered theories for why national governments should leave markets alone. Despite this advice, however, many nations subsequently attempted to develop using government policies that interfered with the free market. At different times during the 19th century, the United States, Germany, and France protected their domestic industries from foreign competition. During the 20th century, underdeveloped countries experimented with socialism and developmentalism, both of which involved government interference with markets.

Times have changed, however. In the 1990s, underdeveloped countries around the world—from Latin America to Africa to Asia to the former Socialist Bloc—have returned to the ideas of Smith and Ricardo. Mexico constitutes an excellent example of this recent move to free markets. Since the 1980s, Mexico has privatized its state-owned industries, made its laws more favorable to private agriculture and foreign investment, and eliminated government subsidies of consumer goods. Perhaps most important, in 1994, NAFTA went into effect, eliminating Mexican tariffs on imports from the United States and Canada and creating more favorable conditions for foreign investors. In defending NAFTA against its critics in 1993, President Clinton claimed that the agreement would stem illegal immigration from Mexico to the United States by raising Mexican levels of economic development:

> What does Mexico get out of this . . .? [T]hey have 90 million people there now producing for themselves. What they want is American investment in Mexico to hire Mexicans to produce goods and services for Mexicans so

they can grow their economy from within. . . . [T]he more people down
there . . . have jobs and the better the jobs are, the more they can buy American products and the less they will feel a compulsion to become part of
America's large immigration problem today. (Clinton 1993)

Why have free market ideas been revived by countries around the
world? This is a question that sociologists and political scientists are still
trying to answer. Part of the explanation, however, is that mounting evidence of problems resulting from government intervention in the economy (beginning in the 1970s) led to the election of governments more
favorable to free markets, such as that of Margaret Thatcher in England
in 1979 and Ronald Reagan in the United States in 1980. The policies implemented under the Reagan administration actually relied on a tremen-
dous amount of government intervention in the economy through military spending. But at the rhetorical level, the Reagan and the Thatcher
revolutions were a victory for the free market and a defeat for the idea of
government intervention in the economy. This victory of free markets in
the developed world set a precedent for the underdeveloped countries—
both through the power of persuasion and through the pressure of international organizations such as the World Bank and the International
Monetary Fund (IMF), which essentially told developing countries that
they could receive loans only if they opened their economies to market
forces.

Such advice also found support in underdeveloped regions of the
world, in part because economists, policymakers, and everyday people
in these countries became aware of long-standing problems with developmentalism and socialism. Where developmentalism was concerned, there was growing skepticism that protecting domestic entrepreneurs from foreign competition would lead underdeveloped countries to
industrial self-sufficiency. To achieve self-sufficiency in nondurable consumer goods such as candy bars and underwear was relatively easy. But
graduating to heavier and more technology-intensive industries such as
automobiles and computers was much more difficult because these industries required levels of capital and technology that local entrepreneurs did not possess (Ranis 1990:214). To solve this problem, Latin
American governments made arrangements with foreign investors to
build manufacturing plants in industries such as automobiles (Stallings
1990:74-5). Nevertheless, and despite high levels of growth, the Latin
American countries practicing protectionism suffered from a number of
persistent economic problems, including inflation, large-scale unemployment, and rising levels of social inequality.

Another problem observed with developmentalism was that it created a self-perpetuating collusion between domestic firms on the one hand and government officials on the other. Government officials were interested in staying in power; at the same time, domestic firms were interested in maintaining their privileges—in particular, the tariffs and other forms of protection that insulated them from foreign competition. Some of these firms became quite inefficient, but government officials refused to threaten them with taking away their protection and privilege. Why? Because these government officials relied heavily on domestic firms both for political support and for unofficial forms of support (such as bribes). So although both the firms and the officials benefited from their mutual support, domestic consumers were forced to buy lower-quality, higher-priced goods from companies that would have been put out of business if only they had been exposed to competition.

While developmentalist governments in Latin America faced the problem of how to deal with corrupt bureaucracies and inefficient domestic companies, socialist governments faced the even more intractable problems of how to run economies in the absence of market incentives. In state-socialist economies, prices were not determined by the market at all but, rather, by government bureaucrats. A Hungarian economist named János Kornai developed a theory for explaining something that was obvious to any Eastern European by the 1970s—namely, that state-run firms were not as efficient as privately owned ones. In fact, the images of Eastern Europeans waiting in endless lines for basic consumer goods was not just Cold War propaganda: It was based in the reality of everyday life for the millions of people living under state-socialist economies.

Why did state-socialist economies fail to perform as well as capitalist ones? Kornai's answer had to do with the structure of incentives under different forms of ownership. The central and defining feature of state-socialist economies was government ownership; in contrast, capitalist economies were defined by private ownership. A capitalist firm owned by a private entrepreneur faced what Kornai called **hard budget constraints,** which essentially meant that the owner had to face directly the consequences of his or her own mistakes. If one's calculation of risks was incorrect—if, for example, there turned out to be no market for what one was manufacturing—the firm would go bankrupt. On the other hand, the government managers responsible for making firm decisions under state socialism had only **soft budget constraints.**

Kornai likened the relationship between firm managers and the government under state socialism to the relationship between a child and his or her parent: The parent exerts authority over the child and provides the child with pocket money. In a scenario familiar to many college students who have emptied their checking accounts, Kornai described the result: "The manager has absolute safety. He is sure he will be bailed out. He knows the state will act as a kind father. So the brake on expansion doesn't operate. He says to himself: Why not ask for more money?" (Kornai quoted in Minard 1983:66). The most important result of soft budget constraints, according to Kornai, was constant shortages of consumer goods; these shortages, in turn, meant that state-socialist economies were "sellers'" rather than "buyers'" markets, which meant that there were few incentives to innovate.

In the end, state socialism appeared to be reasonably good at some things—such as keeping everybody fed and educated—and bad at others—such as creating innovative, dynamic economies that kept people's standards of living on the rise. This was particularly apparent when comparing state-socialist and capitalist countries starting out with similar levels of development, such as East and West Germany and North and South Korea. Moreover, by the 1970s, it was becoming clear that the Soviet Union's economy was falling farther behind that of the United States, making it increasingly difficult for the Soviets to keep up with the United States in the arms race (Chirot 1991). In the 1980s, Gorbachev's plan to open his country politically as well as economically ultimately led to the breakup of the Soviet Union and its satellites and the abandonment of state socialism throughout Eastern Europe.

With the collapse of the Communist Bloc in 1989, state socialism joined developmentalism as an abandoned experiment in economic development. If neither of these two models worked, what hope was there for poor countries to provide better lives for their citizens? A growing number of economists and policymakers returned to the original advice of Smith and Ricardo and looked to free markets for economic development.

For lack of a better term, we will refer to these pro-free market economists and political leaders as neoliberals. Whereas in the United States, we associate the world liberal with big government and social welfare policies, in most other countries, it refers to the exact opposite idea—namely, free markets and *laissez-faire* policies. Thus, neoliberals are the new free marketeers—as opposed to the old free marketeers such as Adam Smith. The quintessential neoliberal economists are Chicago School figures such as Milton Friedman and Robert Lucas; the quintessential neoliberal politicians are Margaret Thatcher and Ronald Reagan. But today, neoliberalism has spread well beyond the borders of the University of Chicago and the Republican Party: Free markets have come back into fashion throughout the discipline of economics, and even a Democrat like President Clinton has neoliberal elements in his platform, such as his endorsement of free trade through NAFTA.

Economic development has come full circle. Since the era of Smith and Ricardo, many national governments have ignored the advice to leave the invisible hand of the market alone, relying instead on government policy to help stimulate growth and development. In contrast, today, from Eastern Europe to Latin America, poor countries are having free market revivals: They are privatizing, deregulating, liberalizing, and hoping for the market to work its magic—all under the supervision of approving economists (Babb 1998). But is the free market really the solution to the problems of underdeveloped countries?

Toward a New Sociology of Development

One of the reasons that there can be so much controversy over how to achieve economic development is that development is not immediately visible to the naked eye. As a result, different observers may disagree about whether or not development is occurring in a given time or place. For example, Tijuana is not a beautiful city. The houses where the factory workers live look like shacks to North American eyes. Some beaches in Tijuana have signs to warn visitors not to swim, because the unprocessed sewage that drains into the water creates a dangerous health risk. Nevertheless, although border cities such as Tijuana and Ciudad Juárez are far less attractive than Mexico's scenic colonial towns and beach resorts, the foreign-owned factories located there create jobs for thousands of Mexican workers and contribute greatly to Mexico's GDP.

Known as *maquiladoras*, these factories were originally attracted to Mexico's border towns by a mid-1960s trade agreement that created a "free trade zone" on the border. Within this zone, foreign firms could invest freely and did not have to pay tariffs on the materials that they used in processing. Since then, thousands of firms have brought raw and semiprocessed materials over the U.S.-Mexico border to places such as Tijuana, used Mexican labor to process it, and shipped the finished products back to the United States. Moreover, since the more recent adoption of NAFTA, even more foreign firms have been drawn to Mexico by the promise of being able to sell their finished products to Mexican consumers. In a sense, NAFTA has made all Mexico into a free trade zone like

Tijuana, with the added bonus of making it possible for U.S. and Canadian firms to sell their wares on Mexican markets.

How are we to interpret what we see in Tijuana? Are the Mexican border towns that were at the vanguard of Mexico's move to free trade in the midst of an industrial revolution that will bring a better standard of living to all Mexicans? Or is Tijuana destined always to be ugly and poor? In broader terms, is the application of the free market model to Mexico going to lead to economic development?

Part of what makes these questions so difficult to answer is that economic development is a *dynamic process* rather than a *stable condition*. This means we cannot discern development with the "snapshot" approach, because a single observation cannot identify change—either in a positive or a negative direction. Moreover, even if we make "movies" instead of snapshots—in other words, make several observations over time rather than just making a single observation—it is often difficult to make definitive statements about whether economic development is occurring in any given place. This is because development is a very long-term process, which may often be interrupted by short-term economic crises and stagnation in growth.

While the United States was industrializing in the late 19th century, for example, it also had several serious economic recessions. Ultimately, however, these periods of stagnation did not prevent the United States from growing into a major industrial power. During the early 1990s, an economic recession made it seem as if the United States was "falling behind" its major industrial rivals, Germany and Japan. As this book goes to press, however, Germany is suffering from problems of unemployment, Japan is in the midst of a major financial crisis, and some people are perhaps prematurely talking in triumphalistic terms about a "Second American Century," with the United States as the world's economic leader (Zuckerman 1998).

To judge among the development strategies of different countries, it is wiser to look at long-term historical evidence rather than the latest growth statistics. For example, the long-term failures of socialism in countries such as the Soviet Union and developmentalism in countries such as Mexico might suggest that certain forms of government intervention are not conducive to economic development. On the other hand, in recent years, much attention has been paid to a group of countries in Southeast Asia—the "Asian Tigers," or Hong Kong, South Korea, Taiwan, and Singapore—as examples of development success. For example, Exhibit 6.5 illustrates how economic growth in South Korea has consistently outstripped that of Mexico since the mid-1960s—a trend that has

EXHIBIT 6.5

Economic Growth in Mexico and South Korea, 1965 to 1995

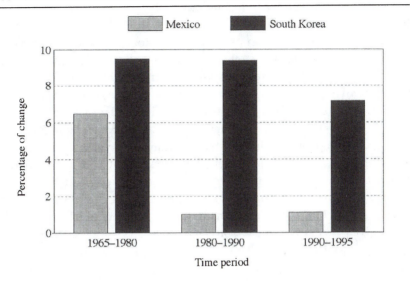

Note: Figure shows percentage of change in real gross domestic product.
Sources: Gereffi (1990b) and World Bank (1995).

brought South Korea into an entirely different national income category. Unlike Mexico, which is still considered a medium-income developing country, as of 1997, South Korea has been categorized with the upper-income countries by the World Bank.

Despite the recent Asian financial crisis, the Asian tigers are widely acknowledged to be relatively successful developers. But what lessons does East Asia's development success have for other developing countries? The moral that neoliberal economists and policymakers draw from the Asian Tigers is that development should be largely left to the invisible hand of the market. According to a recent article by two economists, "In a fundamental sense, the system of market capitalism, which first appeared in Western Europe, has finally become a global—and in particular, Asian—instrument of economic development" (Radelet and Sachs 1997:57). In their view, two main features of the Asian Tigers' economic strategy enabled them to grow and prosper since the 1960s. The first was free trade: By opening up their markets to foreign competition, East Asian industries were forced to become internationally competitive, which helped stimulate demand for East Asian products abroad, thereby increasing domestic growth. The second crucial element was the Asian Tigers' opening to foreign investment, which gave East Asian countries access to foreign capital and technology that domestic firms were unable to provide.

The broader implication of East Asian experience, according to the neoliberals, is that underdeveloped countries should rely on free trade and foreign investment rather than try to make development happen through government intervention. In this view, development is a natural process that occurs when markets are left alone. The case presented by today's neoliberals for development sounds as logical and compelling as the arguments presented by Smith and Ricardo 200 years ago. The problem is, do these theoretical prescriptions really make sense in practice? The sociological approach to economic development differs from the neoliberal approach in looking at the political, cultural, and social *preconditions* for markets—rather than assuming that markets function by themselves. As a result, the lessons that sociologists draw from the Asian Tigers, as well as other historical examples, are different from those drawn by economists.

The State and Markets

One obvious source of potential disagreement between sociologists and economists concerns the role of the government in the economy. What is the best way for governments to foster growth and bring higher standards of living for underdeveloped countries? Even the most pro-free market economists admit that development has to have a role for the state. This is because governments solve all kinds of problems that markets cannot solve on their own. In fact, even Adam Smith recognized that certain fundamental government interventions were required to make capitalism work, including national defense, public works (e.g., roads and highways), and education.

Governments also make markets work by providing institutions, or "rules of the game," within which capitalism can function: Governments make laws for governing the market, provide regulatory agencies and courts for enforcing rules and adjudicating conflicts, and penalize those who violate the rules. Although many economists take the role of institutions in economic development for granted, Douglass North (1981, 1990) and other economists of the neoinstitutionalist school specify institutions as a key determinant of the success or failure of development. One of the institutions most stressed by North is property rights, which historically were a key ingredient in economic development.

In medieval Europe, private property rights were notoriously insecure, and kings and other feudal powers routinely and arbitrarily seized the property and the profits of entrepreneurs. One of the reasons for England's early success in capitalist development, according to North, was its ability to create a more stable environment through property rights. North's work complements earlier scholarship by an anthropologist named Karl Polanyi (1944), who shows that the rise of capitalism in England was made possible by large-scale government intervention to establish private property rights and terminate the traditional rights that interfered with them.

One of these interventions was known as the "enclosures"; beginning in the 16th century and continuing even into the 19th century, English landowners got Parliament to pass legislation privatizing the common lands that peasants had by tradition used as pasture for their livestock; this was accomplished by literally fencing in or "enclosing" the commons. In England, 20.9% of all the land, or about 30% of agricultural land, was enclosed by act of Parliament between 1750 and 1820 (Neeson 1993:329). Without a state to establish and enforce landlords' private property rights, capitalist agriculture in England could never have progressed.

Secure property rights create the certainty that capitalists need to make long-term investments, but they cannot be provided by markets alone. Rather, property rights must be imposed and enforced by governments. These rights have important consequences for development. Imagine if you were a developer who bought a piece of land on which to build a factory and that the land was subsequently taken over by drug dealers from a local gang. Your first impulse would probably be to call the police to expel the invaders from your private property. Without a state willing and able to establish and enforce private property rights, you would either have to write off the land you purchased as a loss or hire your own expensive private security force to do battle with the trespassers. While this example might sound far-fetched to Americans, it is familiar to the inhabitants of many underdeveloped countries, where governments fail to provide even the most basic institutional frameworks for economic growth. Indeed, in some countries, the local government might even be in cahoots with the drug dealers! Without the certainty of secure property rights, economic development cannot progress.

Intellectual property rights are also important to economic development. For example, patents serve as a guarantee to innovators and their financial backers that they will be able to reap the profits on their investment without competition—at least initially. In a truly free market, any individual would be able to copy any other individual's idea, thus dramatically lowering the profit to be extracted from that idea and removing much of the incentive to innovate in the first place. Patent legislation represents a government restriction on free markets that rewards innovators and thereby serves to further economic development.

Another institution provided by governments with important consequences for development is antimonopoly legislation. History suggests that some industries, such as railroads, are natural monopolies. Without government regulation to break up such monopolies or to put restrictions on their profits, such industries can raise costs throughout the economy (as when a monopolistic railroad charges high prices for the transportation of goods). Antimonopoly legislation thus constitutes another example of a government restriction on free markets that helps promote growth and development. Such legislation plays the crucial role of lowering transaction costs so that economies can function more efficiently.

Thus, economists recognize some kinds of government intervention as helpful—and even necessary—for economic development. The real development controversy today is not an *absolute* one about whether we should have government or markets. Rather, it is a *relative* debate about the *degree and kind* of government intervention needed for economic growth. Today's neoliberal economists and policymakers prescribe minimalist interventions, such as the provision of property rights, infrastructure, defense, and education. In contrast, they reject more activist interventions, such as protection for domestic industries and state-owned firms.

Economics and sociology are descendants of very different intellectual lineages, which explains their divergent approaches to economic development. Economists trace their ancestry to Adam Smith, the 18th-century economist who noticed the extraordinary potential of individual self-interest to be used in the service of generalized prosperity. The main character in Smith's *The Wealth of Nations* is *homo economicus,* an abstract self-interested individual who relentlessly pursues his individual welfare. In contrast, sociology has always looked at people as occupying different social roles in different institutional settings—families, bureaucracies, political parties. Sociology does not posit an abstract human nature; it holds that people behave differently in different settings. Even different organizations of the same type—such as government bureaucracies—can produce different sorts of human behavior and different outcomes for development.

Government Bureaucracies

Sociologists have a radically different view of bureaucracy from that of economists. One group of economists (the "public choice" school) sees government bureaucracies as inherently problematic for economic development (Buchanan, Tollison, and Tullock 1980). Their models assume that people behave as self-interested, atomistic individuals in all spheres of their lives; a government official is just another example of Adam Smith's *homo economicus.* Given a trade-off between his own personal good and the greater good, he will generally choose the former; thus, for example, given the choice between awarding protective tariffs to an inefficient industry (and being rewarded with a bribe or campaign contribution) on the one hand and exposing the industry to foreign competition (and forgoing the monetary reward) on the other, he will put his own individual good over the greater good of economic development.

Max Weber, a founding father of sociology, studied bureaucracies of many nations and came up with an "ideal type" (roughly, an abstract model) of bureaucracy as a hierarchical, meritocratic organization in which bureaucrats performed tasks in the organizational interest. Of course, Weber knew about corruption and recognized his "ideal type" for what it was—an ideal model of bureaucracy rather than one matched by all actually existing bureaucracies. Some bureaucracies adhere more closely to this ideal type than others. In more ideal-typical bureaucracies, officials pursue organizational goals because of formal and informal sanctions but also because of organizational legitimacy: They believe in the organization and therefore take the good of the organization as their own.

Government bureaucracies working toward economic development in underdeveloped countries, therefore, have the potential to be powerful forces for the promotion of economic development. The question is how to realize this potential. In his recent studies on development, Peter Evans (1992, 1995) examines a range of different kinds of governments in underdeveloped countries, from "predatory states" to "developmental states." Quintessential examples of predatory states were the governments of Zaire (before its revolution in 1997) and Haiti (before the end of its military government in the mid-1990s). Predatory states are those that behave exactly as economic theory predicts that they should: They are collections of self-interested actors who use coercion and corruption to obtain material rewards. Such states bleed local economies dry and cause economic stagnation rather than development.

Developmental states behave quite differently: They help remove obstacles to development that markets cannot remove on their own, providing institutional frameworks and systems of incentives that encourage entrepreneurs to take risks. One particularly good example of a developmentalist state is that of postwar Japan, which played a crucial role in providing capital to expanding industries. Overseeing postwar industrial policy in Japan was its Ministry of International Trade and Industry (MITI), which as a highly efficient organization staffed by some of Japan's most talented university graduates came close to Weber's ideal type of bureaucracy (Evans 1995:47-8). During the postwar period, Japanese government bureaucracies successfully used government interventions to go beyond the minimalist standards endorsed by the neoliberals (Gao 1997). These included protective tariffs for domestic industries and tight control over foreign investment, which was allowed to enter only under strict conditions (Evans 1995:100). As a result, the Japanese government was able to *create* comparative advantage in industries such as computers rather than merely relying on the comparative advantages it already had, as neoliberal economists would prescribe.

What is the key to having successful government organizations such as MITI to oversee economic development and create comparative advantage? Evans's answer is that they must first be autonomous enough from the entrepreneurs they are supervising so as not to become the corrupt government patrons of favored private sector clients—as in the *homo economicus* model. To this end, government bureaus should be insulated from politics and consist of stable, meritocratic hierarchies that individual bureaucrats can climb through their careers regardless of what party happens to be in power. This form of organization is known as a career civil service. But such autonomy is not enough. They must also be *embedded* in society in ways that facilitate the informal exchange of information between government bureaucrats and the private sector. In Japan, informal social networks among elite university graduates—some of whom went on to be government bureaucrats and others of whom became leading industrialists—were particularly important (Evans 1995:49).

Foreign Investment

Contrary to Evans's notion of embedded autonomy and its role in economic development, economists of the "public choice" school see development as resulting naturally from the combined decisions of individual entrepreneurs operating within the framework of a minimalist state. A similar view has become common currency among economists and policymakers, who recommend that capital- and technology-poor under-developed countries rely on foreign investment rather than big government: "The trick is to bring multinational production enterprises and their technologies into the poorer economies to link them to the engines of growth of the advanced economies" (Radelet and Sachs 1997:50). Rather than risk corruption under protectionist policies, underdeveloped countries would be better off simply to attract foreign investors. Capital is capital; so why does it matter where it comes from?

In abstract economic models, foreign and domestic investments are seen as perfect substitutes. But some sociologists have called this assumption into question. In his study of economic development in Brazil, Peter Evans (1979) found that foreign firms suffer from problems of information that domestic firms do not: "A rational profit maximizer who grew up in Kansas City and works in Chicago brings different information to a decision from one who grew up in São Paulo and works there" (p. 36). In other words, foreign investors act within the constraints of bounded rationality, which heavily influences the kinds of investment decisions they make and thereby influences economic development.

Problems of information and uncertainty, Evans argues, meant that foreign firms in Brazil were unwilling to take the same risks as domestic investors with the same amount of capital; as a result, these firms made only minimal contributions to economic development. Foreign firms tended to use "tried and true" production methods from the home country rather than adapting to local conditions; this meant using capital-intensive techniques developed in countries where wages were high rather than applying labor-intensive techniques that took advantage of the huge pool of unemployed Brazilian labor. As a result, the presence of foreign firms had a minimal impact on Brazilian unemployment.

In addition, foreign firms tended to try to persuade Brazilian consumers to buy products developed for the home country rather than address the particular demands of local consumers. Because Brazilians were on average much poorer and their incomes distributed more unequally than First World consumers, expensive products such as automobiles had to be oriented toward a tiny elite market rather than a mass market—again, limiting employment possibilities. And most important, foreign firms in Brazil were unwilling to invest in locally generated technologies, hire local professionals, or use more than a minimum of local inputs and equipment. As a result, foreign firms did not have as positive impact in creating Hirschman's forward-and-backward linkages as domestic firms would have had, and their contribution to local economies was limited to job creation for a small number of workers (Evans 1979).

Do Evans's findings imply that underdeveloped countries should reject foreign investment? Because underdeveloped countries are capital and technology poor, if they are going to pursue capitalist development it seems that foreign investment is inevitable. Moreover, since the collapse of communism, only a handful of scholars of development still call for socialism as a viable option. However, Evans's analysis suggests that foreign investment best contributes to capitalist development where domestic firms are also present; this implies a role for the state to encourage *domestic* firms—perhaps through more activist measures than the neoliberal orthodoxy implies.

For example, a comparison of Taiwan and South Korea (development successes) on the one hand with Brazil and Mexico (development failures) on the other shows that economic development in the first two cases relied more heavily on domestic rather than foreign firms (see Exhibit 6.6). In fact, although Korea and Taiwan started out the postwar period with more foreign investment (as a percentage of total investment), by the late 1980s, they had substantially less foreign investment than Latin America (Haggard 1990a:193; Stallings 1990).

It is important for development that developing countries use foreign investors for their own ends rather than the reverse. As Stallings (1990) observes,

> The purpose of foreign capital is to further the interests of those who provide it. Development of the host country is a fortuitous side effect at best, which will only come about if the host government maintains enough autonomy and control to guarantee that the benefits are shared between providers and recipients of foreign capital. (p. 84)

In this view, the governments of underdeveloped countries need to provide incentives for foreign investment, such as stable institutional environments and reliable information. But governments also need to drive hard bargains with foreign investors to get concessions such as technology transfers. For example, in 1995, China "very successfully played off General Motors against Mercedes-Benz over which company would give China the most technology in return for the right to manufacture and sell in China for fixed periods of time. Both ended up giving to China sophisticated technology to design and build new models" (Johnson 1997:26). Another example of developmentalist terms that an underdeveloped country can negotiate is local content requirements, forcing foreign firms to use local suppliers and thereby forge backward links into local economies. Yet another requirement for foreign investment is that foreign firms produce for export rather than simply for internal markets.

EXHIBIT 6.6

The Five Largest Companies in Mexico and South Korea, 1987

Mexico

Rank/ Company	Main Industry	Sales (US $ millions)	Employees	Ownership
Petroleos Mexicanos	Petroleum	13,115.7	210,157	State
Chrysler de México	Motor vehicles	1,216.6	15,412	Foreign
General Motors de México	Motor vehicles	1,129.6	9,793	Foreign
Teléfonos de México	Communications	1,081.1	44,700	State
Ford Motor Company	Motor vehicles	1,054.4	5,344	Foreign

South Korea

Rank/ Company	Main Industry	Sales (US $ millions)	Employees	Ownership
Samsung	Electronics	21,053.5	160,596	Local private
Lucky-Goldstar	Electronics	14,422.3	88,403	Local private
Daewoo	Electronics	13,437.9	94,888	Local private
Sunkyong	Petroleum refining	6,781.6	17,985	Local private
Sangyong	Petroleum refining	4,582.9	16,870	Local private

Source: Gereffi (1990a).

Evidence suggests that the ability of different countries to place conditions on foreign investment partially accounts for development success. For example, one of the factors benefiting South Korea and Taiwan in their negotiations with foreign investors was that they were recipients of large quantities of bilateral aid from the U.S. government—money that could be used directly by the government to fulfill its own economic policy objectives and that made them less dependent on foreign investment. Another set of factors benefiting the East Asian cases was the "dual hegemony" of United States and Japanese investors, which gave East Asian governments more leeway to negotiate with foreign investors until they achieved acceptable terms, such as export and local content require- ments. In contrast, Latin American governments were never as successful in harnessing foreign investment to their own developmentalist objec- tives (Evans 1995:122; Haggard 1990b:199; Stallings 1990).

Of course, the willingness and ability of a government to negotiate with foreign firms to pursue developmental goals depends on a very dif- ferent kind of government official than the *homo economicus* model sup- poses. For one thing, such officials must be willing to turn down the fi- nancial rewards associated with colluding with foreign firms. For another, the pursuit of developmental goals means that government offi- cials must not merely favor the domestic firms with the best government connections. Japan's experience in fostering the computer industry is in- structive in this regard: In the 1960s, Japan persuaded IBM to license its technology not to a single favored government client but to 15 competing local firms (Evans 1995:100). Finally, a recent study shows that foreign investment in underdeveloped countries is not homogeneous but, rather, comes in a number of varieties and subvarieties, corresponding to differ- ent organizational forms (Gereffi 1994). Government ministries need to evaluate the costs and opportunities of these different models of the role of foreign investment and make policy choices reflecting their own factor endowments and development goals.

Minimalist Versus Developmentalist States

A second difference between neoliberals and sociologists over the role of the state in economic development has to do with what "medicine" to prescribe for underdeveloped countries. Since the Reagan and Thatcher revolutions, neoliberal orthodoxy has prescribed minimal interventions. More activist interventions, such as government ownership of industries and protectionism for domestic entrepreneurs, are opposed by this view. Free markets and free trade governed by minimalist interventions are presumed to be good for all countries alike, regardless of level of development.

We saw earlier in this chapter that several of the nations that success- fully developed in the 19th century—namely, the United States, Ger- many, and France—used tariffs to protect domestic industries. Of course, as a large country with an enormous internal market, the United States may have enjoyed an advantage with respect to protectionism that most underdeveloped countries do not enjoy today. Because of the size of the

U.S. market, protected industries did not need to worry about being competitive in other countries; moreover, there was room in the U.S. economy for multiple competitors in any given industry, forcing domestic firms to become competitive even without foreign rivals.

It is certainly true that one of the lessons to be learned from East Asian development success is the importance of exports for development success in small countries. Exhibit 6.7 illustrates the difference in export performance between Mexico and South Korea. Aided by their ability to export to foreign markets, the Asian Tigers were able to industrialize more successfully than Latin American countries: Between 1965 and 1990, industries' share of GDP grew by only 3% in Latin America; it grew by 13% in East and Southeast Asia. Clearly, East Asia was more successful in achieving its industrial revolution (Gereffi 1994:217).

Success in exports is an important element of development success for small countries. But do the Asian Tigers really prove that protectionism is a bad strategy and incompatible with creating competitive exports? A closer look at the history of postwar economic policy in the East Asian countries shows that this view is questionable. With the exception of Hong Kong (which, properly speaking, was a British Colony rather than a country), all the Asian Tigers had important phases of import substitution. During these periods, domestic industries were protected from foreign competition and economic policy was oriented toward satisfying domestic rather than international markets; only later did policy shift to open these protected economies—a policy shift from import substitution to export-oriented industrialization (Gereffi and Wyman 1990; Haggard 1990b).

Our reading of the history of East Asian development differs from a neoliberal account in several respects. First, rather than viewing import substitution as a sort of misguided prologue to real development success, both could be seen as complementary phases of the same process: Protectionism was the *foundation* for later export success. For example, in Taiwan and South Korea, the domestic firms that were initially protected and nurtured by the state later became successful exporters that led economic growth (Hyundai is a well-known example). In this view, import substitution in both East Asia and Latin America made sense as a policy from the 1930s through the 1950s, given the context of the international economy: Export opportunities were greatly diminished by the Great Depression and later by World War II and the reconstruction of Europe (Ramos 1993:63). Good development policies are made by governments that monitor and respond to changing domestic and international conditions to achieve the most favorable outcome. The shift from import substitu-

EXHIBIT 6.7

Exports as Percentage of GDP, Mexico and South Korea, 1965 and 1987

	1965	*1987*
Mexico	5	15
South Korea	7	39

Source: Gereffi (1990a).

tion to export orientation in East Asia is a good example of this kind of flexibility.

A second difference between sociological and neoliberal accounts is that the former recognizes that the move to export-oriented industrialization did not represent a shift to unfettered markets but, rather, to a different kind of government involvement in the economy—not *less state intervention* but *different state intervention.* Taiwan's and South Korea's opening to foreign competition did not represent the triumph of markets over government but, rather, a shift in government roles in a context of ongoing intervention to "a direct role for government in institutional/ organizational change" (Ranis 1990:226).

For example, starting in the 1960s, the Taiwanese government aggressively sought out U.S. electrical and electronics companies to invest in its new export processing zones (EPZs), and "formed an electronics working group to assist in marketing, coordinating production with the demands of foreign buyers, procuring raw materials, training personnel, improving quality, and speeding up bureaucratic approval procedures" (Wade 1990:95). In South Korea, the government provided heavily subsidized loans (with interest rates often below the rate of inflation) to help promote "the entrepreneurs who had already proven their mettle through good export records, the risk-takers who entered into heavy and chemical industries, and the faithful who plunged into the untried sea of international competition with new products, relying on the state's good offices to rescue them" (Woo 1991:148-59).

Local Institutions and Multiple Development Paths

Another fundamental difference between the neoliberal and sociological accounts of development is that whereas neoliberals emphasize the single "recipe" that leads to economic success, sociologists point out that economic development has occurred in different ways at different times and places. In this view, there is neither a single recipe for economic development nor a single form of capitalism; rather than speaking of "capitalism" in the singular, some sociologists have begun to emphasize "capitalisms" in the plural (Hollingsworth and Boyer 1997).

The diversity of capitalisms is illustrated quite well by the fact that among the richest, most highly developed countries in the world, there are some striking and persistent differences. Capitalism in the United States, for example, is quite different from capitalism in Germany or from capitalism in Japan. For example, whereas industry in the United States tends to rely on a large, relatively unskilled workforce with a general education, in Germany, workers are highly trained for jobs in specific areas through a system of apprenticeships. Whereas in the United States, workers move from job to job with great frequency, the Japanese economy rests on a system of reciprocal commitment between workers and employers: The workers are loyal to the company, and the company guarantees them lifetime employment. The resulting commitment of workers to the firm is often invoked as a reason that many Japanese firms can manufacture products of such high quality (Hollingsworth 1997).

If there are so many different forms of capitalism, which capitalism should a developing country select? There are certainly many ways of going about answering this question, but two stand out for the purposes of this chapter. First, research in the history of economic development suggests that relative backwardness—that is, how far an underdeveloped country has to go to catch up—needs to play a role in determining development strategy. The fundamental difference in circumstances faced by economic "leaders" and "followers" was noted by Alexander Gerschenkron in his study of economic development in Western Europe. Gerschenkron (1962) found that "late developers"—that is, nations such as Germany and France—found special ways of compensating for their "relative backwardness." The more backward the country, the more it had to compensate. As a result, "Industrialization processes, when launched at length in a backward country, showed considerable differences, as compared with more advanced countries" (p. 7). For example, activist government has played an important part in bringing about industrialization in most late developers.

In addition to relative backwardness, recent research suggests that development, where it occurs, takes advantage of the particular social features of the country in which it is occurring. Rather than trying to copy complete development "recipes" from other places, each developing nation should try to draw on its own unique array of social endowments, including culture, social networks, organizations, the educational system, and the political system. Taken together, these groupings of social resources make up a country's social system of production—a system that should be used in the development process.

Culture and Institutions in East Asia

The East Asian "Tigers" are often cited by economists as examples of how the neoliberal "recipe" of free market capitalism can lead to development success. In fact, however, there were some very important differences in the development experiences of different East Asian countries, based on unique features of each country's social system of production. In their study of Japan, South Korea, and Taiwan, Hamilton and Biggart (1988) found striking variations in the kinds of economic organization that evolved in the three countries—despite the fact that South Korea and Taiwan started from approximately the same initial "level" of underdevelopment in the postwar period. South Korean development success has been dominated by a group of large, hierarchical firms known as *chaebol*, which use their close ties to the government to obtain financing and other benefits. In contrast, Taiwanese economic growth has been dominated by small-to-medium family firms, which instead of growing into large incorporated companies, split up and diversify as they get larger (Hamilton and Biggart 1988:S59-S66). Despite these differences, both South Korea and Taiwan are generally considered to be successful developers.

Hamilton and Biggart suggest that political and cultural embeddedness explains the difference between Taiwanese and South Korean economic organizations. The South Korean postwar economy developed within the context of a strong, centralized state, which encouraged the formation of large conglomerates as its partners in economic development. In contrast, the postwar Taiwanese state was much less directly involved with business, following a philosophy of "planning within the context of a free economy" (Hamilton and Biggart 1988:78).

Rather than posing their explanation solely at the level of state involvement, Hamilton and Biggart also show how state involvement in the economy evolved according to local culture. Whereas the Korean government was constructed in the model of the strong Confucian state with a central ruler, the Taiwanese government was shaped by the need of Chiang Kai-shek (the mainland Chinese nationalist leader who ruled Taiwan after the Chinese revolution) to avoid problems with the native Taiwanese; the result in Taiwan was a model of "a state that upholds moral principles . . . that explicitly [allow] no corruption and unfair wealth, and that 'leaves the people at rest' " (Hamilton and Biggart 1988:S83). This left the Taiwanese economy to develop along lines that suited Taiwanese culture, in which there was a long-standing tradition of splitting up the family inheritance among the sons of a household.

Hamilton and Biggart's study implies that economic arrangements in different national contexts are embedded in both culture and local political systems. It also suggests that economic success is best achieved when it builds on local culture and institutions, which give economic arrangements legitimacy. Of course, not all social institutions are formalized; they also include informal, unwritten social rules of behavior. Only with reference to such unwritten rules can we understand the differences between Taiwanese and South Korean economic organization—as well as Taiwanese and South Korean developmental success.

The Big Bang and Transitions from Socialism

The idea that capitalist growth and economic development proceed in culturally and institutionally specific ways holds important lessons for underdeveloped nations, particularly for the formerly state-socialist countries. Conventional neoliberal wisdom holds that state-socialist countries in transition should shed their failed socialist institutions as quickly as possible and replace them with Western capitalist ones, a prescription commonly known as the "Big Bang" approach. "Rather than piecemeal incremental reform, the plan instead was to follow guidelines derived from textbook economics to dismantle the economic institutions of state socialism and replace them with a full set of market institutions in rapid order" (Nee and Matthews 1996:415). What does the experience of postsocialist countries with economic development thus far suggest regarding this prescription?

A complete review of all the countries undergoing socialist transitions is beyond the scope of this book, but as of early 1999, China has by far the most successful economy among the formerly socialist countries, with growth rates averaging (until the recent Asian financial crisis) over 10% per year. The Central Intelligence Agency (CIA) estimated that China's GDP will exceed that of the United States before the year 2020 (Johnson 1997:24). Chinese economic success has occurred in the wake of a series of reforms since 1978 designed to improve economic performance through harnessing the power of markets: Cooperative farms were placed under the "household responsibility system" so that peasant families could directly reap the rewards of their efforts, and centralized control of state industries was devolved to provincial and local governments (Nee and Matthews 1996:401-5).

However, China's success in the area of economic development does not fit easily into conventional neoliberal wisdom. Some sociologists have pointed out that the model of development adopted in China is actually a "hybrid" model in which strong elements of the old state-socialist system remain (Nee 1992; Nee and Matthews 1996; Walder 1995). First, although China has lowered its formal tariff barriers, it still relies heavily on the nontariff forms of protection that are more difficult to monitor and control through international organizations such as the World Trade Organization (WTO) (Johnson 1997:26). An example of a nontariff barrier would be a regulation with differential effects on foreign and domestic firms—for example, a requirement that the parts in all cars have labels in Chinese. These sorts of covert protectionist measures have infuriated U.S. government officials, who want to lessen the huge U.S. trade deficit with China.

Second—and more important—although Chinese industry has clearly been marketized (i.e., made to produce for private markets), it has definitely *not* been privatized (i.e., sold by the state to individual capitalists). In fact, some public industries have played a critical role in China's recent economic success. In his study of the public industrial sector in China, Walder (1995) found that public rural industries managed by county, township, and village governments have had growth rates well above the already high national average. He concludes that neoliberals' blanket condemnation of state-owned industries is unwarranted. Given the proper organizational incentives, government managers can behave in ways that lead to growth and development.

Given what we know about the real-life organization of capitalist firms (discussed in Chapter 4), we should not be surprised by Walder's findings. In fact, the managers of the industries in Walder's study are analogous to the managers of large private corporations in the capitalist world; their motivations should be familiar to anyone who has ever worked in management at IBM or Ford. Unlike the idealized entrepreneur of economic models, managers in capitalist corporations are generally not owners and do not benefit directly from the increased profitability of the firms they manage; rather, they have other incentives, such as promotion and salary increases, to make firms more profitable.

Similarly, local public industries in China today operate under a system of fiscal contracting, obliging them to give the government a fixed financial return, a system that allows managers to keep any residual financial return—an indirect incentive to increase profitability. Local public industries in China differ from national public industries in having harder budget constraints, because their managers can very clearly stand to lose in case of industry failure. Moreover, they benefit from a large margin of organizational autonomy, because they are under the control of local officials rather than distant bureaucrats in Beijing. Therefore, they do not suffer from the same problems of information as national industries; local officials can immediately spot problems and opportunities and act on them (Walder 1995).

The lesson of Walder's study is that public bureaucracies can be made to function quite efficiently. The local public firms that function so successfully in China result from a policy in which the Chinese government has "fixed its course to remake the economic institutions of state socialism not by revolution but by reform" (Nee 1992:1). This stands in marked contrast to the Big Bang approach that many economists have recommended for Eastern Europe. As a result of Big Bang policy, a large number of viable state-owned enterprises in Eastern Europe have been allowed to collapse, without government intervention to help restructure them and make them more competitive (Amsden, Kochanowicz, and Taylor 1994:10).

Some sociologists believe that as Chinese economic reform proceeds and Western capitalist institutions (such as property rights and contract law) are adopted, purely private firms will emerge that are more efficient than China's hybridized public sector (Nee 1992). Nevertheless, if China makes the move to a full-fledged capitalist system, the form of capitalism that emerges is likely to have a particularly Chinese flavor. Boisot and Child (1996) observe that the markets in China are evolving along the lines placed by long-standing institutional and cultural arrangements, leading to a form of "network capitalism." Many business transactions seem to be settled within the context of networks based on interpersonal reciprocal obligations known as *guanxi*.

Thus, a future Chinese capitalism might resemble Taiwanese capitalism in relying on informal social ties to a much greater extent than prevails in the West. But Chinese capitalism will probably also differ from that of Taiwan because of the institutional legacy of socialism. Some observers think that China may even be in the process of developing a form of capitalism that regulates and restricts property rights much more than in any existing capitalist country (Boisot and Child 1996:615). Stark (1996) similarly observes a unique form of "recombinant property," including both private and public elements emerging in Hungary today.

Conclusion

In the 1950s, a dialogue between economists and sociologists on the subject of economic development would sound very different than it would today. In sociology departments in the 1950s, modernization theorists asserted that economic development was rooted in the transition from traditional to modern values (assumed to be Western values) and that what held developing countries back was their failure to undergo this cultural transformation: All countries were assumed to be on the same "path" to development, and underdeveloped countries simply needed to do what developed countries had done before them (Toye 1989:32). In contrast to this sociological approach to development, many economists of the 1950s were open to the idea that different nations had different paths to follow and that poor countries should use the power of the state to help compensate for the imperfections of markets.

Today, these positions have been essentially reversed. More than 200 years after Adam Smith, a free market revival among economists and policymakers has led to the prescription of a single "recipe" for economic development for the poorer countries of the world. Now that free markets have come back into fashion, there has been a return among economists to what Hirschman (1981) refers to as "monoeconomics"—or the belief that there is a single set of economic laws applicable at all times and in all places. Among economists today, free markets, free trade, foreign investment, and private ownership are generally seen as good for *all* countries, no matter how poor. They point to historical evidence that rather than promoting economic development, government intervention under developmentalism and state socialism led to economic stagnation. If economists had a motto about economic development today, it would probably be "markets good, government bad."

In contrast, the new sociological approach is generally more friendly toward government intervention and more cautious about unfettered markets. It opposes the view that there is a single path to economic development for all countries, regardless of differences in local and international context. Underdeveloped countries can and should learn from the experiences of successful developers, but each country also faces a unique set of international and local constraints and opportunities. Rather than following a single recipe, underdeveloped countries need carefully to study the varied experiences of successful developers and come up with their own individually tailored programs for economic development.

7

Globalization

Have you ever looked at the labels on your jeans, your T-shirt, or your athletic shoes? If you do, you know that most of the clothes we wear in the United States are manufactured someplace else—usually in a less developed country where labor costs are cheaper. Although the headquarters of companies such as "the Gap," "Nike," or "DKNY" are in the United States, their factories are located in countries such as Malaysia, Vietnam, El Salvador, and Macao. This kind of international production can cause political controversy, because companies often move their production offshore to benefit from lower wages, lower taxes, and lax labor safety and environmental regulations.

While international production is bringing Third World labor to First World consumers, international consumption is spreading First World cultural icons all over the world. Michael Jordan, for example, has become the world's best-known athlete, and today it is possible to buy posters of the famous basketball player in Europe, South America, and China. English is widely touted as the global language. Today, people can watch minute-by-minute coverage of international events on the Cable News Network—not only throughout the United States but also in New Delhi, Moscow, and Montevideo. In London, England, a new genre of music called *bhangra* blends South Asian and Western disco sounds in a cultural melding of the musical traditions of the native British and recent generations of Indian immigrants. And today, McDonald's hamburgers are available to customers from Beijing to Buenos Aires.

All these different phenomena are part of a larger trend known as "globalization," or "the intensification of worldwide social relations which link distant localities in such a way that local happenings are shaped by events occurring many miles away and vice versa" (Giddens 1990:64). This concept refers both to *objective* changes in the world around us—for example, advances in communications and globalized production—and in *subjective* changes in the way we perceive ourselves in the world (Robertson 1992:8). Today, we are connected by multiple links to diverse parts of the world, and we think of ourselves as world citizens more than at any other time in history.

Globalization is a process that encompasses three interconnected dimensions: *economic globalization, cultural globalization,* and *political globalization.* The best known of these dimensions is economic globalization, which refers to internationalization of production, consumption, distribution, and investment; the purchase of clothing made in Thailand by U.S. consumers or the marketing of Coca Cola in Brazil are examples of this. Cultural globalization refers to the displacement, melding, or supplement of local cultural traditions by foreign or international ones; the popularization of U.S. rock and roll music throughout the world is a well-known example. Finally, political globalization refers to the internationalization of "relations for the concentration and application of power," exemplified by the deployment of United Nations peacekeeping troops in the former Yugoslavia (Waters 1995:7).

Although this chapter takes all three dimensions of globalization into account, it focuses mostly on *economic* globalization—arguably, the most important of the three dimensions and the driving force behind the other two. As we outline the history of economic and related forms of globalization, we will make three main arguments. The first is that economic globalization is not a recent phenomenon but, rather, is part of a process that has been going on for centuries. The second argument is that economic globalization has always been subject to various forms of extra-economic control: Nations have decided how much globalization was compatible with national goals and regulated it accordingly. The third and final argument is that economic globalization has recently grown to such an extent that it poses a threat to the ability of nonmarket institutions—particularly nation-states—to regulate markets.

The Origins of Globalization

In just the past few years, the widespread availability of new technologies such as the Internet and international satellite television have made globalization a household word. But is globalization itself actually new, or is it just a new name for something old? In fact, the political, economic, and cultural unification of the people of different regions under the umbrella of large empires is nothing new. The ancient histories of the European, Asian, American, and African continents are filled with stories of shifting boundaries between competing kingdoms and empires and the subjugation of militarily weaker peoples by stronger ones. The biblical book of Exodus documents the enslavement of the Israelites by the Egyptians. Later, an Egyptian city was named Alexandria, to honor Alexander the Great, the Macedonian who conquered Egypt in the fourth century B.C. About four centuries later, Egypt became a province of Rome and served as a breadbasket for feeding Romans in times of domestic grain shortages. Ancient Empires such as Rome also led to the spread of uniform cultural patterns over large geographical areas, as the elite in subjugated territories came to adopt the religion, language, law, dress, and consumption patterns of their conquerors.

If cross-regional economic, political, and cultural relations among different peoples have existed for thousands of years, does this mean that globalization has existed for thousands of years as well? We believe that a useful distinction can be made between the kinds of interregional ties that were made in ancient times and those that exist today. For the purposes of this chapter, therefore, we will use the term *globalization* to refer to those kinds of cross-regional economic, political, and cultural relations that have occurred in conjunction with modernity.

Ordinarily we use the word *modern* to mean "current" or "up-to-date," but sociologists have a more specific meaning in mind. **Modernity** refers to a historical period beginning in Western Europe sometime around the year 1500 and that, depending on the scholar you ask, either continues through the present or has ended very recently (which is why some scholars speak of "postmodernity"). Modernity is associated with a number of social characteristics that distinguish it from any previous social systems. Two of its most distinctive features are the economic system of industrial capitalism and the political institution of the nation-state. Why did these features appear first in Western Europe rather than someplace else? It was certainly not because Western Europe was any more civilized than other regions of the world. While Europe was languishing in what are sometimes called "the Dark Ages," Islamic civilizations of the Middle East and Northern Africa were making important advances in mathematics and science. Chinese civilization at the time was even more impressive and was responsible for inventions such as paper, gunpowder, and the printing press.

Sociologists continue to disagree about the relative importance of different catalysts of social change in late medieval Europe. However, they agree that one of the most important catalysts was the emergence of the modern nation-state in Western Europe (Tilly 1990). Although the process of nation building led to the consolidation of power and an increase in the size of political units (which were highly fragmented during the Middle Ages), this process led to a decentralized network of relatively small and competing political entities (compared with the huge empires of ancient times). Military competition among these different governments led to organizational and technological innovations, particularly in the areas of transportation and weaponry—much in the same way that competition between the United States and the Soviet Union led to advances in satellite and communications technology later on.

The emerging nation-state system also turned out to be remarkably compatible with the new capitalist economic system that was beginning to take shape. By 1500, a new class of merchant capitalists was becoming wealthy through a developing European trade network. In England, feudal agriculture was replaced by commercial or capitalist agriculture. With the support of Parliament, property rights changed as common lands, a form of public property, were enclosed and privatized. The emergence of a class of landless rural workers meant that wage labor was available to those who wanted to hire it. Private ownership of the means of production (the land, raw materials, capital, and equipment used in economic activity) in combination with wage labor were the foundation of Western European **capitalism,** which became an extraordinary catalyst for innovation and social change and eventually led to the industrial revolution of the 18th and 19th centuries.

These central features of modernity evolved in conjunction with Western European expansion across the globe from the 16th to the 19th centuries, an expansion known as **colonialism.** The year 1492 marked the "discovery" of America by Christopher Columbus; soon afterward, the Americas were divided up among competing European powers (Spain, Portugal, England, France, and Holland), and their native populations were put to work, displaced, or exterminated. West African slaves were imported to plantations in the West Indies and South America to provide the labor to cultivate and harvest lucrative cash crops such as cotton, indigo, and sugar.

In the centuries that followed, European colonies were established in much of Asia and all of Africa. Ironically, the same European culture that took credit for science and the ideals of progress, rationality, and individual rights also generated the horrors of slavery and colonial occupation, which characterized the first phase of globalization; this was the dark side of modernity.

Colonialism and slavery were enormously powerful forces for the promotion of economic globalization. In the earliest centuries, gold and silver mined in Latin America was sent to Spain, where it was coined and used to pay government debts and purchase imports from other countries; this accumulated capital was later used by French or British entrepreneurs to invest in the transport of slaves between Africa and America. While it was bringing about increasing levels of global economic integration, colonialism also fueled the growth of European capitalism and modernity more generally. The riches of the New World flowed across the Atlantic Ocean to strengthen and solidify emerging nation-states, which used these resources to build bigger bureaucracies and stronger armed forces. This accumulated wealth also helped strengthen and expand a new class of entrepreneurs whose wealth eventually financed European industrialization. Moreover, the colonies became a crucial source of both the raw materials that served as inputs for industry in Europe and a captive market for finished products.

European modernity, therefore, was based on a form of economic globalization, or what some sociologists call the creation of a **modern world system**—a system qualitatively different from anything that had been seen on Earth before. The modern world system differed from previous sorts of interregional economic relations in two principal respects. First, unlike the empires that the world had known for over 5,000 years, the modern world system was not unified under a single government but, rather, encompassed multiple nation-states unified by economic ties. The fact that the world system was not confined within the bounds of a single government was precisely what made it so dynamic (Giddens 1990:69; Wallerstein 1974:15). Second, unlike the world empires of before, this new world order was truly global and came to span every habitable continent.

Today, we still live in a world system but one that has changed a great deal since its first centuries. For one thing, the wealthiest and most powerful countries are no longer the European powers that originally colonized the globe. Today's economic powerhouses are the United States, Germany, and Japan—not England, France, and Spain—and the United States is the world's only remaining military superpower. For another thing, slavery has been abolished, and the kind of direct political control of Third World countries that characterized colonialism has almost completely disappeared. Most recently, the British colony of Hong Kong was returned to the Chinese government in 1997, in a peaceful transition of power that demonstrated the contemporary irrelevance of colonial rule. However, the elimination of slavery and formal colonial domination have not led to a world system made up of a club of "equal partners": Just as at other times in history, today's globe is divided between the haves and the have-nots, and between the powerful and the powerless.

Globalization Today

In the late 1960s, Marshall McLuhan wrote a book titled *War and Peace in the Global Village* (McLuhan and Fiore 1968). This book gained widespread acclaim because of its recognition of the way that technological advances in media have changed people's lives. The notion of a global village encompasses several ideas at once. One is smallness: Because of improvements in transportation and communications, the world feels less large than it used to, and distances that once seemed insurmountable have been made insignificant by air travel and the Internet. Another idea conveyed by the imagery of the global village is the idea of community and collective interest. The commonly held (if somewhat inaccurate) stereotype of the village is of a premodern collectivity in which there is a shared culture, relatively little difference between the richest and poorest, and a communitarian sense of mutual obligation and common interest.

In the previous section, we saw that globalization is not, in fact, anything new: The forces of modernity have been making the world into a unified whole for several centuries. Nevertheless, McLuhan's book implies that there *is* something new about globalization. Certainly, the world *feels* a lot more like a "global village" today than it did 50 years ago. Three decades after the publication of McLuhan's book, we notice that even more of the products we buy are manufactured in foreign countries, that more of our tastes are influenced from abroad, and that ordinary people are much more likely to have lived in or visited a foreign country.

What accounts for this general feeling today that we are all part of "one world"? In this section, we will examine some of the technological developments that have strengthened our sense of being part of a global village in the late 20th century. Most of these developments can ultimately be attributed to the remarkable innovative powers of capitalism, which has turned out to be the most powerful engine for social and technological change that the world has ever seen. Capitalism is like the proverbial shark that has always to move forward or sink to the bottom: It brings progress and technical innovation because its very existence depends on them. It is therefore largely (although not entirely) responsible for the technical innovations that have facilitated the integration of the globe in ways that would have been unimaginable three centuries ago. The three major areas of technical innovation we will discuss in this section are the use of token money, advances in communications, and advances in transportation (Waters 1995:145-46).

Capitalism has brought about technological and organizational innovations, which have in turn contributed to globalization. Nevertheless, although technical advances have been necessary conditions for globalization, we also argue that they were not sufficient. Rather, *at all times, political decisions have influenced the way that these technical resources have been used, thereby determining their role in globalizing processes.* This is because people have disagreed about the ways that globalizing technologies should be used. Should nations be able to trade freely among themselves, or should international trade be restricted? Should money be allowed to flow freely around the globe, or should there be limits placed on capital mobility? Should people be able to immigrate at will, or should there be barriers to the free flow of immigration? Different answers to these kinds of questions have resulted in periodic cycles in the levels of *political control* applied to globalization. Technology is not destiny; rather, social, cultural, and political factors have always determined which kinds of technologies get developed and how they will be used in the globalizing process.

Money and the International Monetary System

One of the most important technological advances generated by hundreds of years of capitalism is one that most people do not think of as technological—namely, the invention and use of token or fiat money. This money has value by virtue of social agreement only rather than because it is made out of something with value—such as gold or silver (Carruthers and Babb 1996). Many premodern societies did not have money at all, because their members lived in nonmarket economies. Barter was often sufficient for these societies' needs; in other cases, relatively rare and coveted items such as cowry shells (in Africa) or cacao beans (in pre-Columbian Mexico) were used as money, particularly for trade among the peoples of different regions.

It has generally been true in human history that whenever a society has developed more complex and more regionally expansive economic systems, it has also had to develop more sophisticated forms of money. For example, barter is obviously too cumbersome for payments within an empire spanning a large geographical area. The empires of ancient and early modern times therefore had money in the form of gold, silver, and copper coins minted by the central government. These coins were accepted as payment because the materials out of which they were made had value that was *universal* (for all practical purposes); this meant that they were always and everywhere accepted in exchange for goods. The role of the central government was to certify that coins contained a certain amount of precious metals. However, a recurring problem with this form of money is that people could "clip" or shave off pieces of metal from the edges, leading to *de facto* devaluation and to rather oddly shaped coins!

The colonization of the Americas led to a massive influx of gold and silver into the European economy in the 16th century—and consequently both to inflation and to the "capital accumulation" that helped fuel European capitalism (Wallerstein 1974:83). But ultimately, it turned out that specie money (or money made of precious metals) was an inadequate medium of circulation for a vigorous and expanding capitalist economy. Gradually, modern economies made the transition to a fractional reserve system. So, for example, while a bank might have only $1,000 worth of gold in its vaults, it could issue $5,000 in the form of "banknotes," or promises to pay the bearer a certain amount of gold. This allowed a bank to issue more paper money than it had gold. Therefore, it is easy to see why the fractional reserve system was better for economic growth and capitalism.

The system worked as long as people with bank notes didn't all try to cash them in for gold at the same time. Unfortunately, this happened periodically when people lost confidence in the system; the result was usually a "credit crunch" and even an economic recession or depression. Central banks, such as the Federal Reserve System in the United States, were founded throughout the modern world to keep such "panics" and their negative side effects from occurring.

Central banks are interesting institutions because they are technological inventions and political institutions at the same time. A central bank can be thought of as a technical and organizational innovation for the creation of money and the administration of monetary policy. But the whole idea of "monetary policy" is based on a highly political presupposition—namely, that governments have an active role to play in the economy and that maintaining monetary stability is something that a government should do for the better good of its citizens. When this idea was first proposed explicitly, it generated a lot of suspicion and controversy. Today, almost everybody agrees that central banks are necessary. However, because monetary policy has different consequences for different groups of people, the way they should be run is still a political issue.

The Bretton Woods system that originated in 1944 was based on the notion that monetary stability was not just a national but also an *international* affair. This was because by the mid-20th century capitalism had been truly globalized. The Great Depression of the 1930s was not just something that happened in the United States but, rather, all over the world. Bretton Woods replaced individual countries' gold reserve system with an international fixed exchange rate system: All currencies were convertible to U.S. dollars, which were ultimately convertible into gold, and exchange rates among currencies were fixed at a certain level. To help maintain these fixed exchange rates, the International Monetary Fund— or IMF—was founded as a sort of international lending agency for supporting national central banks.

As money was adapted to more advanced forms of capitalism and a more globalized economy, it became more and more abstract. Bretton Woods led to the adoption of very abstract forms of money throughout the world, because no currency but the dollar represented a claim on precious metals. But in the early 1970s, the Bretton Woods system collapsed, which meant the transition to floating exchange rates determined by international markets rather than fixed exchange rates determined by international agreement.

The collapse of Bretton Woods also meant the dissolution of the last, tenuous link of the international monetary system to the gold standard. Today, the money you have in the bank is nothing more than a string of electronic "bits" on a computer chip! Furthermore, financial markets have become increasingly global, which has meant that today money can travel more or less freely around the world—in other words, capital is extremely mobile. On a technological level, the globalization of financial markets and increasing capital mobility has been facilitated both by advances in communications and by decisions by governments to allow for more capital mobility.

Communications and the Globalization of Finance

When the American colonies of Great Britain rebelled little more than 200 years ago, news of the rebellion had to travel back to England by boat across the Atlantic Ocean, a journey of several months. The invention of the telegraph in the mid-1800s made international politics more immediate, as well as more accessible to the citizens of nation-states around the world; by the time of the Civil War, people in Great Britain could read in their newspapers about American battles only a day after they occurred (Waters 1995:146). More recent inventions, such as the telephone, the television, satellite communications, and the Internet, have made information even more accessible worldwide. The Persian Gulf War provided striking evidence of how far the globalization of communications has come: Through live satellite coverage, U.S. citizens were able to watch the war from their living rooms as entertainment on their televisions.

The globalization of communications has had economic, political, and cultural implications. One economic consequence has been to facilitate international **capital mobility** (the free movement of money across national borders) through **foreign portfolio investment** (purchases of securities by foreign nationals). Globalized communications facilitated the growth of foreign portfolio investment in two principal ways. First, the act of investing in a foreign financial instrument is vastly simplified by global telecommunications and computing. Second, these same technological advances have made information to foreign investors much more accessible than it was previously. One hundred years ago, even investing in a neighboring country such as Mexico was a leap into the unknown. Today, it is possible for U.S. citizens to invest in exotic faraway places such as Thailand, with far more information than was available about Mexico in the past century. Through the Internet, using services such as Reuters and others an investor can keep abreast of daily developments in markets around the world and make informed decisions about his or her investments.

Thanks to advances in communications (as well as the abstraction of money), today an investment banker in New York can buy Mexican bonds by hitting the "return" key on a computer—and can sell them just as easily. What most people don't know, however, is that *political decisions* have also been involved in the globalization of capital flows. At the beginning of the 20th century, capital was mobile, and foreign portfolio investment was common. But after World War I, governments began to implement legal controls on capital flows, and foreign portfolio investment declined (also as a result of the Great Depression) (Evans 1979:77).

In the 1970s, this "deglobalizing" tendency was reversed, and the governments of the industrialized countries decided to get rid of existing capital controls—leading to a "reglobalization" of capital movement and the renewed vigor of foreign portfolio investment (Eichengreen 1996). Political interests have been involved in the move toward greater capital mobility; recently, Wall Street financial firms have been pushing for the U.S. government to put pressure on foreign governments to open their financial markets (Bhagwati 1998).

Another political factor encouraging international capital mobility is that since the 1970s, multilateral organizations such as the IMF, as well as certain governments, have consistently acted as lenders of last resort when it looks like investors are going to lose a lot of money. For example, the IMF and the U.S. Treasury offered Mexico huge loans in 1995 to help stabilize the peso. Without these kinds of bailouts, investors would probably view foreign investment as much more risky and would decide to invest at home rather than abroad (Helleiner 1994:1-12).

Although it is true that this kind of last-resort lending is one way of averting global financial disaster, politicians of both the left and the right have objected that such interventions subsidize mostly rich investors at the cost of ordinary taxpaying citizens. Or to put it another way, existing international mechanisms for dealing with financial crises socialize the risk incurred by private individuals. National financial systems are insulated from instability by deposit insurance and reserve requirements, but the emerging international system as yet has no such systems to fall back on (Krugman and Obstfeld 1991:613).

Transportation and the Movement of Goods and People

Innovations making transportation cheaper and faster have a number of economic and cultural effects. Two of the most visible and important of these effects are the globalization of production and its counterpart—the globalization of consumption. Two other potentially globalizing consequences of transportation revolutions have to do with the movement of *people* rather than the movement of *goods and capital*—namely, international migration and international tourism.

Gradually, the consolidation of nation-states improved the prospects for global trade and capitalist expansion (Tilly 1990). In the 15th century, the "square-rigged" ship, capable of ocean navigation, emerged in Europe, thereby making possible the voyages that brought slaves from Africa to the New World, precious metals and raw materials from the New World to the Old, and textiles and spices from the Far East to Europe (Georgano 1972:131-33).

One key technological development in the area of transportation was the invention of the steam engine in the 1800s, which improved transportation by water and brought far-flung landlocked provinces all over the world into the modern world system through the invention of the railroad. The enormous effect of this transportation revolution is illustrated in García Márquez's (1970) novel *One Hundred Years of Solitude*, in which the isolated Latin American village of Macondo is suddenly brought into the modern world by the arrival of its first train, which would bring "so many ambiguities and certainties, so many pleasant and unpleasant moments, so many changes, calamities, and feelings of nostalgia" (p. 228). In keeping with Latin American history, the railroad integrates Macondo into the world economy, making possible great plantations of bananas for export to the United States. Other technological innovations that facilitated worldwide economic integration were 19th- and 20th-century advances in shipping and, of course, the development of the internal combustion engine, which gave access by road to areas not on railroad lines. So, for example, today in Mexico it is possible to buy consumer goods imported from China, not only in Mexico City but also in small provincial towns, serviced by truck rather than by train.

While some globalizing innovations in transportation have been *technological* in nature, others have had to do with the *organization* of different technologies. Some good examples of this are the recent innovations of containerization and mixed-mode transportation. Once upon a time, cloth had to be unloaded from boats by longshoremen, bolt by bolt, to be transferred to trucks. Today, the cloth is placed in huge containers specially designed to fit the ship, the truck, and the crane used to shift them from one form of transportation to the other. Intermodalism is a related transportation technology, using a combination of air and ground transportation—a faster, cheaper method used by companies such as Federal Express ("Thinking about Globalisation" 1997:13).

Another recent globalizing innovation in transportation has been the rise of transcontinental air travel, pioneered in the 1920s and commercialized shortly thereafter. The first commercial airliners were designed to serve the very wealthy and often served elaborate and luxurious meals that could include lobster, assorted cheeses, and drinks that included champagne and red and white Bordeaux (Hudson 1972:27). After the Second World War, air travel gradually became less costly and more accessible to ordinary people. Whereas a trip from the United States to Europe had once taken almost a week on a ship with meals and sleeping accommodations, air travel made such trips both quicker and cheaper and made routine tourism and transcontinental business travel more feasible.

Free Trade versus Protection

Thanks in part to the technological advances in transportation over the past 150 years or so, both production and consumption are far more globalized than they used to be. While apple orchards in Washington State export fruit to Asia and Latin America, teenagers in New York City wear athletic shoes manufactured in Vietnam, and children in Mexico City play with plastic toys made in China. However, technological advances explain only part of these forms of globalization. At the same time, political decisions about the way economies should be organized have critically determined the role of transportation technology in economic globalization.

One important political factor affecting the impact of transportation on globalization is whether countries have *free trade* or *protectionist* regimes. Under a free trade regime, foreign imports are allowed to flow into a country with relatively few restrictions; under a protectionist regime, imports are subject to *tariffs* (taxes on imports) or other restrictions, to help keep them from competing with domestic firms.

Since the dawn of capitalism, free trade has been a political issue. In the 19th century, the United States had a protectionist policy that was supported by some groups and opposed by others. On the side of import substitution were northern industrialists and workers, who benefited from tariff protection; on the side of free trade were southern plantation owners and western farmers, who would have benefited from free trade. This bitterly divisive issue was one important reason for the Civil War. After World War I, U.S. industries were advanced enough to face foreign competition, and many industrialists switched their support to free trade (Bensel 1984:104). Today, the United States advocates free trade not only for itself but for the rest of the world as well. However, some less developed countries—notably China—continue to maintain protectionist policies, for virtually the same reasons that the United States did in the 19th century.

Free trade has gone in and out of fashion over the years and has been applied unevenly in different places. As the world's first industrial power, England adopted a relatively unrestricted trade policy during the first half of the 19th century and encouraged other countries to do the same. However, countries such as the United States and Germany that were trying to develop their own domestic industries adopted more protectionist policies during the second half of the 19th century (when England reverted to protectionism as well) (Hobson 1997; Yarbrough and Yarbrough 1988:322).

After World War I, there was a worldwide shift toward protectionism. For example, in the United States, the Great Depression stimulated protectionist sentiments, leading to the enactment of the famous Smoot-Hawley tariff legislation. This trend reversed in 1947, the year of the first round of negotiations of the General Agreement on Tariffs and Trade (GATT), which committed its participants to lowered trade barriers. Since the 1970s, there has been an accelerated globalization of trade, and many new countries have entered GATT, which was replaced by the World Trade Organization (WTO) in 1995. There have also been numerous regional trade agreements, which promote freer trade among the partners in a particular region. The North American Free Trade Agreement (NAFTA) and the European Union (EU) are examples of this.

NAFTA presents a good example of how international free trade is related to the globalization of production through foreign direct investment. NAFTA makes it more attractive for U.S. firms to move their manufacturing operations to Mexico, both by committing Mexico to more explicit legal guarantees for private investors and by lowering tariffs on both sides of the border. For example, under NAFTA, it is easier for Ford to produce automobiles in Mexico for sale in the United States because it no longer faces the tariff and nontariff barriers that previously inhibited reimportation of finished products (Faux and Lee 1993:101-2). Today, it is easier than ever for U.S. companies to ship raw or semifinished materials over the border to Mexico and use low-cost Mexican labor to make them into finished products to be sold back home. The kind of offshore production that has flourished under NAFTA is made possible by foreign direct investment, which involves complete or controlling ownership of a firm by a foreign company (unlike foreign portfolio investment, discussed in the previous section).

The companies that carry out foreign direct investment are known as transnational companies, or TNCs. Transnational companies have a long history, dating back at least to colonialism. The classic 19th-century foreign enterprise used local low-wage workers (or even slave labor) to extract minerals, foodstuffs, and raw materials and then shipped them overseas to be used in industry. However, an important change since the 1960s has been that TNCs no longer use local labor just to extract minerals and primary commodities such as sugar and coffee; rather, a growing proportion of foreign direct investment is directed toward the production of *industrial goods*, such as cars and refrigerators.

Foreign direct ownership can generate political opposition in the country receiving the investment. This is because although such investment may provide needed employment, it fosters the impression that the national economy is being "bought out" by foreigners—who unlike domestic owners have no nationalistic interest in "giving back" to the country from which they made their profits. Even in the United States, there was a flurry of concern a decade ago that the Japanese were "taking over" the United States—a scenario dramatized in Michael Crichton's 1992 science fiction novel, *Rising Sun*. In Crichton's somewhat xenophobic novel, Japanese investors are depicted as sinister invaders quietly buying up factories, patents, and real estate in the United States. Such nationalist responses to foreign investment are much more common in underdeveloped countries, where there have been many nationalizations of foreign-owned industries since the beginning of this century.

Migration and Tourism

Like the movement of capital and goods across national borders, the movement of people has been affected both by technological improvements and by social and political factors. The large-scale movement of populations from one region to another is as old as humanity itself, but modernity increased both the *scale* of the movement of people across regions and the *rapidity* with which that movement occurred. Both the African slaves who survived the Middle Passage and the European colonists who crossed the Atlantic made a permanent impact on the New World populations. Whereas in some parts of the New World indigenous populations were exterminated, in Mexico, Central America, South America, and the Caribbean, a mixing of races sometimes known as *mestizaje* brought a new group into existence. As Juan Luis Guerra, a popular singer from the Dominican Republic put it poetically, "We are a wormhole between the sea and the sky, 500 years after the Conquest, an illuminated race, black, white, Taino[1]—but who discovered whom?" (Guerra 1992). The result of these sometimes involuntary migrations was cultural globalization and the creation of new racial and ethnic identities.

Just as technological improvements in the 19th and 20th centuries increased the movement of capital and goods across borders, it also facilitated the movement of people. Cheaper and faster transportation can affect the movement of people in two ways: It can increase *tourism*, or temporary movement, and it can increase *migration*, or permanent movement. International tourism has indeed become a multibillion-dollar business, and by the early 1980s, it accounted for about 5.2% of world exports. Among the causes of the spectacular increase of international tourism are the technological advances that make low-cost air travel possible and higher standards of living in industrialized countries, which put international travel within the economic means of more people; whereas "globe-trots" and "grand tours" used to be a luxury only for the very wealthy, today, even college students can get special travel packages to go to Cancún for spring break (Böröcz 1996:1-51). International tourism has some obvious implications for cultural globalization, because it brings millions of people from different parts of the globe into face-to-

---

[1] An indigenous Caribbean nation.

EXHIBIT 7.1

International Tourist Arrivals Worldwide, 1970 to 1993

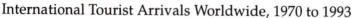

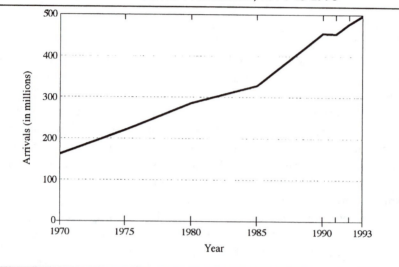

Source: Vellas and Bécherel (1995).

face contact. Exhibit 7.1 shows how international tourism has increased dramatically since 1970. Like other aspects of globalization, international tourism has some controversial aspects, such as the threat it poses to the environment in some regions and the rise of sexual tourism in countries such as Thailand and Cuba.

International tourism and international migration are both similar and different. On the one hand, they both consist of international movements of people, facilitated by the technological improvements in transportation. On the other hand, they differ in that international migration *is a much more politicized issue* than international tourism. For example, around the turn of the century in the United States, racist legislation excluded the immigration of Chinese nationals (Clifford 1997:48-55). Relatively liberal toward the end of the 19th century, immigration policies around the world began to become more restrictive at about the time of the First and Second World Wars. After 1945, however, labor shortages made more liberal policies politically palatable, because native-born workers were not so worried about losing their jobs. The result was an increased flow of immigrants from the Third World to the industrialized countries.

Since the 1970s, slower economic growth and rising unemployment have made immigration politically unpopular, and countries have been closing their borders once again ("Thinking about Globalisation" 1997:8). The United States—which unlike the nations in Europe and Oceania, shares a long border with a much poorer country—has recently implemented laws restricting the rights of even legal immigrants. Meanwhile, xenophobic social movements have appeared throughout Western Europe. As a consequence of such political opposition, the mobility of labor has decreased substantially in the past 20 years, while the mobility of capital has followed the exact opposite trend! Nevertheless, in the world today, it is easier to find political movements opposed to immigration than it is to find movements opposed to free trade: Today, the mobility of labor generates more opposition than the mobility of capital. Theoretically, however, both the globalization of trade and the globalization of labor should be expected to lower domestic wages.

If free trade and the free flow of immigrants both tend to push down the wages of domestic workers, why does the latter tend to generate more social movements, whereas the former is generally ignored? One possible explanation for the varied political salience of the two issues is that immigration is visible and often causes obvious cultural friction (e.g., when people move into an area with a different language or religion). Capital mobility, on the other hand is largely invisible, and even when it becomes visible (as when an automobile factory in Michigan closes to move operations to Mexico), it is usually too late to do anything about it.

Globalization and the Future of Market Embeddedness

Throughout this book, we have looked at the many different ways that markets are embedded in nonmarket social relations and institutions. Markets have all sorts of preconditions that can be provided only through nonmarket means, such as the state, social networks, or organizations. In the chapter on economic development (Chapter 6), we saw that, historically, different countries have drawn on their varying strengths to come up with different solutions to the problems of markets. Moreover, markets in different sectors and in different nations tend to be embedded in different nonmarket arrangements. For example, whereas social networks might provide the organizing logic in some cases, highly bureaucratized organizations might provide the logic in others. Whereas in some countries, certain key industries might be directly controlled by the government, in other countries, the same industries might be subject to more arm's-length government regulation. Every nation has a unique social system of production, a set of cultural, political, and social institutions in which its economy is embedded.

Although it is still unclear what their ultimate outcome will be, the forces of globalization have affected these different forms of market embeddedness in various ways, three of which we will examine here. First, economic globalization has contributed to the globalization of culture, creating internationally shared systems of cultural meaning that exist alongside the national ones. Second, economic globalization has favored the emergence of new forms of economic organization—forms that draw more heavily on networks and less heavily on formal bureaucratic organizations. Third—and perhaps most important—economic globalization has tended to undermine the role of national governments in providing the institutional frameworks within which markets have been embedded.

The Globalization of Culture

The increased availability of products manufactured or invented in other countries has provided the impetus for the growth of a new set of more or less internationally understood cultural meanings. The "golden arches," a decades-old familiar American symbol, is today recognizable in major cities around the world, where the McDonald's corporation is successfully marketing its products. However, sometimes the products of one culture do not "translate" well into another, leading to the kinds of adaptations and accommodations discussed in Chapter 2—such as the vegetarian McDonald's hamburger sold to Hindu customers in India. To help deal with problems in cultural translation, business schools and corporations have put new emphasis on international marketing, based on techniques for selling goods from one nation and cultural milieu in another culture. "Micromarketing" is a technique through which U.S. firms identify the market segment within a foreign country that is most likely to buy their products so that their advertising program can cater specifically to that segment (Roach 1997).

In addition to tangible commodities, such as food and footwear, a substantial portion of today's globalized market is for informational products, such as software, movies, and television programs. Although we do not yet live in a world in which everybody speaks the same language, the rise of transnational mass media has done a lot to foster the rise of an internationally shared set of meanings. Perhaps the best example of this is the worldwide recognition of media celebrities, facilitated by widespread dissemination of movies and television. An Argentine traveling to North Africa will likely encounter many questions about one of his fellow countrymen: the world famous soccer star Diego Maradona, who was disqualified from the 1994 World Cup tournament for his use of drugs.

The country with the highest number of globally recognizable media figures, however, is not Argentina, but the United States. For example, Michael Jordan has risen to become a global media icon and is adored by sports fans all over the world (see Andrews et al. 1996). In fact, it seems that much of what is referred to as the globalization of culture is actually the Americanization of culture. In economists' language, the United States seems to have "comparative advantage" in cultural exports. What would underachieving Bart Simpson say if he knew how important he had become to our national balance of payments?

Part of the U.S. advantage derives from a certain international appeal that American culture seems to have around the world: We seem to inspire a love-hate reaction of "love the product, hate the producer" (Spark 1996:83). But another big advantage is that the United States is a very big and very rich country that can invest more in the media. For example, whereas the average investment for a feature film is $6 million in Britain and $5 million in France, the average in the United States is $12.3 million. American film producers can afford to spend more on making a movie for the simple reason that more people will see it; the internal U.S. market is enormous. Thus, by the time *Terminator 2* or *Titanic* is distributed in France, the huge costs of making the film have already been recovered.

International television is another medium in which the United States has been more successful than other countries. Like the technology that gave birth to the Internet, global satellite communications are the descendant of a technology originally used during the Cold War. Two innovations—the declining costs of launching satellites and the miniaturization of the equipment used to receive their signals—made relatively inexpensive, global, multichannel television a possibility ("Thinking about Globalisation" 1997:16). In part because U.S. companies had a head start in cable broadcasting, this has mostly meant the worldwide dissemination of American channels, such as CNN and MTV.

How do people in other countries view U.S. cultural hegemony? In one sense, the success of U.S. media throughout the world provides an answer in itself: Our cultural products wouldn't enjoy such success if people around the world didn't enjoy them. However, the global success of U.S. cultural products has sometimes generated a backlash in other countries and accusations that U.S. companies use their enormous re-

---

SIDEBAR 7.1

Diabolique and the Globalization of Culture

Americans who have lived abroad know that U.S. movies have international appeal: From India to South Africa to Germany, we can always find the comforting presence of American culture on the silver screen. However, in some countries, the ubiquity of U.S. films has generated a fierce debate about cultural imperialism and the importance of preserving local culture. For example, the French are very nationalistic about their film industry and try to protect it from competing U.S. films, which are made by studios that can spend millions of dollars more than their French counterparts on production and marketing. In France and some other countries, many people support limiting U.S. films and television programs. In the words of the president of a French film company, "This is not a trade war, it is an identity statement. All we want is to preserve a world in which grandchildren have the same national identity as their grandparents" (Gubernick 1994:118). In 1993, Hollywood films accounted for 60% of movie tickets sold in France (Echikson 1993:16).

Particularly galling to the French is the U.S. practice of remaking classic French films with slicker, more expensive production—and then remarketing them back to French audiences. One of the best known of these was the 1993 film *Point of No Return*, starring Bridget Fonda, which was a remake of the 1990 French release, *La Femme Nikita*. In 1996, the widow of French director Henri-Georges Clouzot tried legally to block the release of the movie *Diabolique*, a 1955 French classic that had been remade starring Sharon Stone—a remake done without Mrs. Clouzot's permission and about which she reportedly found out only from reading a magazine at a beauty parlor (Luscombe 1996:79).

---

sources to overwhelm local cultural products through marketing and advertising (see Sidebar 7.1).

One industrialized country that has put up particularly strong resistance to U.S. cultural invasions has been France. If you wanted to speak a language which would be understood around the world 150 years ago, you learned French, which was then the official language of diplomacy. Today, English is the world's most universally spoken language and may even become more widely spoken thanks to the Internet. Through U.S.-dominated media, English words have found their way into many other languages, including French. The "franglais" words that have made their way into French have been omitted by *La Dictionnaire de l'Académie Française*, one of France's most important dictionaries, for reasons of cultural nationalism (Akrill 1993:14). The French government has an official policy for protecting France's historically prestigious film industry from more popularly oriented American imports.

Of course, not *all* cultural globalization is Americanization. Some countries have been able to use their own comparative advantages in the media industry to carve out niches in the global mass media industry. One good example of this is the Hong Kong film industry, which produces top-quality martial arts films viewed all over the world, including in the United States. Who knows? Perhaps someday, English dictionary publishers will ban words borrowed from Chinese.

Whatever nations' cultural products become internationally dominant in the future, cultural globalization is changing the set of meanings within which local markets are embedded. This has led to a certain amount of convergence in consumer preferences around the world and the creation of a global culture. But while local cultures are being molded and remolded by the forces of global capitalism, marketers and advertisers are also increasingly seeing the value of *adapting* their strategies to local cultures. The new global culture is thus homogeneous and heterogeneous at the same time.

New Forms of Production in the Global Economy

As we saw in Chapter 4, a great deal of economic activity under modern capitalism has been carried out under the auspices of large, bureaucratic organizations. For example, a company such as IBM can either buy its microchips from an array of competing outside suppliers or it can manufacture the chips "in-house." By manufacturing its own chips, IBM is saved from having constantly to monitor the quality of the microchips provided by outside vendors. The idea that apparently inefficient large, bureaucratic corporations exist because they minimize transaction costs is an important revision of classical economic thinking and one that has been accepted by economists for several decades.

Times have changed, however. Today, IBM users see the label "Intel Inside" on the casing of their computers. In fact, the processor used in IBM computers today is not manufactured by IBM, a company with its headquarters in the United States, but by Intel, a corporation that has its manufacturing located in Malaysia. Today's personal computers are truly global commodities. A computer may have a Pentium processor manufactured by Intel, a U.S. company with operations in Malaysia, a monitor made by Tatung in Taiwan, and pieces assembled into the final product by Mitsubishi workers in Japan; after completion, the computer

may be marketed to consumers in the United States. Thanks to these globalizing trends, ordinary consumers around the world are thoroughly
enmeshed in a web of economic connections to workers in countries
throughout the globe.

Manufacturing within global commodity chains is not precisely new.
Transnational corporations have been a common phenomenon for decades. However, unlike the old transnationals, the new form of global production is increasingly based on complex *networks* rather than on centralized *organizations*. Under older production arrangements, a company
such as Ford would set up production in a country such as Mexico. The
workers in the Mexican plant were Ford employees, and the automobiles
they assembled would be sold under the Ford label. In contrast, the new
style of global production is much more decentralized and involves multiple smaller firms rather than a single large one. While one firm acts as
the buyer-retailer, other firms act as subcontractors, and still other firms
as sub-sub-contractors.

Organizing economic activity through networks rather than bureaucratic hierarchies can be a more efficient, and hence more competitive,
way of doing business in many sectors. While hierarchical organizations
tend to proliferate in industries in which firms are principally competing
on the basis of lowering cost, networks seem to work better for competition on the basis of quality and innovation. Networks encourage greater
experimentation and hence have a higher propensity to innovate than
large organizations (Powell and Smith-Doerr 1994:382). After all, it is
considerably easier for a firm to cancel orders to its subcontractors than
for it to close an entire subdivision and lay off its workers. Today, firms
must compete not only with other firms in the same nation but with companies in the same business all over the world. By eliminating cumbersome bureaucracies and relying on networks instead, many firms may be
become more competitive than their rivals, thereby surviving and prospering in the new global economy. Therefore, global economic integration can be cited as an important factor contributing to the recent prolif-
eration of network-based production.

One additional effect of globalization has been to make people *more*
aware that capitalism has multiple forms, which fosters emulation across
nations. For example, the presence of Japanese multinational auto manufacturers in the United States in the 1980s made American managers
aware of the Japanese "team system"—a form of factory organization
very different from the vertical bureaucratic hierarchies traditionally
used by companies such as Ford and GM. Japanese firms also have different forms of industrial relations at the shop floor level from the Fordist

model of mass production familiar in the United States. Under the Japanese *kanban* system, retailers can call on the manufacturer at a moment's notice to produce and ship specific items. Since the 1980s, this "just-in-time" system of production has increasingly been emulated in the United States (Piore and Sabel 1984:201). The just-in-time system takes advantage of the flexibility of network-based production and obviously reduces the cost of maintaining large inventories of materials, intermediate goods, or unsold products. It often relies on a workforce with a different profile from the low-skill worker that proliferated under Fordism. Workers in flexible production systems must possess more training to be flexible themselves; if a firm must suddenly "switch gears" and produce something new, a skilled worker with a broad base of training will perform better than an unskilled one (Piore and Sabel 1984).

Another common and long-standing feature of the Japanese economy that makes it different from the U.S. economy is its reliance on production networks, embodied in the business groups known as *keiretsu*. Examples of network-based production prospering under economic globalization can be found in many regions of the world. In Northern Italy, there are entire regions oriented around production in specific industries, such as shoes or high-fashion clothing. Production is carried out within small firms linked by family and other informal ties. Even more interesting than these regional economic links is the increased presence of transnational or global networks. Some of the best-known examples can be found in the computer industry (Intel inside), but global production networks have also become common in other industries—most notably, the garment industry. Whenever you buy an item of clothing from a store such as The Limited or The Gap, you are actually purchasing a product created by a vast global production network rather than by a single company. Of these sorts of garment retailers, one sociologist observes,

> Technically, they are not "manufacturers" because they have no factories. Rather, these companies are "merchandisers" that design and/or market, but do not make, the branded products they sell. These firms rely on complex tiered networks of overseas production contractors that perform almost all their specialized tasks. Branded merchandisers may farm out part or all their activities—product development, manufacturing, packaging, shipping, and even accounts receivable—to different agents around the world. (Gereffi 1994:221)

Unlike traditional corporations, which solve information and coordination problems through a formal bureaucratic chain of command, networks solve these problems through trust. While it is easy to understand how such trust can be established within a family that lives in a certain region or among the business elite of a certain nationality, much research remains to be done regarding how the trust underlying *international networks* can be established. It is possible that global commodity chains are bound together by family ties, such as those that exist among the ethnic Chinese families scattered throughout Southeast Asia (Landa 1981). Some authors have suggested that common language and historical legacies can forge the basis for trust. For example, Hong Kong firms like to have relationships with suppliers in Jamaica, perhaps because they share the English language and the experience of being a British colony (Gereffi 1994:225).

However such trust is formed, once established, it amounts to a re-source—a form of "social capital," in the words of some sociologists—on which firms and the nations in which they operate can draw (Portes 1998). For example, manufacturers in the East Asian "NICs" (newly in-dustrializing countries) benefit from long-standing relationships of trust that they have with U.S. buyers, who prefer to rely on the manufacturers they have done business with in the past, to ensure standards in terms of price, quality, and delivery schedules. These East Asian firms may not actually manufacture these products themselves but instead purchase them from firms in other countries where labor is even cheaper, such as Sri Lanka or China. Although it would seem to make sense for U.S. buy-ers to save money by "bypassing the middleman," relying on known and trusted intermediaries in East Asia solves problems of information and transaction costs (Gereffi 1994:224).

The Obsolescence of the Nation-State?

Earlier in this chapter, we saw that two of the defining characteristics of modernity were capitalism and the nation-state. Capitalism has always been embedded in political institutions, such as the legal framework that protects property rights. During the 20th century, however, the role of government in regulating capitalism expanded considerably, as ex-panded voting rights and democratic institutions gave ordinary people more of a say in the way governments were run. As a result, people in countries such as the United States, England, and Germany increasingly held governments accountable for economic and social issues such as employment, health care, and social welfare. Governments used eco-nomic policy tools such as monetary and fiscal policy to promote eco-nomic growth and social welfare; if they could not satisfy the demands of their constituents, these governments were voted out of office.

With the recent rise of economic globalization, however, many social scientists have been discussing the growing obsolescence of the nation-state (Eichengreen 1996; Keohane and Nye 1977; Sassen 1996; Western 1997). Economic globalization seems to have led to a steady erosion in the ability of ordinary people to control the circumstances of their lives through national governments. For example, in the decades following World War II, governments would routinely lower interest rates as a way of stimulating economic growth. But today, thanks to capital mobility, such a move may result in capital flight, as investors move to countries offering higher interest rates.

Another example: In the industrialized countries during the postwar period, organized labor was able to demand a larger share of the economic pie. But today, if workers in a factory threaten to strike, the owners of the factory may simply decide to move operations to Indonesia, where wages are a fraction of what they are in the United States and workers have weaker unions.

Yet another example: Governments used to tax corporations as a way of financing social spending. Today, however, corporations can escape such taxes by moving overseas; they may use a similar strategy to avoid paying the cost of environmental regulations.

In other words, as long as economies were national, national governments could exercise some control over them, and people could hold these governments accountable through democratic institutions. Today, however, economic globalization has meant a loss of political control at the level of the nation-state, which has not been effectively replaced by global political institutions: *Political and economic globalization have occurred at different rates.* In the words of one observer, "When the economy is thoroughly internationalized, it cannot be regulated by a national government. Yet there is no international government" (Macewan 1994:9). This section explores some of the issues and controversies surrounding the role of the nation-state in the face of globalization.

The High Costs of Global Capital Mobility

In the previous section, we saw that both technological developments and political decisions have contributed to a globalization (or more accurately, a reglobalization) of finance and capital flows since the 1970s. The result has been worldwide capital market integration, the beneficial consequences of which are often pointed out by economists. Theoretically, the globalization of finance should lead to a more efficient allocation of global capital, because instead of having to invest in whatever country you happen to live in, today, you can invest in whatever country gives you the best rate of return. Moreover, it should give the governments and businesses of Third World countries access to resources that they could not tap before—and that in the long run might help backward economies develop.

There is, however, a negative side to global capital market integration. One problem is that just as it has become easier for people to put their money into foreign countries, it has also become easier for them to take their money out—a phenomenon known as capital flight. The increased threat of capital flight limits governments' autonomy to formulate and implement economic policy; governments must worry more about not "scaring off" investors and, consequently, worry less about their political constituents. This is particularly true in the smaller, poorer countries that depend heavily on foreign investment.

Sometimes, foreign investors panic and begin to take their money out of a country all at the same time if they believe that there is likely to be an event (such as devaluation) that will hurt their investments. This kind of financial stampede is often caused by a self-fulfilling prophecy: Investors believe there will be a devaluation and as a result remove their money from the country, which in turn causes a devaluation. In recent years, capital flight has had severely negative consequences for countries such as Mexico, South Korea, and Indonesia.

Furthermore, because economies have become so globalized, these episodes of capital flight can have a "ripple effect" throughout the world. The Mexican peso crisis caused financial problems throughout Latin America (jokingly referred to as the "tequila effect"). Financial crises in Hong Kong, Indonesia, and Korea in 1997 affected stock markets in Asia, Australia, and even Europe. Moreover, the devaluation of Asian currencies subsequently had a negative impact on the economy of the West Coast of the United States, because many firms there make a high proportion of their sales in Asia.

Thus, the instabilities inherent in global financial markets can undermine even healthy national economies and inhibit the ability of national governments to make economic policies. Moreover, the international institutions capable of helping underdeveloped countries to deal with financial crises sometimes do more harm than good: Their cure is worse than the disease. The IMF has recently been criticized from many sides for the conditions that it places on the governments of developing countries in return for loans to bail them out from financial crises. The IMF usually requires that countries change their economic policies to prioritize the goals of low inflation and monetary stability and to abandon the goals of high employment and economic growth. So if a country such as Mexico wants to be rescued by the IMF, it must implement policies such as lowering government spending, laying off government workers, and raising taxes—policies that will essentially send the economy into a recession. After implementing this kind of IMF austerity program in 1995, the Mexican economy had an annual gross domestic product (GDP) growth rate of *negative 6%*—its worst since the Great Depression.

One of the fundamental problems with the IMF as an organization for the regulation of the global economy is that it is not a democratic institution representing the interests of the citizens of the countries it influences with its policies. The governments of some developing countries have recently been considering whether IMF bailouts are worth the high price of sacrificing national economic sovereignty. In the face of its financial crisis in 1997, the Malaysian government simply refused both the IMF's resources and its advice. Other countries are considering the possibility of instituting controls on the entry and exit of short-term capital, thereby lowering the probability of needing to turn to the IMF in the first place; Chile has a system of capital controls in place that has been relatively successful at helping prevent financial crises ("Of Take-offs and Tempests" 1998:88). Today, even some mainstream economists who favor other forms of globalization (such as free trade) are beginning to question the desirability of free global capital mobility. In a recent article, an economist who otherwise opposes protectionism in developing countries wrote that "the weight of evidence and the force of logic point . . . toward restraints on capital flows. It is time to shift the burden of proof from those who oppose to those who favor liberated capital" (Bhagwati 1998:12).

Free Trade and Foreign Direct Investment

Some economists today see the globalization of the production, distribution, and consumption of goods as an inevitable process that will lead to the industrialization of the Third World and the equalization of per capita national incomes around the world. Although some sociologists see this prediction as overly optimistic, it is clear that free trade and foreign direct investment have had an enormous transformative impact on the world in the past 20 years—for better or for worse.

Postwar foreign direct investment (see Exhibit 7.2) has tended to concentrate in the developed rather than the developing world. Even today,

EXHIBIT 7.2

Net Flows of Foreign Direct Investment to Developing Countries

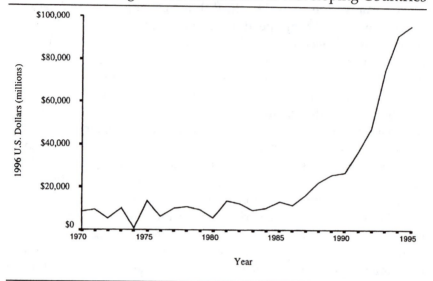

Source: Bouton and Sumlinski (1996).

U.S. firms still have more money invested in countries such as Japan, Germany, and France than they have in countries such as Mexico, El Salvador, and Vietnam. Since 1970, however, foreign direct investment in underdeveloped countries has grown dramatically. In part, this has resulted from the opening of Third World markets to free trade, which has facilitated the spread of transnationals by making it easier to import and export products and has brought about more complicated, globalized commodity chains. Thanks to transnationals, domestic consumers can buy products manufactured at home by a foreign company (as when Mexicans buy Ford cars manufactured near Mexico City) or those manufactured abroad by a domestic company (as when American consumers buy computers manufactured by Mexican workers for Texas Instruments).

In addition to providing access to foreign markets, offshore production allows firms to set up factories in countries where wages are lower, which lowers their costs of production. Often, firms will abandon one Third World country with low but rising wages for another Third World country with even lower wages. For example, Nike's athletic shoe production was once located in South Korea, but rising wages in that country led Nike executives to decide to locate to poorer Southeast Asian countries such as Indonesia, China, and Vietnam. In 1997, the minimum wage in Vietnam was $42 a month—a rate that means that Nike was able to limit its production cost to about 1% of the retail price of a pair of shoes (Ballinger 1997:21).

Obviously, then, globalization is good for the companies that succeed in lowering their production costs. But is it good for the rest of us? The broader benefits of this kind of globalized production processes are clearest if we think of people around the world as *consumers:* If companies can lower the production costs they devote to wages, this means cheaper products available to more people. The garment industry is one example of a labor-intensive industry in which lowered production costs can have a significant effect on the prices paid by consumers.

However, the example above of Nike suggests that the benefits to consumers do not occur automatically: Nike is clearly not passing along all the benefits of globalized production to the consumer. Partly, Nike has been able to market itself as a unique brand with no perfect substitute: I may be able to buy similar footwear at a quarter of the price at Payless, but discount footwear would not confer the same social status as Nike footwear (recall the discussion of product differentiation in Chapter 2). The cultural meaning attached to Nike products is essentially created through marketing, which invokes associations with celebrity endorsers. One has to pay more to benefit from the cultural meaning attached to Nike. The reluctance of consumers to substitute Nike footwear with a cheaper brand means that Nike has no reason to pass along its lower labor costs.

If the benefits to consumers of globalized production aren't automatic, they seem even more problematic if we consider people as potential *producers.* In the decades following World War II, workers in developed countries such as the United States, France, and Sweden benefited from industrial jobs paying relatively high wages for unskilled labor (Western 1997). But recently, companies around the world have been sending their manufacturing operations to Third World countries where wages are lower. The result has been the *industrialization* of the periphery and the *de-industrialization* of the core.

Economists claim that such offshore production is the first step toward the elevation of Third World countries to First World living standards. Regardless of whether offshore industrial investment will bring long-term benefits to Third World countries, however, nobody argues that these benefits are going to arrive tomorrow; rather, they will come through a gradual process of rising real wages. In the meantime, the globalization of production has created an array of collateral social and environmental problems with which national governments are incapable of dealing. For the workers of industrialized countries such as the United States, globalized production has meant the replacement of industrial jobs with service sector jobs. Exhibit 7.3 illustrates the increasing importance of services in the employment of U.S. workers.

So if industrial jobs have been replaced with service jobs, what's the big problem? The problem is that service jobs are characterized by *wage polarization*. On the one hand, there are high-paying service sector jobs reserved for highly educated college graduates who can work as doctors, lawyers, and marketing researchers. On the other hand, there are low-wage, low-skill "McJobs" flipping burgers or cleaning office buildings. So the unskilled laborer who made $15 an hour working in a factory 10 years ago is now making $5.50 at McDonalds, leading to an increase in what is known as "education wage differentials" (Mishel and Bernstein 1994:140-53). As we saw in Chapter 5, wages for poorly educated or unskilled workers have declined over the last two decades.

Economic globalization allows companies to shop around the world, not only for the lowest wages but also for the lowest taxes, the lowest rate of unionization, and the most lax environmental and worker safety standards (see Sidebar 7.2). One of the advantages for a corporation to invest in many Third World countries is that their political and regulatory systems are often corrupt and/or authoritarian. For example, that labor organizers can be thrown in jail or even killed makes it very difficult for Mexican workers to organize. And although NAFTA imposes environmental standards on U.S. companies that invest in Mexico, the enforcement mechanisms in Mexico are often so corrupt that with a relatively small bribe, a U.S.-owned company can avoid spending a large sum on a proper environmental cleanup.

Sometimes it is easy to demonize an individual company for its unfair labor practices and poor environmental record. For example, the Nike athletic shoe company has recently been at the center of a growing scandal around its factories in Indonesia, China, and Vietnam, where workers in a mostly female industry have charged that they were subjected to corporal punishment, sexual abuse, and inhumane working hours (Ballinger 1997:21). But scapegoating Nike misses the point: Capitalism is an economic system based on the profit motive, and a company that can increase its profit margin by manufacturing overseas will naturally do so unless political restrictions are imposed. Nike has become an important political symbol of the negative effects of economic globalization, but it is only one among many. While most of us would like to see companies invest in democratic countries, respect human rights, and have a good environmental record, competitive markets can encourage the oppo-

EXHIBIT 7.3

Percentage of U.S. Labor Force Employed in Different Industries

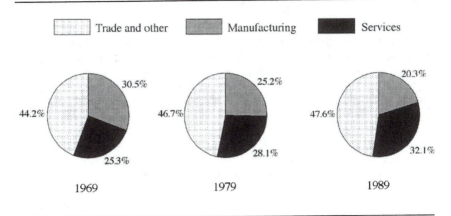

Source: Mishel and Bernstein (1994).

site—and can even drive a firm that does not follow the unethical invest-ment practices of its competitors out of business.

A similar set of disincentives exists for the governments of Third World countries, which want foreign investment to provide jobs for their constituents and to help support the international value of their domestic currencies. For example, a foreign firm might approach the government of Thailand with a proposal to build factories in Bangkok, but only on the condition that it can dump toxic waste without having to pay fines. If the Thai government refuses, the foreign firm can find an even more desper-ately poor country—say, Bangladesh—where the government agrees to accept the environmental damage (or to ignore worker safety standards or to refrain from imposing taxes). Thus, political officials following their own short-term interests can behave in ways that hurt the long-term in-terests of their populations, particularly in countries with shaky demo-cratic traditions.

What is the solution to the social, economic, and environmental prob-lems associated with economic globalization? One common response to the negative incentives created by markets is to impose government regulation. For example, 100 years ago, young children worked in facto-ries, sometimes as much as 12 to 15 hours per day; later, legislation was passed banning child labor and imposing stiff penalties for companies that broke the law. Today, as a consequence, it is relatively rare to find even very poor children working for wages in the United States. Another

---

SIDEBAR 7.2

Trouble on the Mexican Border?

The *maquiladora* system was introduced into towns along the Mexican border with the United States in the mid 1960s; it allows non-Mexican companies to employ Mexican workers in factories on the Mexican side of the U.S.-Mexico border and then ship the finished products back to be sold in the United States without being subject to tariffs. NAFTA and the peso devaluation have both encouraged the *maquiladora* industry to grow dramatically in recent years. Some critics of the program point out that the *maquiladoras* offer few positive benefits for the local economies in which they are located, beyond the provision of jobs. Foreign firms in these zones pay little or nothing in taxes and contribute very little to improving the local economy. Although they may employ local (mostly female) workers, the materials they use are not purchased from Mexican suppliers but are imported; transportation, professional services, and management are similarly imported. Although competitive by Mexican standards, *maquiladora* wages are much lower than even minimum wages over the border in the United States. For example, *Forbes* magazine reports that in and around the Mexican city of Tijuana, *maquiladora* wages run around US$14 per day ("Maquiladora-ville" 1996:111).

Another problem with *maquiladoras* is that they take advantage of weaknesses in the Mexican political system. Corrupt local politicians often allow foreign companies to violate environmental and worker safety regulations. Whereas some environmental violations are visible, others have invisible but deadly long-term effects. For example, a closed battery-recycling plant in the border town of Chilpancingo has left large concentrations of lead and other heavy metal deposits. In 1993, six children were born without brains—a rare birth defect known as anencephaly; in 1994, there were 13 children born with this defect. Fearing bad publicity, a local political official prevented activists from making a new count in 1995 (Bacon 1997:30).

Economists argue that foreign direct investment in Third World countries can help foster economic development and raise local standards of living. But unless it respects human rights and the effective political participation of the people affected by it, offshore investment offers temptation for abuse.

---

way of dealing with the inadequacies of markets is collective bargaining through labor unions, which levels the playing field between workers and their employers and allows workers to demand better conditions and higher wages.

Unfortunately, economic globalization makes both government regulation and collective bargaining much more problematic. As we previously noted, economic globalization means that a government imposing regulations can be punished by capital flight. Similarly, the efficacy of collective bargaining is dramatically reduced when corporations can simply exit countries where unions become too troublesome. To take just one among hundreds of potential examples, in 1993 Hoover Europe (a subsidiary of the U.S. company) removed its operations from France to Scotland, because Scottish unions were more flexible than French (Rodrik 1997:44). Today, it seems that capital must be assiduously courted on all sides by countries falling over each other to offer the lowest taxes, the fewest regulations, and the least troublesome labor movements. The result has been what some sociologists call the "hollowing-out" of the capacity of governments around the world to carry out their traditional functions and the weakening of labor unions in many countries (Western 1997).

Although economists argue that weaker governments and unions will contribute to greater competitiveness and market efficiency, a more embedded view of markets raises the possibility that globalizations may undermine the institutional foundations of capitalism itself. At the macroeconomic level, economic globalization detracts from the efficacy of some of the most fundamental forms of government intervention in the economy, such as the regulation of financial markets and monetary policy aimed at balancing the goals of growth and inflation. At the level of individual nations, globalization could hurt institutions on which local production systems depend, such as tax-funded public education systems and stable bargaining arrangements between unionized workers and their employers. As a result, economic globalization might turn out to be carrying the seeds of its own demise.

Conclusion

Have we arrived at the global village envisioned by Marshall McLuhan? The evidence laid out in this chapter has both confirmed and contradicted McLuhan's vision. On the one hand, we do seem to live in a world that has become "smaller" in terms of time and space—in which global and local cultures coexist side by side. Some say that today we have outgrown modernity: We have become so global that we can no longer adopt the Western European point of view as universal and that the idea of "national interest" has become obsolete. The apparent obsolescence of the nation-state in a global age leads some scholars to conclude that we have gone beyond the "modern" age and now live in a "postmodern" one.

However, there are also reasons to be very skeptical of the notion that we have become "one world." In particular, globalization seems to have sharpened the distinction between the haves and the have-nots—for example, between those who have money to invest anywhere in the world, on the one hand, and those whose standard of living depends on a factory moving its operations offshore, on the other. There is no doubt that we have become global *consumers* and participate in intricate commodity chains that span the planet. But it is much harder to argue that we are global *citizens*, because our ability to control the circumstances of our lives through political means seems to be diminishing steadily.

What can we do to restore the ability of people to have control over their lives above and beyond their participation in markets? Different observers suggest two possible solutions to the problems with reconciling democracy and globalization. One is to deglobalize—to reimpose political controls on capital mobility, trade, and immigration—as a way of revitalizing the control that governments can exert over national economies. Another possibility is to work toward more global forms of political participation. Rather than a world of social policies made by individual nation-states, perhaps we can envision a more decentralized system of political decision making through worldwide nongovernmental organizations (NGOs), unions, human rights groups, local governments, and regional governments, such as that of the European Union.

Related to the question of the future of democratic participation in a global economy is what effect globalization may have on the multiplicity of capitalisms that have evolved in different parts of the world. By forcing domestic firms to compete internationally, globalization might be making what was once a diversity of national capitalisms more homogeneous. An example of this would be the increased adoption of the Japanese team system of management in U.S. workplaces. On the other hand, some sociologists have suggested that heightened competition will reinforce national differences, as different regional and national brands of capitalism carve out niches in the global marketplace (Hollingsworth and Streek 1994). Thus, there is evidence that network-based systems of production tend to flourish in some industrial sectors more than others and in some national and regional contexts better than others. If economic globalization continues, perhaps the world economy might continue to evolve toward a global division of labor—one in which each country specialized in the production of goods and services to which it was most culturally, institutionally, and politically suited.

There are also, however, good reasons to believe that the global economy might be evolving toward more homogeneity rather than more diversity. Although global capitalism leads to greater competitiveness and increased experimentation with new ways of organizing production, it also displays a troubling tendency to undermine many of the institutions in which local capitalisms are embedded. Thus, for example, the Japanese model of production is fundamentally based on the guarantee of lifetime employment—a tradition now being put under pressure by the global financial community, which shows a marked preference for U.S.-style, flexible labor markets. In other countries, local systems of production may rest on systems of public education, which could potentially be gutted by the decreasing ability of governments to tax mobile capital. Ultimately, the future of local and national social systems of production may depend on the ability of ordinary people to reassert their right to participate in forms of political control over economies—forms of control that can emerge only through making economies less globalized or through the creation of supranational forms of political participation.

8

Conclusion

More than two centuries after Adam Smith claimed that markets and economic self-interest could benefit society, markets have apparently conquered the world. On the outskirts of Moscow, the Izmailovo market sprawls as a monument to Russia's transition to capitalism. In the words of two foreign observers who visited the market,

> The past and future were simultaneously on sale. Oil paintings of snowy villages and religious icons, many of dubious origin, were commingled with South Korean electronics and cheap videocassettes. . . . The favored mode of payment for all of this was the dollar—the same dollar whose possession only a few years earlier could have resulted in a stiff prison term. (Yergin and Stanislaw 1997:9)

Today, markets seem to be the only game in town, and many people think this is a good thing. Markets apparently don't suffer from some of the most prominent defects of other ways of organizing economic activity. Market transactions are voluntary rather than coerced: When you go to the market to buy or sell, you may not like the price, but it's your choice whether or not to trade. Moreover, when we add up all the billions of individual choices across an entire economy, market prices can provide more accurate and timely information about supply and demand than a centralized plan ever could. And markets seem to have an almost irrepressible quality as they break out all over the world.

We have tried in this book to offer some measured reflections on markets, even in the face of the triumphant rhetoric heard so often today. One message of this book has been that markets, for all their merits, have some detrimental consequences. Even with markets there is, in the words of Milton Friedman, "no free lunch." In particular, markets can perpetuate rather than ameliorate economic inequality. We have also shown that markets don't appear or flourish on their own, however ubiquitous they seem these days. Politicians and economists celebrate "laissez-faire" markets, but no market exists without rules, institutional foundations, or social regulation (Weber 1981). Markets function only in the presence of nonmarket social institutions, the nature of which makes markets in different places look very different.

Markets and Their Side Effects

The recent "wave" of democratization around the world coincided with the decline of socialism and the global spread of markets, contributing to a general impression that democracy and capitalism are like Siamese twins: You can't have one without the other. This idea has a strong appeal to many Americans, because democracy in the United States was founded on a fundamental regard for the rights of private property holders. However, the cross-national and historical evidence regarding this connection is rather mixed. Over centuries of development, capitalism has been associated with a variety of political regimes, from democracy to despotism. Generally speaking, markets are simultaneously associated with some outcomes that are positive and socially beneficial and with another group of less desirable outcomes.

On the positive side, free markets involve mutually advantageous, voluntary choices made by pairs of individuals, unlike some of the other ways to organize economic life. People who wish to trade with each other can do so, and mutual consent underpins market exchange. But the rise of large organizations within an economy undercuts this happy picture of freedom and voluntarism. Authority structures within corporate hierarchies give some people (the bosses) the power to dictate what others will do. Employees are free to quit their jobs, but as employees, their economic activities are anything but free.

People who trade in markets also abide by certain rules and are subject to particular restrictions. When you bring your goods to sell in a market, for instance, you are supposed to either accept the price offered, try to bargain for a higher price, or refuse to sell. You are not supposed to pull out a gun and force buyers to pay a higher price than they wish for your goods (in the United States, such illegal coercive action is termed *racketeering*). In most modern societies, people generally see the rules for conducting market transactions as fair and legitimate.

Their general legitimacy notwithstanding, markets also have consequences that some people in modern societies view as unfair. People bring their goods to market and accept the market price as determined by supply and demand. Sometimes, however, people don't regard the market price as a fair price. The cause may be "unfair competition" (as in the case of domestic textile manufacturers facing cheap foreign imports), "price gouging" (as when sellers take advantage of a temporary increase in demand to "jack up" their prices), or wage or price discrimination (as when different people are charged different prices for the same good or receive different wages for the same job). In such cases, there will be public pressure on governments to intervene in the market and remedy the situation.

Moreover, if we look closely at capitalist markets, we find that they are undemocratic in some important respects. One of these, discussed at length in Chapter 5, is inequality. Democratic countries may be founded on the principle of equality of political representation (one person, one vote), but no such principle informs markets. No rule stipulates one person, one dollar. Rather, markets engender substantial inequality.

Inequality starts with the resources and endowments that people possess. Some can offer more valuable goods, services, or skills to the market than others. Some people have large portfolios of stocks and bonds, and others have no financial assets at all. Some people have large endowments of "human capital" (high levels of education and training); others have very little. Some people possess abilities that the market rewards (such as the ability to persuade people to buy things); other people's abilities (such as skill in providing child care and homemaking services) are not so highly valued in the marketplace. People who bring highly valued goods to the market will be highly rewarded for these goods; these are the winners of the market system. Conversely, those who come to the market with goods that are not valued or undervalued will receive far fewer rewards; these are the market's losers.

Do these inequalities mean that markets are evil institutions that must be abandoned? For centuries, radical political thinkers have suggested that the abolition of markets was the only way to achieve a truly moral society. But for most of us living in modern, industrialized countries, less radical solutions to the dilemmas of markets exist all around us. For example, consider that in countries such as the United States, Japan, and Germany, primary and secondary education is provided by the government, regardless of an individual's ability to pay. In a pure market system, a good education would be an investment in human capital purchased by the wealthy and middle class for their children; lacking sufficient income, the children of the very poor simply wouldn't go to school. But in the United States and other countries, citizens do not believe that it is fair for educational opportunities to be provided solely through the market. Free, public education funded by taxes is legitimate, something we view as the necessary basis for equality of opportunity.

Indeed, in today's advanced industrialized countries, there are many such modifications and ameliorations of the pure market system (Esping-Andersen 1990). Protective labor legislation, government regulation of industries, publicly funded old age pensions, minimum wage laws, public unemployment insurance, income assistance for the poor, consumer protection laws, progressive income tax systems, health and safety laws, and similar programs all help to protect or insulate citizens from the forces of the marketplace. Such policies help to manage the social costs of markets. Of course, not all countries ameliorate the inequalities of markets to the same extent. Americans, for example, live with levels of economic inequality that would be politically unacceptable in Sweden or Denmark. But even in the United States, free market forces are tempered by nonmarket protections and supports.

Recently, these national systems of protections and supports have been placed under pressure as market forces become more global and more powerful (Western 1997:176-90). In Chapter 7, we saw that although economic globalization is not entirely new, in recent decades it has become an unusually strong force with profound political, social, and cultural consequences. Globalization has meant higher mobility of capital so that investors can pick and choose among different countries for the one that offers the best financial prospects. Increasingly, national governments compete among themselves for investment so they can encourage economic growth and high employment. Competing in this way, national governments may find themselves sacrificing certain programs and regulations; multinational corporations may be enticed to come, for example, only if labor regulations are loosened or taxes are lowered. For instance, in the period between the mid-1970s and the mid-1980s, personal income taxes in developed countries have generally become less progressive (Garrett 1998:91).

Economic globalization leads not only to competition among the governments of different nations but also among the workers of different nations. Some of these workers have large amounts of human capital and continue to sell their skills for significant financial rewards. For workers with fewer skills, however, the effects of globalization can be devastating. As we saw in Chapter 5, unskilled, poorly educated American workers have been hard hit by globalization as they are now competing with similar workers in developing countries earning very low wages. In the words of former Labor Secretary Robert Reich, the new global economy bestows "ever greater wealth on the most skilled and insightful, while consigning the less skilled to a declining standard of living" (Reich 1992:3).

Heightened competition alone would be enough to put these workers in a more difficult bargaining position. But matters are made worse by the truly enormous differences that exist between the wages and regulations governing labor in different countries—between the United States and Thailand, for example. In the words of U.S. labor representative Thomas R. Donahue, it seems that "the world has become a huge bazaar with nations peddling their work forces in competition against one another, offering the lowest prices for doing business" (Donahue quoted in Rodrik 1997).

Economic globalization has brought benefits to the consumers of the world, who now enjoy a greater range of products sold at lower prices than ever before. It has also benefited the workers of some less developed countries, where foreign investment has led to more jobs and higher standards of living. But economic globalization has brought people around the world face-to-face with some of the social costs of markets—costs that were previously managed through national institutions.

The winners in the new global marketplace are people who have fortunes to invest or people with skills that are highly valued on international labor markets. But unless new solutions to the problems of globalized markets are devised, everybody else is likely to lose out. Too much economic inequality, too great a distance between the haves and the have-nots, threatens to unleash the kind of distributional political struggles that in the long run undermine economic growth.

One economist observed in a recent study of globalization that "the broader challenge for the 21st century is to engineer a new balance between market and society, one that will continue to unleash the creative energies of private entrepreneurship without eroding the social basis of cooperation" (Rodrik 1997:85). Rodrik argues that abstract principles such as "free trade" should be tempered by democratic institutions, to ensure that broadly shared national values are not sacrificed to market efficiency. For example, if the citizens in a given country agree that free trade in shoes with Thailand violates a national consensus against child labor, that nation should be able to restrict its trade in shoes with Thailand. Rodrik's (1997) argument assumes that markets are a social institution and that their stability depends on notions of legitimacy or social conceptions of right and wrong (p. 71). This insight is consistent with one major theme of this book: the concept of economic embeddedness.

The Embeddedness of Markets

"Neoliberalism," an ideological trend that essentially updates the economic liberalism advocated by Adam Smith, has accompanied this most recent wave of economic globalization. It is a perspective that favors decision making by markets rather than by governments and pushes for less government intervention in the economy. But the term *neoliberal* actually encompasses a spectrum of beliefs. At the left of this spectrum are politicians such as President Clinton in the United States and Prime Minister Tony Blair in England, who believe that the liberation of the forces of market competition is mostly beneficial but that certain limits (such as minimum wages) should be imposed. At the right of the spectrum are the "market fundamentalist" economists of the old Chicago school, such as Milton Friedman, who believes in the full marketization of many aspects of social life.

Neoliberalism is not a coherent ideology but, rather, a much more diffuse "spirit" of our times. Social scientists disagree about where neoliberalism came from and why it has lasted so long. In part, it grew out of the failures of big-government policies in countries such as the United States and England in the 1970s and developments in economic theory that centered on economists at the University of Chicago. Today, the discipline of economics has drifted far beyond the original Chicago school paradigm, but the influence of neoliberal ideas is apparent in the policies of governments around the world, which have privatized government industries, liberalized trade, and eliminated government regulations. The assumptions behind these policies are that capitalism is good and that free markets can be harnessed for the greater good of society.

One of the central questions that this book has brought to these assumptions is, which capitalism? The evidence presented here shows how rare a "pure" or "ideal" market is. Markets depend for their very existence on nonmarket social institutions, and they are shaped in various ways by their social context. If I wish to buy a used car, what guarantee do I have that the car is not a lemon? How do people in markets deal with problems of trust and uncertainty? Sometimes, we can solve this kind of classical problem of information through the use of informal social networks: By purchasing the car from a family member, I can ensure that I am getting what I paid for. Or sometimes, we rely on formal social institutions backed by government sanction; problems of inadequate information are addressed through laws that require sellers to disclose all known problems with their cars.

Markets are always embedded in different sorts of nonmarket social relations and institutions, whether formal or informal. These relations and institutions vary greatly depending on time, place, and sector of the economy. Sometimes, there can even be different forms of market embeddedness within the same economic sector. In the United States, capital markets allocate capital from those who have it (savers and investors) to those who seek it (borrowers). Some segments of the capital market are dominated by large organizations (e.g., commercial banks, investment banks, pension funds) that operate within a legal regulatory framework (e.g., the Securities and Exchange Commission or SEC, Comptroller of the Currency, Federal Reserve System). Others involve informal arrangements built around social relationships, such as the rotating credit associations discussed in Chapter 3. Here, there is no government oversight, no compliance with formal laws.

In some cases, the problems associated with markets are solved through the use of hierarchies. We saw in Chapter 4 that a great deal of economic activity under modern industrial capitalism occurs within hierarchical organizations. Most American workers do not wake up every morning and proceed to a marketplace to sell their labor power to that day's highest bidder. A far more typical experience is for people to go to work within a bureaucratic organization—whether it be a university, a manufacturing plant, or a government office. Even professionals are increasingly working within organizations. Physicians, once renowned for their self-employed status, now work as salaried employees within health maintenance organizations (HMOs), which have complex bureaucratic procedures for regulating costs and constraining the medical decisions of their professional staff. The omnipresence of bureaucracy throughout the economy calls into question simplistic notions that private markets are necessarily more efficient than public bureaucracies at providing certain goods or services. Anyone who has been placed on hold by an HMO administrator can attest to the fact that private sector organizations can be every bit as "bureaucratic" as government organizations.

The main point about bureaucracies is to set aside oversimplified assumptions that they are all inefficient and should be eliminated. Rather, bureaucracies exist because they can help solve problems that markets on their own cannot solve. Large corporations such as Ford and IBM exist partly because hierarchies can help to reduce transaction costs (other reasons matter as well, as Roy [1997] and Freeland [1996] point out).

A recent trend in some industries is to divide production among networks of smaller organizations. This trend is exemplified by the "Intel

Inside" label that we see on most computers today, which indicates that the microprocessor inside was manufactured by the Intel Corporation, although the body of the computer as well as many of the other components may have been manufactured by any one of a number of computer companies. An international network of companies, big and small, design, manufacture, and assemble computers and write the software to operate them. This trend should caution us against any simple generalizations about the superior efficiency of markets or organizations.

Within the economy of any single country, we can find examples of formal and informal institutions, of networks and hierarchies, and of private and public sector involvement in the economy. At the same time, if we look at different countries we can distinguish different *national traditions* of institutional embeddedness. One of the best-known differences lies in the ways that governments intervene in the economy. There is no country in the world in which the government plays no role in the economy; in fact, governments typically provide the *preconditions* for markets through the provision of various collective goods. But national differences in government intervention can be seen in the *forms* of intervention that governments undertake. In countries such as Germany, France, and Sweden, the government has historically tended to intervene more directly in the economy, through means such as government ownership of firms. In the United States, in contrast, the government has intervened more indirectly, through the promulgation and enforcement of laws (Campbell and Lindberg 1990).

The role of government in national economies is only the tip of a very large iceberg of institutions that influence markets—institutions that include formal organizations, social networks, and cultural values. One example of divergent national institutions can be seen in the different structures of large Japanese and American firms. At the shop floor level, Japanese firms are known for their famous "team system" of worker participation in the day-to-day running of production—a system very different from the "Fordist" assembly line technique traditionally used in the United States. Unlike an American factory worker, who can expect to work in several or even many firms in his or her lifetime, the Japanese factory worker enjoys lifetime employment at a single firm; in return, the worker is expected to be loyal to the company and to deliver a higher-quality product (Hollingsworth 1997). Long-term loyalty is also encouraged by a pay scale that rewards seniority and by less inequality between ordinary workers and management (compared with the U.S. workplace). If we move from the shop floor to the macro level, we find that large Japanese firms are organized into the intercorporate networks known as *keiretsu*—again, unlike the prevailing forms of corporate organization in the United States (Hamilton and Biggart 1988).

There was a time when many social scientists thought of modernization and capitalist development as a single path along which all countries would travel. But in Chapters 6 and 7, we suggested that there are multiple forms of capitalism and a diverse number of historical paths to economic development rather than a single one. If we are right, then we should also take neoliberal prescriptions with a grain of salt, especially when considering what developing countries should do to "catch up" to developed ones. Rather than simply adopt American or Western models of development, developing countries should draw on and exploit their own local institutional strengths—whether they be social networks, styles of firm organization, government structures, or cultural institutions.

The Future of Economy and Society

Economic globalization has brought markets to every corner of the world. For all its attendant problems, one benefit of economic globalization has been that it has made us more aware of the diversity of forms of market embeddedness in different national settings. For example, only when Japanese multinationals began coming to the United States, and vice versa, did people in the United States realize that the American model of shop floor management was neither universal nor necessarily the best way of running things.

Ironically, just as we are becoming aware of the diversity of "capitalisms" across the globe, economic globalization seems to be threatening this diversity, by putting pressure on local systems of market embeddedness. As governments and firms around the world scramble to compete in today's global economy, it may be that these organizations will converge on a single model that "works best" in this economy—one that will likely include a reduced role for government in ameliorating the most harmful side effects associated with markets. One of the biggest challenges today is to keep the forces of economic globalization from destroying those forms of market embeddedness that are most compatible with human welfare.

References

Abu-Lughod, Janet. 1989. *Before European Hegemony: The World System A.D. 1250–1350*. New York: Oxford University Press.

Akrill, Josephine. 1993. "An Outbreak of Franglais Fever." *Times Literary Supplement* 4688:14.

Amenta, Edwin. 1998. *Bold Relief: Institutional Politics and the Origins of Modern American Social Policy*. Princeton, NJ: Princeton University Press.

Amsden, Alice H., Jacek Kochanowicz, and Lance Taylor. 1994. *The Market Meets Its Match: Restructuring the Economies of Eastern Europe*. Cambridge, MA: Harvard University Press.

Andrews, David L., Ben Carrington, Zbigniew Mazur, and Steven J. Jackson. 1996. "Jordanscapes: A Preliminary Analysis of the Global Popular." *Social Science Journal* 13:428-57.

Appadurai, Arjun. 1986. "Introduction." Pp. 3-63 in *The Social Life of Things*, edited by Arjun Appadurai. Cambridge, UK: Cambridge University Press.

Arhin, Kwame. 1976. "The Pressure of Cash and Its Political Consequences in Asante in the Colonial Period." *Journal of African Studies* 4:453-68.

Atack, Jeremy. 1986. "Firm Size and Industrial Structure in the United States during the Nineteenth Century." *Journal of Economic History* 46:463-75.

Ayres, Ian and Peter Siegelman. 1995. "Race and Gender Discrimination in Bargaining for a New Car." *American Economic Review* 85:304-21.

Babb, Sarah L. 1998. "The Evolution of Economic Expertise in a Developing Country: Mexican Economics 1929–1998." Ph.D. dissertation, Northwestern University, Evanston, IL.

Bacon, David. 1997. "Evening the Odds: Cross-Border Organizing Gives Labor a Chance." *The Progressive* 61(7):29-32.

Baker, Wayne E. 1984. "The Social Structure of a National Securities Market." *American Journal of Sociology* 89:775-811.

———. 1990. "Market Networks and Corporate Behavior." *American Journal of Sociology* 96:589-625.

Ballinger, Jeff. 1997. "Nike Does It to Vietnam." *Transnational Monitor* 18(3):21.

Bassett, William F., Michael J. Fleming, and Anthony P. Rodrigues. 1998. "How Workers Use 401(k) Plans: The Participation, Contribution, and Withdrawal Decisions." *Federal Reserve Bank of New York Staff Reports* 38.

Becker, Gary S. 1968. "Economic Discrimination." Pp. 209-10 in *International Encyclopedia of the Social Sciences*, edited by D. L. Sills. New York: Macmillan.

———. 1971. *The Economics of Discrimination*. 2d ed. Chicago: University of Chicago Press.

———. 1993a. "The Evidence against Banks Doesn't Prove Bias." *Business Week*, April 19, p. 18.

————. 1993b. "Nobel Lecture: The Economic Way of Looking at Behavior." *Journal of Political Economy* 101:385-409.

Belk, Russell W. and Gregory Coon. 1991. "Can't Buy Me Love: Dating, Money and Gifts." *Advances in Consumer Research* 18:521-27.

Bensel, Richard Franklin. 1984. *Sectionalism and American Political Development: 1880–1980.* Madison: University of Wisconsin Press.

Berkovec, James A., Glenn B. Canner, Stuart A. Gabriel, and Timothy H. Hannan. 1994. "Race, Redlining, and Residential Mortgage Loan Performance." *Journal of Real Estate Finance and Economics* 9:263-94.

Berle, Adolph A. and Gardner Means. 1968. *The Modern Corporation and Private Property.* New Brunswick, NJ: Transaction Books.

Bernstein, Lisa. 1992. "Opting out of the Legal System: Extralegal Contractual Relations in the Diamond Industry." *Journal of Legal Studies* 21:115-57.

Bhagwati, Jagdish. 1998. "The Capital Myth: The Difference between Trade in Widgets and Dollars." *Foreign Affairs* 77(3):7-12.

Bian, Yanjie. 1997. "Bringing Strong Ties Back In: Indirect Ties, Network Bridges, and Job Searches in China." *American Sociological Review* 62:366-85.

Bianchi, Suzanne M. 1995. "Changing Economic Roles of Women and Men." Pp. 107-54 in *State of the Union: America in the 1990s.* Vol.1, edited by Reynolds Farley. New York: Russell Sage.

Biernacki, Richard. 1995. *The Fabrication of Labor: Germany and Britain, 1640–1914.* Berkeley: University of California Press.

Biggart, Nicole Woolsey. 1989. *Charismatic Capitalism: Direct Selling Organizations in America.* Chicago: University of Chicago Press.

Blank, Rebecca M. 1997. *It Takes a Nation: A New Agenda for Fighting Poverty.* Princeton, NJ: Princeton University Press.

Blau, Francine D. 1998. "Trends in the Well-Being of American Women, 1970–1995." *Journal of Economic Literature* 36:112-65.

Boisot, Max and John Child. 1996. "From Fiefs to Clans and Network Capitalism: Explaining China's Emerging Economic Order." *Administrative Science Quarterly* 41:600-28.

Böröcz, József. 1996. *Leisure Migration: A Sociological Study on Tourism.* Tarrytown, NY: Pergamon.

Bouton, Lawrence and Mariusz A. Sumlinski. 1996. *Trends in Private Investment in Developing Countries: Statistics for 1970-95.* Washington, DC: World Bank.

Brainerd, Elizabeth. 1998. "Winners and Losers in Russia's Economic Transition." *American Economic Review* 88:1094-1116.

Bruce, Scott and Bill Crawford. 1995. *Cerealizing America: The Unsweetened Story of American Breakfast Cereal.* Boston: Faber & Faber.

Buchanan, James M., Robert D. Tollison, and Gordon Tullock, eds. 1980. *Toward a Theory of Rent-Seeking Society.* College Station: Texas A&M University Press.

Burt, Ronald S. 1992. *Structural Holes: The Social Structure of Competition.* Cambridge, MA: Harvard University Press.

Campbell, John L. and Leon N. Lindberg. 1990. "Property Rights and the Organization of Economic Activity by the State." *American Sociological Review* 55:634-47.

Caplow, Theodore. 1982. "Christmas Gifts and Kin Networks." *American Sociological Review* 47:383-92.

Carr, James H. and Isaac F. Megbolugbe. 1993. "The Federal Reserve Bank of Boston Study on Mortgage Lending Revisited." *Journal of Housing Research* 4:277-313.

Carroll, Glenn R. and Karl Ulrich Mayer. 1986. "Job-Shift Patterns in the Federal Republic of Germany." *American Sociological Review* 51:323-41.

Carruthers, Bruce G. 1996. *City of Capital: Politics and Markets in the English Financial Revolution.* Princeton, NJ: Princeton University Press.

Carruthers, Bruce G. and Sarah Babb. 1996. "The Color of Money and the Nature of Value: Greenbacks and Gold in Postbellum America." *American Journal of Sociology* 101:1556-91.

Carruthers, Bruce G. and Terence C. Halliday. 1998. *Rescuing Business: The Making of Corporate Bankruptcy Law in England and the United States.* Oxford: Clarendon.

Carter, Michael J. and Susan B. Carter. 1985. "Internal Labor Markets in Retailing: The Early Years." *Industrial and Labor Relations Review* 38:586-98.

Caskey, John P. 1994. *Fringe Banking: Check-Cashing Outlets, Pawnshops, and the Poor.* New York: Russell Sage.

Chandler, Alfred D. 1977. *The Visible Hand: The Managerial Revolution in American Business.* Cambridge, MA: Harvard University Press.

Cheal, David. 1988. *The Gift Economy.* London: Routledge.

Chirot, Daniel. 1991. "What Happened in Eastern Europe in 1989?" Pp. 3-32 in *The Crisis of Leninism and the Decline of the Left: The Revolutions of 1989,* edited by Daniel Chirot. Seattle: University of Washington Press.

Clifford, Elizabeth. 1997. "Racing the Nation: Immigration Policy, Race, and National Identity in Canada and the United States, 1905–1925." Ph.D. dissertation, Northwestern University, Evanston, IL.

Clinton, William Jefferson. 1993. "Remarks on Endorsements of the North American Free Trade Agreement." *Weekly Compilation of Presidential Documents* 29(45):2303-9.

Coase, R. H. 1937. "The Nature of the Firm." *Economica* 4:386-405.

Collins, Randall. 1986. *Weberian Sociological Theory.* Cambridge, UK: Cambridge University Press.

———. 1992. "Weber's Last Theory of Capitalism: A Systematization" Pp. 85-109 in *The Sociology of Economic Life,* edited by Mark Granovetter and Richard Swedberg. Boulder, CO: Westview.

———. 1997. "An Asian Route to Capitalism: Religious Economy and the Origins of Self-transforming Growth in Japan." *American Sociological Review* 62:843-65.

Cornelius, Peter K. and Beatrice S. Weder. 1996. "Economic Transformation and Income Distribution: Some Evidence from the Baltic Countries." *IMF Staff Papers* 43:587-604.

Cowherd, Douglas M. and David I. Levine. 1992. "Product Quality and Pay Equity between Lower-level Employees and Top Management." *Administrative Science Quarterly* 37:302-20.

Crichton, Michael. 1992. *Rising Sun.* New York: Knopf.

Cross, Gary. 1993. *Time and Money: The Making of Consumer Culture.* London: Routledge.

Danziger, Sheldon and Peter Gottschalk. 1995. *American Unequal.* Cambridge, MA: Harvard University Press.

Darity, William A. Jr. and Patrick L. Mason. 1998. "Evidence on Discrimination in Employment: Codes of Color, Codes of Gender." *Journal of Economic Perspectives* 12(2):63-90.

Davies, Margery W. 1982. *Woman's Place Is at the Typewriter: Office Work and Office Workers 1870–1930.* Philadelphia: Temple University Press.

Davis, Gerald F. 1991. "Agents without Principles? The Spread of the Poison Pill Takeover Defense through the Intercorporate Network." *Administrative Science Quarterly* 36:583-613.

DiMaggio, Paul and Hugh Louch. 1998. "Socially Embedded Consumer Transactions: For What Kinds of Purchases Do People Most Often Use Networks?" *American Sociological Review* 63:619-37.

DiPrete, Thomas A. and Whitman Soule. 1986. "The Organization of Career Lines: Equal Employment Opportunity and Status Advancement in a Federal Bureaucracy." *American Sociological Review* 51:295-309.

Dobbin, Frank. 1992. "The Origins of Private Social Insurance: Public Policy and Fringe Benefits in America, 1920–1950." *American Journal of Sociology* 97:1416-50.

———. 1994. *Forging Industrial Policy: The United States, Britain, and France in the Railway Age.* Cambridge, UK: Cambridge University Press.

Douglas, Mary and Baron Isherwood. 1978. *The World of Goods: Towards an Anthropology of Consumption.* Harmondsworth, UK: Penguin.

Earle, Peter. 1989. *The Making of the English Middle Class: Business, Society and Family Life in London, 1660–1730.* Berkeley: University of California Press.

Echikson, William. 1993. "Sacre bleu! American dinosaurs." *Fortune* 128(14):16.

Eckes, Alfred E., Jr. 1995. *Opening America's Market: U.S. Foreign Trade Policy since 1776.* Chapel Hill: University of North Carolina Press.

Edelman, Lauren. 1990. "Legal Environments and Organizational Governance: The Expansion of Due Process in the American Workplace." *American Journal of Sociology* 95:1401-40.

———. 1992. "Legal Ambiguity and Symbolic Structures: Organizational Mediation of Civil Rights Law." *American Journal of Sociology* 97:1531-76.

Edin, Kathryn and Laura Lein. 1997. *Making Ends Meet: How Single Mothers Survive Welfare and Low-Wage Work.* New York: Russell Sage.

Eichengreen, Barry. 1996. *Globalizing Capital: A History of the International Monetary System.* Princeton, NJ: Princeton University Press.

Epstein, Richard A. 1992. *Forbidden Grounds: The Case against Employment Discrimination Law.* Cambridge, MA: Harvard University Press.

Esping-Andersen, Gøsta. 1990. *The Three Worlds of Welfare Capitalism.* Princeton, NJ: Princeton University Press.

Evans, Peter. 1979. *Dependent Development: The Alliance of Transnational, State, and Local Capital in Brazil.* Princeton, NJ: Princeton University Press.

———. 1992. "The State as Problem and Solution: Predation, Embedded Autonomy and Adjustment." Pp. 139-81 in *The Politics of Economic Adjustment: International Constraints, Distributive Politics, and the State,* edited by Stephan Haggard and Robert Kaufman. Princeton, NJ: Princeton University Press.

———. 1995. *Embedded Autonomy: States and Industrial Transformation.* Princeton, NJ: Princeton University Press.

Faulkner, Robert R. and Andy B. Anderson. 1987. "Short-Term Projects and Emergence Careers: Evidence from Hollywood." *American Journal of Sociology* 92:879-909.

Faux, Jeff and Thea Lee. 1993. "The Road to the North American Free Trade Agreement: Laissez-Faire or a Ladder Up?" Pp. 97-115 in *The North American Free Trade Agreement: Labor, Industry, and Government Perspectives,* edited by Mario F. Bognanno and Kathryn J. Ready. Westport, CT: Praeger.

Feagin, Joe R. and Nikitah Imani. 1994. "Racial Barriers to African American Entrepreneurship: An Exploratory Study." *Social Problems* 41:562-84.

Feenstra, Robert C. 1998. "Integration of Trade and Disintegration of Production in the Global Economy." *Journal of Economic Perspectives* 12(4):31-50.

Fein, Ellen and Sherrie Schneider. 1997. *The Rules II.* New York: Warner.

Feinman, Jay M. 1976. "The Development of the Employment at Will Rule." *American Journal of Legal History* 20(1):118-35.

Fernandez, Roberto and Nancy Weinberg. 1997. "Sifting and Sorting: Personal Contacts and Hiring in a Retail Bank." *American Sociological Review* 62:883-902.

Fischer, Eileen and Stephen J. Arnold. 1990. "More Than a Labor of Love: Gender Roles and Christmas Gift Shopping." *Journal of Consumer Research* 17:333-45.

Fligstein, Neil. 1990. *The Transformation of Corporate Control.* Cambridge, MA: Harvard University Press.

———. 1996. "Markets as Politics: A Political-Cultural Approach to Market Institutions." *American Sociological Review* 61:656-73.

Florida, Richard and Martin Kenney. 1991. "Transplanted Organizations: The Transfer of Japanese Industrial Organization to the U.S." *American Sociological Review* 56:381-98.

Fortin, Nicole M. and Thomas Lemieux. 1997. "Institutional Changes and Rising Wage Inequality: Is There a Linkage?" *Journal of Economic Perspectives* 11(2):75-96.

Fowles, Jib. 1996. *Advertising and Popular Culture.* Thousand Oaks, CA: Sage.

Freeland, Robert F. 1996. "The Myth of the M-Form? Governance, Consent, and Organizational Change." *American Journal of Sociology* 102:483-526.

Freeman, Richard B. 1993. "How Much Has De-Unionization Contributed to the Rise in Male Earnings Inequality?" Pp. 133-63 in *Uneven Tides: Rising Inequality in America,* edited by Sheldon Danziger and Peter Gottschalk. New York: Russell Sage.

Friedman, Milton. 1962. *Capitalism and Freedom.* Chicago: University of Chicago Press.

Fullerton, Don. 1994. "Tax Policy." Pp. 165-208 in *American Economic Policy in the 1980s,* edited by Martin Feldstein. Chicago: University of Chicago Press.

Gao, Bai. 1997. *Economic Ideology and Japanese Industrial Policy: Developmentalism from 1931 to 1965.* Cambridge, UK: Cambridge University Press.

Garrett, Geoffrey. 1998. *Partisan Politics in the Global Economy.* Cambridge, UK: Cambridge University Press.

Gates, Henry Louis Jr. 1998. "Net Worth: How the Greatest Player in the History of Basketball Became the Greatest Brand in the History of Sports." *New Yorker,* June 1, pp. 48-61.

Georgano, G. N. 1972. *A History of Transport.* London: J. M. Dent and Sons.

Gereffi, Gary. 1990a. "Big Business and the State." Pp. 90-109 in *Manufacturing Miracles: Paths of Industrialization in Latin America and East Asia,* edited by Gary Gereffi and Donald L. Wyman. Princeton, NJ: Princeton University Press.

———. 1990b. "Paths of Industrialization: An Overview." Pp. 1-31 in *Manufacturing Miracles: Paths of Industrialization in Latin America and East Asia,* edited by Gary Gereffi and Donald L. Wyman. Princeton, NJ: Princeton University Press.

———. 1994. "The International Economy and Economic Development." Pp. 206-33 in *The Handbook of Economic Sociology,* edited by Neil J. Smelser and Richard Swedberg. Princeton, NJ: Princeton University Press.

Gereffi, Gary and Donald L. Wyman eds. 1990. *Manufacturing Miracles: Paths of Industrialization in Latin America and East Asia.* Princeton, NJ: Princeton University Press.

Gerlach, Michael L. 1992. *Alliance Capitalism: The Social Organization of Japanese Business*. Berkeley: University of California Press.

Gerschenkron, Alexander. 1962. *Economic Backwardness in Historical Perspective*. Cambridge, MA: Belknap.

Giddens, Anthony. 1990. *The Consequences of Modernity*. Cambridge, UK: Polity.

Goldin, Claudia. 1990. *Understanding the Gender Gap: An Economic History of American Women*. New York: Oxford University Press.

———. 1997. "Career and Family: College Women Look to the Past." Pp. 20-58 in *Gender and Family Issues in the Workplace*, edited by Francine D. Blau and Ronald G. Ehrenberg. New York: Russell Sage.

Goldman, Robert. 1992. *Reading Ads Socially*. London: Routledge.

Gottfried, Heidi. 1991. "Mechanisms of Control in the Temporary Help Service Industry." *Sociological Forum* 6:699-713.

Gottschalk, Peter. 1997. "Inequality, Income Growth, and Mobility: The Basic Facts." *Journal of Economic Perspectives* 11(2):21-40.

Gottschalk, Peter and Sheldon Danziger. 1993. "Family Structure, Family Size and Family Income." Pp. 167-93 in *Uneven Tides: Rising Inequality in America*, edited by Sheldon Danziger and Peter Gottschalk. New York: Russell Sage.

Gottschalk, Peter and Timothy M. Smeeding. 1997. "Cross-National Comparisons of Earnings and Income Inequality." *Journal of Economic Literature* 35:633-87.

Gramlich, Edward M., Richard Kasten, and Frank Sammartino. 1993. "Growing Inequality in the 1980s: The Role of Federal Taxes and Cash Transfers." Pp. 225-49 in *Uneven Tides: Rising Inequality in America*, edited by Sheldon Danziger and Peter Gottschalk. New York: Russell Sage.

Grandy, Christopher. 1989. "New Jersey Corporate Chartermongering, 1875–1929." *Journal of Economic History* 49:677-92.

Granovetter, Mark S. 1974. *Getting a Job: A Study of Contacts and Careers*. Cambridge, MA: Harvard University Press.

———. 1985. "Economic Action and Social Structure: The Problem of Embeddedness." *American Journal of Sociology* 91:481-510.

———. 1994. "Business Groups." Pp. 453-75 in *The Handbook of Economic Sociology*, edited by Neil J. Smelser and Richard Swedberg. Princeton, NJ: Princeton University Press.

Grierson, Philip. 1959. "Commerce in the Dark Ages: A Critique of the Evidence." *Transactions of the Royal Historical Society* 6th ser. 9:123-40.

Gubernick, Lisa. 1994. "No Trade War Here." *Forbes* 153(5):118.

Guerra, Juan Luis. 1992. "El costo de la vida." Soundtrack on *Areito*. Mexico: Karen Records.

Guillén, Mauro F. 1994. *Models of Management: Work, Authority, and Organization in a Comparative Perspective*. Chicago: University of Chicago Press.

Gulati, Ranjay. 1995a. "Does Familiarity Breed Trust? The Implications of Repeated Ties for Contractual Choice in Strategic Alliances." *Academy of Management Journal* 38:85-112.

———. 1995b. "Social Structure and Alliance Formation Patterns: A Longitudinal Analysis." *Administrative Science Quarterly* 40:619-52.

Gunder Frank, Andre. 1978. *World Accumulation, 1492–1789*. New York: Monthly Review Books.

Hacker, Andrew. 1997. *Money: Who Has How Much and Why*. New York: Simon & Schuster.

Haggard, Stephan. 1990a. "How Societies Change Developmental Models or Keep Them: Reflections on the Latin American Experience in the 1930s and the Postwar World." Pp. 110-38 in *Manufacturing Miracles: Paths of Industrialization in Latin America and East Asia*, edited by Gary Gereffi and Donald L. Wyman. Princeton, NJ: Princeton University Press.

————. 1990b. *Pathways from the Periphery: The Politics of Growth in the Newly Industrializing Countries*. Ithaca, NY: Cornell University Press.

Hamilton, Alexander. [1791] 1961–1987. "Alexander Hamilton's Final Version of the Report on the Subject of Manufactures." Pp. 230-40 in *The Papers of Alexander Hamilton*, Vol. 10 (December 1791–January 1792), edited by Harold C. Syrett and Jacob E. Cooke. New York: Columbia University Press.

Hamilton, Gary G. and Nicole Woolsey Biggart. 1988. "Market, Culture, and Authority: A Comparative Analysis of Management and Organization in the Far East." *American Journal of Sociology* 94 Suppl.:S52-S94.

Hamper, Ben. 1991. *Rivethead: Tales from the Assembly Line*. New York: Warner.

Han, Shin-Kap. 1996. "Structuring Relations in on-the-job Networks." *Social Networks* 18:47-67.

Handelman, Howard. 1996. *The Challenge of Third World Development*. Upper Saddle River, NJ: Prentice Hall.

Haunschild, Pamela R. 1994. "How Much Is That Company Worth? Interorganizational Relationships, Uncertainty, and Acquisition Premiums." *Administrative Science Quarterly* 39:391-411.

Heckman, James J. and Brook S. Payner. 1989. "Determining the Impact of Federal Antidiscrimination Policy on the Economic Status of Blacks: A Study of South Carolina." *American Economic Review* 79:138-77.

Helleiner, Eric. 1994. *States and the Reemergence of Global Finance*. Ithaca, NY: Cornell University Press.

Hirschman, Albert O. 1958. *The Strategy of Economic Development*. New York: Norton.

————. 1981. *Essays in Trespassing: Economics to Politics and Beyond*. Cambridge, UK: Cambridge University Press.

Hobson, John M. 1997. *The Wealth of States: A Comparative Sociology of International Economic and Political Change*. Cambridge, UK: Cambridge University Press.

Hollingsworth, J. Rogers. 1997. "Continuities and Changes in Social Systems of Production: The Cases of Japan, Germany, and the United States." Pp. 265-310 in *Contemporary Capitalism: The Embeddedness of Institutions*, edited by J. Rogers Hollingsworth and Robert Boyer. Cambridge, UK: Cambridge University Press.

Hollingsworth, J. Rogers and Robert Boyer, eds. 1997. *Contemporary Capitalism: The Embeddedness of Institutions*. Cambridge, UK: Cambridge University Press.

Hollingsworth, J. Rogers, and Wolfgang Streek. 1994. "Countries and Sectors: Concluding Remarks on Performance, Convergence, and Competitiveness." Pp. 270-97 in *Governing Capitalist Economies*, edited by J. Rogers Hollingsworth, Philippe Schmitter, and Wolfgang Streek. New York: Oxford University Press.

Hudson, Kenneth. 1972. *Air Travel: A Social History*. London: Bath, Adams, & Dart.

Jackall, Robert. 1988. *Moral Mazes: The World of Corporate Managers*. New York: Oxford University Press.

Jacoby, Sanford M. 1984. "The Development of Internal Labor Markets in American Manufacturing Firms." Pp. 23-56 in *Internal Labor Markets*, edited by Paul Osterman. Cambridge: MIT Press.

————. 1985. *Employing Bureaucracy: Managers, Unions, and the Transformation of Work in American Industry, 1900–1945*. New York: Columbia University Press.

———— and Sunil Sharma. 1992. "Employment Duration and Industrial Labor Mobility in the United States, 1880-1980." *Journal of Economic History* 52:161-80.

Jevons, W. Stanley. 1931. *The Theory of Political Economy.* 4th ed. London: Macmillan.

Johnson, Chalmers. 1997. "Breaching the Great Wall." *American Prospect* 30:24-29.

Keohane, Robert O. and Joseph S. Nye. 1977. *Power and Interdependence: World Politics in Transition.* Boston, MA: Little, Brown.

Kim, Marlene. 1989. "Gender Bias in Compensation Structures: A Case Study of Its Historical Basis and Persistence." *Journal of Social Issues* 45:39-50.

Kim, Sunwoong and Gregory D. Squires. 1995. "Lender Characteristics and Racial Disparities in Mortgage Lending." *Journal of Housing Research* 6:99-113.

Kiong, Tong Chee and Yong Pit Kee. 1998. "Guanxi bases, Xinyong and Chinese Business Networks." *British Journal of Sociology* 49:75-96.

Kirschenman, Joleen and Kathryn M. Neckerman. 1991. "We'd Love to Hire Them, But . . .: The Meaning of Race for Employers." Pp. 203-32 in *The Urban Underclass,* edited by Christopher Jencks and Paul Peterson. Washington DC: Brookings Institution.

Konrád, György and Iván Szelényi. 1979. *The Intellectuals on the Road to Class Power.* New York: Harcourt Brace Jovanovich.

Kornai, János. 1992. *The Socialist System: The Political Economy of Communism.* Princeton, NJ: Princeton University Press.

Kotlikoff, Laurence J. 1988. "Intergenerational Transfers and Savings." *Journal of Economic Perspectives* 2(2):41-58.

Krooss, Herman E. 1974. *American Economic Development: The Progress of a Business Civilization.* 3d ed. Englewood Cliffs, NJ: Prentice Hall.

Krugman, Paul. 1990. *The Age of Diminished Expectations: U.S. Economic Policy in the 1990s.* Cambridge: MIT Press.

Krugman, Paul R. and Maurice Obstfeld. 1991. *International Economics: Theory and Policy.* 2d ed. New York: HarperCollins.

Kunda, Gideon. 1992. *Engineering Culture: Control and Commitment in a High-Tech Corporation.* Philadelphia: Temple University Press.

LaBarbera, Priscilla A. 1988. "The Nouveaux Riches: Conspicuous Consumption and the Issue of Self-Fulfillment." *Research in Consumer Behavior* 3:179-210.

Ladd, Helen F. 1998. "Evidence on Discrimination in Mortgage Lending." *Journal of Economic Perspectives* 12(2):41-62.

Lamoreaux, Naomi. 1991. "Information Problems and Banks' Specialization in Short-Term Commercial Lending: New England in the Nineteenth Century." Pp. 161-95, in *Inside the Business Enterprise: Historical Perspectives on the Use of Information,* edited by Peter Temin. Chicago: University of Chicago Press.

————. 1994. *Insider Lending: Banks, Personal Connections, and Economic Development in Industrial New England.* Cambridge, UK: Cambridge University Press.

Landa, Janet T. 1981. "A Theory of the Ethnically Homogeneous Middleman Group: An Institutional Alternative to Contract Law." *Journal of Legal Studies* 10:349-62.

Lebergott, Stanley. 1993. *Pursuing Happiness: American Consumers in the Twentieth Century.* Princeton, NJ: Princeton University Press.

Leidner, Robin. 1993. *Fast Food, Fast Talk: Service Work and the Routinization of Everyday Life.* Berkeley: University of California Press.

Levenstein, Harvey. 1989. "Two Hundred Years of French Food in America." *Journal of Gastronomy* 5:67-89.

Levi-Strauss, Claude. [1949] 1996. "The Principle of Reciprocity." Pp. 15-26 in *The Gift: An Interdisciplinary Perspective*, edited by Aafke E. Komter. Amsterdam: Amsterdam University Press.

Levy, Frank. 1995. "Incomes and Income Inequality." Pp. 1-57 in *State of the Union: America in the 1990s*. Vol. 1, edited by Reynolds Farley. New York: Russell Sage.

Levy, Lester S. and Roy J. Sampson. 1962. *American Economic Development: Growth of the U.S. in the Western World*. Boston: Allyn & Bacon.

Lichter, Daniel T. 1997. "Poverty and Inequality among Children." *Annual Review of Sociology* 23:121-45.

Light, Ivan and Stavros Karageorgis. 1994. "The Ethnic Economy." Pp. 647-71 in *The Handbook of Economic Sociology*, edited by Neil J. Smelser and Richard Swedberg. Princeton, NJ: Princeton University Press.

Light, Ivan, Im Jung Kwuon, and Deng Zhong. 1990. "Korean Rotating Credit Associations in Los Angeles." *Amerasia* 16:35-54.

Lincoln, James R., Michael L. Gerlach, and Peggy Takahashi. 1992. "*Keiretsu* Networks in the Japanese Economy: A Dyad Analysis of Intercorporate Ties." *American Sociological Review* 57:561-85.

Longenecker, Clinton O. and Serguei Popovski. 1994. "Managerial Trials of Privatization: Retooling Russian Managers." *Business Horizons* 37(November):35-43.

Luscombe, Belinda. 1996. "Casting the First Stone." *Time* 147(11):79.

Luo, Jar-Der. 1997. "The Significance of Networks in the Initiation of Small Businesses in Taiwan." *Sociological Forum* 12:297-317.

Macewan, Arthur. 1994. "Markets Unbound: The Heavy Price of Globalization." *Dollars and Sense* 195 (Sept-Oct):8-12.

"The Makings of a Molotov Cocktail." 1997. *The Economist*, July 12, pp. S4-S6.

Maloney, Thomas N. 1998. "Racial Segregation, Working Conditions, and Workers' Health: Evidence from the A. M. Byers Company, 1916–1930." *Explorations in Economic History* 35:272-95.

"Maquiladora-ville." 1996. *Forbes*, May 6, pp. 111-12.

Marchand, Roland. 1985. *Advertising the American Dream: Making Way for Modernity, 1920–1940*. Berkeley: University of California Press.

Márquez, García. 1970. *One Hundred Years of Solitude*. Translated by Gregory Rabassa. New York: Harper & Row.

Martinussen, John. 1997. *Society, State and Market: A Guide to Competing Theories of Development*. London: Zed Books.

Marx, Karl. 1976. *Capital*. Vol. 1, translated by Ben Fowkes. New York: Vintage.

Massey, Douglas S. and Nancy A. Denton. 1993. *American Apartheid: Segregation and the Making of the Underclass*. Cambridge, MA: Harvard University Press.

McKendrick, Neil. 1982. "The Commercialization of Fashion." Pp. 9-194 in *The Birth of a Consumer Society*, edited by Neil McKendrick, John Brewer, and J. H. Plumb. Bloomington: Indiana University Press.

McLean, Paul D. and John F. Padgett. 1997. "Was Florence a Perfectly Competitive Market? Transactional Evidence from the Renaissance." *Theory and Society* 26:209-44.

McLuhan, Marshall and Quentin Fiore. 1968. *War and Peace in the Global Village*. New York: Oxford University Press.

Milkman, Ruth. 1997. *Farewell to the Factory: Auto Workers in the Late Twentieth Century*. Berkeley: University of California Press.

Minard, Lawrence. 1983. "The Problem with Socialist Economics (interview with Janos Kornai)." *Forbes*, August 1, pp. 64-66.

Mintz, Beth and Michael Schwartz. 1985. *The Power Structure of American Business.* Chicago: University of Chicago Press.

Mintz, Sidney. 1993. "The Changing Roles of Food in the Study of Consumption." Pp. 261-73 in *Consumption and the World of Goods,* edited by John Brewer and Roy Porter. Routledge: London.

Mishel, Lawrence and Jared Bernstein. 1994. *The State of Working America 1994–95.* Armonk, New York: M. E. Sharpe.

Mizruchi, Mark S. 1996. "What Do Interlocks Do? An Analysis, Critique, and Assessment of Research on Interlocking Directorates." *Annual Review of Sociology* 22:271-98.

Mooij, Marieke de. 1998. *Global Marketing and Advertising: Understanding Cultural Paradoxes.* Thousand Oaks, CA: Sage.

Moore, Gwen. 1990. "Structural Determinants of Men's and Women's Personal Networks." *American Sociological Review* 55:726-35.

Morrill, Calvin. 1995. *The Executive Way: Conflict Management in Corporations.* Chicago: University of Chicago Press.

Munnell, Alicia H., Lynn E. Browne, James McEneaney, and Geoffrey M. B. Tootell. 1992. *Mortgage Lending in Boston: Interpreting HMDA Data.* Working Paper Series 92-7. Boston: Federal Reserve Bank of Boston.

Murphy, Kevin M. and Finis Welch. 1993. "Industrial Change and the Rising Importance of Skill." Pp. 101-32 in *Uneven Tides: Rising Inequality in America,* edited by Sheldon Danziger and Peter Gottschalk. New York: Russell Sage.

Navin, Thomas R. and Marian V. Sears. 1955. "The Rise of a Market for Industrial Securities, 1887–1902." *Business History Review* 29:105-38.

Nee, Victor. 1992. "Organizational Dynamics of Market Transition: Hybrid Forms, Property Rights, and Mixed Economy in China." *Administrative Science Quarterly* 37:1-27.

Nee, Victor and Rebecca Matthews. 1996. "Market Transition and Societal Transformation in Reforming State Socialism." *Annual Review of Sociology* 22:401-35.

Neeson, J. M. 1993. *Commoners: Common Right, Enclosure and Social Change in England, 1700–1820.* Cambridge, UK: Cambridge University Press.

Nightingale, Carl Husemoller. 1993. *On the Edge: A History of Poor Black Children and Their American Dreams.* New York: Basic Books.

Nimmer, Raymond T. and Patricia Ann Krauthaus. 1992. "Information as a Commodity." *Law and Contemporary Problems,* 55:103-30.

Norris, James D. 1990. *Advertising and the Transformation of American Society, 1865–1920.* New York: Greenwood.

North, Douglass C. 1981. *Structure and Change in Economic History.* New York: Norton.

———. 1990. *Institutions, Institutional Change and Economic Performance.* Cambridge, UK: Cambridge University Press.

"Of Take-offs and Tempests: Can Capital Controls Stop Poor Countries Crashing?" 1998. *The Economist,* March 14, p. 88.

Offer, Avner. 1997. "Between the Gift and the Market: The Economy of Regard." *Economic History Review* 50:450-76.

Ohnuki-Tierney, Emiko. 1997. "McDonald's in Japan: Changing Manners and Etiquette." Pp. 161-82 in *Golden Arches East: McDonald's in East Asia,* edited by James L. Watson. Stanford, CA: Stanford University Press.

Oliver, Melvin L. and Thomas M. Shapiro. 1995. *Black Wealth/White Wealth: A New Perspective on Racial Inequality.* New York: Routledge.

Olney, Martha L. 1991. *Buy Now, Pay Later: Advertising, Credit, and Consumer Durables in the 1920s.* Chapel Hill: University of North Carolina Press.

Olsen, Barbara. 1995. "Brand Loyalty and Consumption Patterns: The Lineage Factor." Pp. 245-81 in *Contemporary Marketing and Consumer Behavior: An Anthropological Sourcebook,* edited by John F. Sherry Jr. Thousand Oaks, CA: Sage.

Ottman, Jacquelyn A. 1993. *Green Marketing.* Lincolnwood, IL: NTC Business Books.

Palmer, Donald, Brad M. Barber, Xueguang Zhou, and Yasemin Soysal. 1995. "The Friendly and Predatory Acquisition of Large U.S. Corporations in the 1960s: The Other Contested Terrain." *American Sociological Review* 60:469-99.

Parker, Robert E. 1994. *Flesh Peddlers and Warm Bodies: The Temporary Help Industry and Its Workers.* New Brunswick, NJ: Rutgers University Press.

Pedersen, Sharon. 1987. "Married Women and the Right to Teach in St. Louis, 1941–1948." *Missouri Historical Review* 81:141-58.

Pérez-Stable, Marifeli. 1993. *The Cuban Revolution.* New York: Oxford University Press.

Perrow, Charles. 1986. *Complex Organizations: A Critical Essay.* 3d ed. New York: Random House.

Persson, Torsten and Guido Tabellini. 1994. "Is Inequality Harmful for Growth." *American Economic Review* 84:600-21.

Petersen, Mitchell A. and Raghuram G. Rajan. 1994. "The Benefits of Lending Relationships: Evidence from Small Business Data." *Journal of Finance* 49:3-37.

Petersen, Trond. 1992. "Payment Systems and the Structure of Inequality: Conceptual Issues and an Analysis of Salespersons in Department Stores." *American Journal of Sociology* 98:67-104.

Piore, Michael J. and Charles F. Sabel. 1984. *The Second Industrial Divide: Possibilities for Prosperity.* New York: Basic Books.

Polanyi, Karl. 1944. *The Great Transformation.* Boston, MA: Beacon.

Pollay, Richard W. 1985. "The Subsiding Sizzle: A Descriptive History of Print Advertising, 1900–1980." *Journal of Marketing* 49:24-37.

Portes, Alejandro. 1998. "Social Capital: Its Origins and Applications in Modern Sociology." *Annual Review of Sociology* 24:1-24.

Powell, Walter W., Kenneth W. Koput, and Laurel Smith-Doerr. 1996. "Interorganizational Collaboration and the Locus of Innovation: Networks of Learning in Biotechnology." *Administrative Science Quarterly* 41:116-45.

Powell, Walter W., Kenneth W. Koput, Laurel Smith-Doerr, and Jason Owen-Smith. Forthcoming. "Network Position and Firm Performance: Organizational Returns to Collaboration in the Biotechnology Industry." In *Networks in and around Organizations,* edited by Steven Andrews and David Knoke. Special volume in the series Research in the Sociology of Organizations. Greenwich, CT: JAI.

Powell, Walter W. and Laurel Smith-Doerr. 1994. "Networks and Economic Life." Pp. 368-402 in *The Handbook of Economic Sociology,* edited by Neil J. Smelser and Richard Swedberg. Princeton, NJ: Princeton University Press.

Radelet, Steven and Jeffrey Sachs. 1997. "Asia's Reemergence." *Foreign Affairs* 76(6):44-59.

Ramos, Joseph. 1993. "Growth, Crises and Strategic Turnarounds." *CEPAL Review* 60:63-79.

Ranis, Gustav. 1990. "Contrasts in the Political Economy of Development Policy Change." Pp. 207-30 in *Manufacturing Miracles: Paths of Industrialization in Latin America and East Asia,* edited by Gary Gereffi and Donald L. Wyman. Princeton, NJ: Princeton University Press.

Reich, Robert. 1992. *The Work of Nations.* New York: Vintage.

Reskin, Barbara and Irene Padavic. 1994. *Women and Men at Work.* Thousand Oaks, CA: Pine Forge.

Reskin, Barbara and Patricia A. Roos. 1990. *Job Queues, Gender Queues: Explaining Women's Inroads into Male Occupations.* Philadelphia: Temple University Press.

Rice, Roger L. 1968. "Residential Segregation by Law, 1910–1917." *Journal of Southern History* 34:179-99.

Roach, Tracey. 1997. "U.S. Companies Go Global with Micromarketing." *Direct Marketing* 59(12):54-5.

Robertson, Roland. 1992. *Globalization.* Newbury Park, CA: Sage.

Rodrik, Dani. 1997. *Has Globalization Gone Too Far?* Washington, DC: Institute for International Economics.

Roy, William G. 1983. "The Unfolding of the Interlocking Directorate Structure of the United States." *American Sociological Review* 48:248-57.

Roy, William G. 1997. *Socializing Capital: The Rise of the Large Industrial Corporation in America.* Princeton, NJ: Princeton University Press.

Rubinstein, Ruth P. 1995. *Dress Codes: Meanings and Messages in American Culture.* Boulder, CO: Westview.

Salmon, Marylynn. 1986. *Women and the Law of Property in Early America.* Chapel Hill: University of North Carolina Press.

Sassen, Saskia. 1996. *Losing Control? Sovereignty in an Age of Globalization.* New York: Columbia University Press.

Schmidt, Leigh Eric. 1995. *Consumer Rites: The Buying and Selling of American Holidays.* Princeton, NJ: Princeton University Press.

Settle, Robert B. and Pamela Alreck. 1986. *Why They Buy: American Consumers Inside and Out.* New York: John Wiley.

Shammas, Carole. 1993. "Changes in English and Anglo-American Consumption from 1550 to 1800." Pp. 177-205 in *Consumption and the World of Goods,* edited by John Brewer and Roy Porter. London: Routledge.

Shammas, Carole, Marylynn Salmon, and Michel Dahlin. 1987. *Inheritance in America: From Colonial Times to the Present.* New Brunswick, NJ: Rutgers University Press.

Smith, Adam. [1776] 1900. *An Inquiry into the Nature and Causes of the Wealth of Nations.* London: George Routledge.

Smith, Vicki. 1990. *Managing in the Corporate Interest: Control and Resistance in an American Bank.* Berkeley: University of California Press.

———. 1994. "Institutionalizing Flexibility in a Service Firm." *Work and Occupations* 21:284-307.

———. 1997. "New Forms of Work Organization." *Annual Review of Sociology* 23:315-39.

Spark, Alisdair. 1996. "Wrestling with America: Media, National Images, and the Global Village." *Journal of Popular Culture* 29(4):83-98.

Spufford, Peter. 1988. *Money and Its Use in Medieval Europe.* Cambridge, UK: Cambridge University Press.

Squires, Gregory D., William Velez, and Karl E. Taeuber. 1991. "Insurance Redlining, Agency Location, and the Process of Urban Disinvestment." *Urban Affairs Quarterly* 26:567-88.

Stallings, Barbara. 1990. "The Role of Foreign Capital in Economic Development." Pp. 55-89 in *Manufacturing Miracles: Paths of Industrialization in Latin America and*

East Asia, edited by Gary Gereffi and Donald L. Wyman. Princeton, NJ: Princeton University Press.

Stark, David. 1996. "Recombinant Property in East European Capitalism." *American Journal of Sociology* 101:993-1027.

Staves, Susan. 1990. *Married Women's Separate Property in England, 1660–1833*. Cambridge, MA: Harvard University Press.

Sterling, Louis. 1995. "Partners: The Social Organisation of Rotating Savings and Credit Societies among Exilic Jamaicans." *Sociology* 29:653-66.

Strang, David and James N. Baron. 1990. "Categorical Imperatives: The Structure of Job Titles in California State Agencies." *American Sociological Review* 55:479-95.

Sundstrom, William A. 1988. "Internal Labor Markets before World War I: On-the-Job Training and Employee Promotion." *Explorations in Economic History* 25:424-45.

———. 1990. "Half a Career: Discrimination and Railroad Internal Labor Markets." *Industrial Relations* 29:423-40.

Sunstein, Cass R. 1991. "Why Markets Don't Stop Discrimination." *Social Philosophy and Policy* 8:22-37.

Swedberg, Richard. 1994. "Markets as Social Structures." Pp. 255-82 in *The Handbook of Economic Sociology*, edited by Neil J. Smelser and Richard Swedberg. Princeton, NJ: Princeton University Press.

Taplin, Ian M. 1995. "Flexible Production, Rigid Jobs: Lessons from the Clothing Industry." *Work and Occupations* 22:412-38.

Taylor, Frederick Winslow. 1947. *The Principles of Scientific Management*. New York: Norton.

"Thinking about Globalisation: Popular Myths and Economic Facts." 1997. *The Economist*, October 25, pp. S1-119.

Tilly, Charles. 1990. *Coercion, Capital, and European States, A.D. 990–1990*. Oxford, UK: Blackwell.

———. 1998. *Durable Inequality*. Berkeley: University of California Press.

Tilly, Chris and Charles Tilly. 1994. "Capitalist Work and Labor Markets." Pp. 283-312 in *The Handbook of Economic Sociology*, edited by Neil J. Smelser and Richard Swedberg. Princeton, NJ: Princeton University Press.

———. 1998. *Work under Capitalism*. Boulder, CO: Westview.

Tittler, Robert. 1994. "Money-lending in the West Midlands: The Activities of Joyce Jefferies, 1638–49." *Historical Research* 67:249-63.

Tocqueville, Alexis de. 1969. *Democracy in America*. Translated by George Lawrence. New York: Anchor.

Tootell, Geoffrey M. B. 1993. "Defaults, Denials, and Discrimination in Mortgage Lending." *New England Economic Review* September/October:45-51.

Toye, John. 1989. *Dilemmas of Development*. 2d ed. Oxford, UK: Basil Blackwell.

Twitchell, James B. 1996. *AdcultUSA: The Triumph of Advertising in American Culture*. New York: Columbia University Press.

United Nations. 1996. *Statistical Yearbook*. New York: United Nations.

United Nations Development Programme. 1996. *Human Development Report*. New York: Oxford University Press.

U.S. Department of Commerce. 1995. *Statistical Abstract of the United States 1995*. Washington DC: Government Printing Office.

———. 1996. *Statistical Abstract of the United States 1996*. Washington DC: Government Printing Office.

U.S. Department of Housing and Urban Development. 1996. *U.S. Housing Market Conditions*. Washington DC: Government Printing Office.

Uzzi, Brian. 1996. "The Sources and Consequences of Embeddedness for the Economic Performance of Organizations: The Network Effect." *American Sociological Review* 61:674-98.

———. 1997. "Social Structure and Competition in Interfirm Networks: The Paradox of Embeddedness." *Administrative Science Quarterly* 42:35-67.

Vallas, Steven P. and John P. Beck. 1996. "The Transformation of Work Revisited: The Limits of Flexibility in American Manufacturing." *Social Problems* 43:339-61.

Vogel, David. 1996. *Kindred Strangers: The Uneasy Relationship between Politics and Business in America*. Princeton, NJ: Princeton University Press.

Wade, Robert. 1990. *Governing the Market: Economic Theory and the Role of Government in East Asian Industrialization*. Princeton, NJ: Princeton University Press.

Waite, Linda J. 1995. "Does Marriage Matter?" *Demography* 32:483-507.

Walder, Andrew G. 1995. "Local Governments as Industrial Firms: An Organizational Analysis of China's Transitional Economy." *American Journal of Sociology* 101:263-301.

Waldfogel, Jane. 1998. "Understanding the Family Gap in Pay for Women with Children." *Journal of Economic Perspectives* 12(1): 137-56.

Wallerstein, Immanuel. 1974. *The Modern World-System*. Vol. 1. New York: Academic Press.

Wank, David L. 1996. "The Institutional Process of Market Clientelism: *Guanxi* and Private Business in a South China City." *China Quarterly* 147:820-38.

Wasserman, Stanley and Katherine Faust. 1994. *Social Network Analysis: Methods and Applications*. Cambridge, UK: Cambridge University Press.

Waters, Malcolm. 1995. *Globalization*. New York: Routledge.

Watson, James L. 1997a. "McDonald's in Hong Kong: Consumerism, Dietary Change, and the Rise of a Children's Culture." Pp. 77-109 in *Golden Arches East: McDonald's in East Asia*, edited by James L. Watson. Stanford, CA: Stanford University Press.

———. 1997b. "Transnationalism, Localization, and Fast Foods in East Asia." Pp. 1-38 in *Golden Arches East: McDonald's in East Asia*, edited by James L. Watson. Stanford, CA: Stanford University Press.

Weatherill, Lorna. 1986. "Consumer Behavior and Social Status in England, 1660–1750." *Continuity and Change* 1:191-216.

Weber, Max. 1946. *From Max Weber*. Edited by H. H. Gerth and C. Wright Mills. New York: Oxford University Press.

———. 1981. *General Economic History*. New Brunswick, NJ: Transaction Books.

Webley, Paul and Stephen E. G. Lea. 1993. "The Partial Unacceptability of Money in Repayment for Neighborly Help." *Human Relations* 46:65-76.

Weems, Robert E. Jr. 1998. *Desegregating the Dollar: African American Consumerism in the Twentieth Century*. New York: New York University Press.

Western, Bruce. 1997. *Between Class and Market: Postwar Unionization in the Capitalist Democracies*. Princeton, NJ: Princeton University Press.

Westphal, James D., Ranjay Gulati, and Stephen M. Shortell. 1997. "Customization or Conformity? An Institutional and Network Perspective on the Content and Consequences of TQM Adoption." *Administrative Science Quarterly* 42:366-94.

Whittelsey, Frances Cerra and Marcia Carroll. 1995. *Women Pay More*. New York: New Press.

Williamson, Oliver E. 1975. *Markets and Hierarchies*. New York: Free Press.

———. 1981. "The Economics of Organization: The Transaction Cost Approach." *American Journal of Sociology* 87:548-77.

———. 1985. *The Economic Institutions of Capitalism.* New York: Free Press.

Wilson, William Julius. 1996. *When Work Disappears: The World of the New Urban Poor.* New York: Vintage.

Wolff, Edward N. 1996. "International Comparisons of Wealth Inequality." *Review of Income and Wealth* 42:433-51.

———. 1998. "Recent Trends in the Size Distribution of Household Wealth." *Journal of Economic Perspectives* 12(3):131-50.

———. 1995. Top Heavy: A Study of the Increasing Inequality of Wealth in America. New York: Twentieth Century Fund.

Woo, Jung-En. 1991. *Race to the Swift: State and Finance in Korean Industrialization.* New York: Columbia University Press.

Wood, Robert G., Mary Corcoran, and Paul N. Courant. 1993. "Pay Differences among the Highly Paid: The Male-Female Earnings Gap in Lawyers' Salaries." *Journal of Labor Economics* 11:417-41.

World Bank. 1997. *World Development Report.* Washington, DC: World Bank.

Yan, Yunxiang. 1997. "McDonald's in Beijing: The Localization of Americana." Pp. 39-76 in *Golden Arches East: McDonald's in East Asia,* edited by James L. Watson. Stanford, CA: Stanford University Press.

Yarbrough, Beth V. and Robert M. Yarbrough. 1988. *The World Economy: Trade and Finance.* Chicago: Dryden.

Yates, JoAnne. 1989. *Control through Communication: The Rise of System in American Management.* Baltimore: Johns Hopkins University Press.

Yergin, Daniel and Joseph Stanislaw. 1998. *The Commanding Heights: The Battle between Government and the Marketplace That Is Remaking the Modern World.* New York: Simon & Schuster.

Yinger, John. 1995. *Closed Doors, Opportunities Lost: The Continuing Cost of Housing Discrimination.* New York: Russell Sage.

Zelizer, Viviana. 1993. *The Social Meaning of Money.* New York: Basic Books.

Zuckerman, Mortimer B. 1998. "A Second American Century." *Foreign Affairs* 77(3):18-31.

Glossary/Index

O

Occupational sex segregation is the
  tendency for women and men to be
  segregated into different kinds of
  jobs. For example, whereas the vast
  majority of kindergarten teachers in
  the United States are women, the
  vast majority of truck drivers are
  men, 127-129

P

Product differentiation is the process
  whereby advertisers distinguish their
  own products from similar products
  available on the market, 35, 36
  (sidebar)
Protectionism is the economic doctrine
  supporting protection of domestic
  producers from foreign competition
  through tariffs, quotas, and other